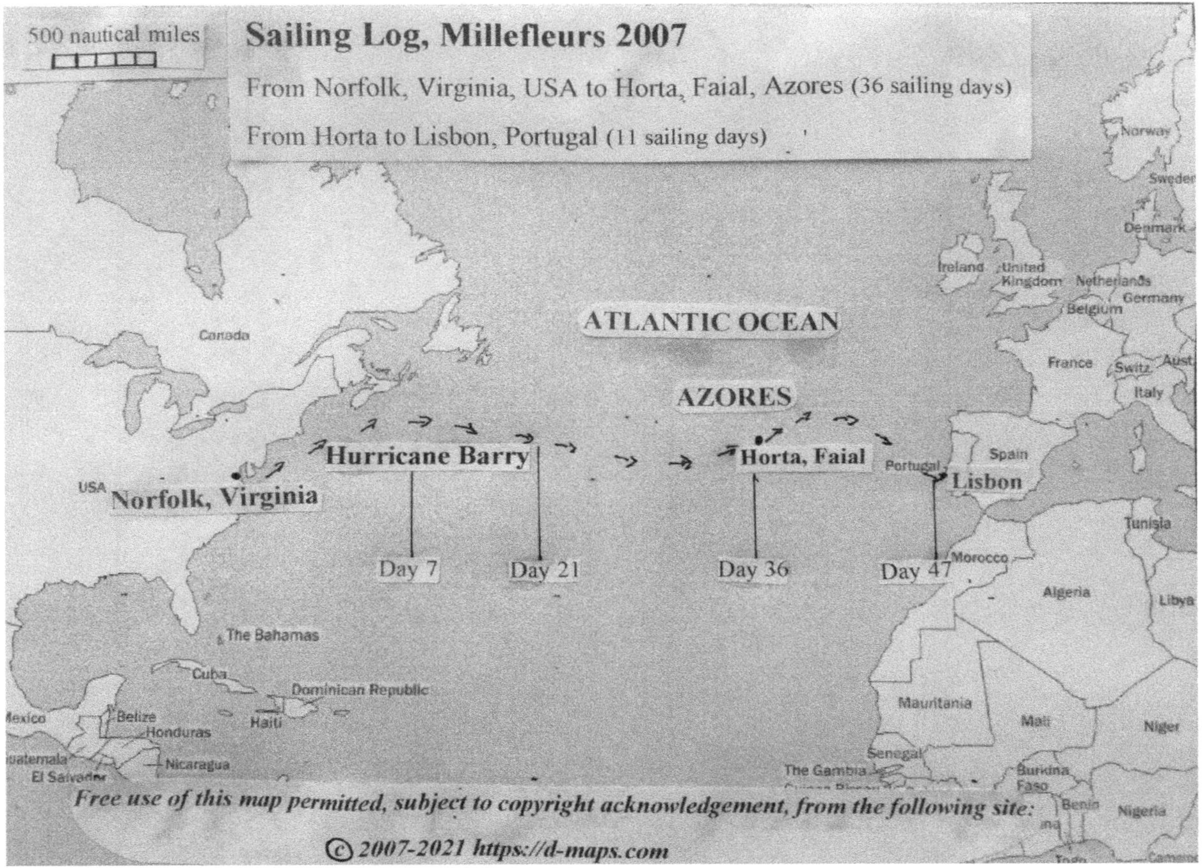

500 nautical miles
Sailing Log, Millefleurs 2007
From Norfolk, Virginia, USA to Horta, Faial, Azores (36 sailing days)
From Horta to Lisbon, Portugal (11 sailing days)
ATLANTIC OCEAN
AZORES
Canada
USA
Norfolk, Virginia
Hurricane Barry
Horta, Faial
Lisbon
Day 7
Day 21
Day 36
Day 47
Norway
Sweden
Denmark
Ireland
United Kingdom
Netherlands
Germany
Belgium
France
Switz.
Italy
Spain
Portugal
Tunisia
Morocco
Algeria
Libya
Mauritania
Mali
Niger
Senegal
The Gambia
Burkina Faso
Benin
Nigeria
The Bahamas
Cuba
Dominican Republic
Haiti
Belize
Honduras
Nicaragua
El Salvador
Free use of this map permitted, subject to copyright acknowledgement, from the following site:
© 2007-2021 https://d-maps.com

Sailing on the Edge

Alone Across the Atlantic

Peter Keating

Copyright © Peter Keating 2021
Published: 2021 by The Book Reality Experience
Western Australia

ISBN: 978-0-6451532-3-1 - Paperback Edition
ISBN: 978-0-6451532-4-8 - EBook Edition

All rights reserved.

The right of Peter Keating to be identified as author of this work has been asserted by him in accordance with sections 77 and 78 of the Copyright, Designs and Patents Act 1988.

This book is a memoir, reflecting the author's present recollections of experiences over time. This means that some details may vary from fact. Some names and characteristics may have been changed, some events have been compressed, and some dialogue has been recreated. Memory can be a fickle thing, so the Author trusts that any minor errors in times, dates and details of particular events will be understood.

Map of Atlantic © 2007-2021 https://d-maps used with permission.
All other images contained within are copyright of the author and all rights are reserved.

No part of this publication may be reproduced, stored in a retrieval system, copied in any form or by any means, electronic, mechanical, photocopying, recording or otherwise transmitted without written permission from the publisher. You must not circulate this book in any format.

*
Cover Design by Luke Buxton | www.lukebuxton.com

To all those
whose tales helped me make it through the nights!

Table of Contents

Introduction 1

Chapter 1 - Oceaning Again 3

Chapter 2 - Arriving USA 9

Chapter 3 - The Dream 13

Chapter 4 - Finding Millefleurs 20

Chapter 5 - Leaving the Chesapeake 31

Chapter 6 - Joining the gulf stream North 34

Chapter 7 - Settling in to the Atlantic 44

Chapter 8 - Hurricane Barry 47

Chapter 9 - Recovering after Barry 68

Chapter 10 - Sam 76

Chapter 11 - Dolphins and more horizons 89

Chapter 12 - Starry, starry nights 96

Chapter 13 - Me and Bobby McGee 107

Chapter 14 - Swimming off 116

Chapter 15 - Sam Revisits 123

Chapter 16 - Gerhardt, the Survivor 126

Chapter 17 - Charlie and Morovo Lagoon 133

Images 148

Chapter 18 - Tired and worn 154

Chapter 19 - Flying fish and dolphins.. 163

Chapter 20 - Message in a bottle 175

Chapter 21 - US Navy 196

Chapter 22 - Diving on the hull 214

Chapter 23 - The 30th day 228

Chapter 24 - Flotsam and life 237

Chapter 25 - Closing land 252

Chapter 26 - Horta ahoy 262

Epilogue 276

About the Author 283

Acknowledgements 284

Glossary 285

Introduction

It is said that "you don't choose a life, you live one" and any adventure is just that. You can't fall to the top of a mountain, you have to literally haul yourself up there and it is in those many thousands of steps taken that the prize is ever valued, as each step is a story in pushing yourself on and on.

So, this crossing of the Atlantic I called Sailing on the Edge, because it was rather 'iffy,' involving many unknowns, like sailing alone through crowded shipping channels, surviving hurricane Barry and those cold nasty seas that could bring me undone at any moment. I had to trust in my ability to stay alert and keep the boat in one piece. I wanted to own that experience before I was too old, regardless of all my doubts and set another of my dreams free, cross it off the list, another storyline created, another tale told.

I believe we are nothing more or less than our stories and in those thousands of long, lonely hours on the helm the stories of others with whom I had sailed and spent time became my constant sources of entertainment. And here within these pages you will meet them, in all their craziness. There was Werner and crocodile surfing, Gerhardt and the Gulag, Charlie from Morova Lagoon and Fred from Fransesca sailing alone with Scorpio over his shoulder. Also featured is the mafia of Malta, Leo from the Chesapeake, the myth of Napoleon on St Helena and many more.

Their stories are weaved into mine as they became my main form of memory entertainment as they hauled along with me day after day, from horizon to horizon. They vicariously helped me change sails and steer, helped me lay it on the line and swim away from *Millefleurs* when all was done and then helped me to survive hurricane Barry.

Then when I was at my lowest, along came the ghost of Sam, a very friendly old sailor who kept me entertained through those long, lonely hours of the dog watch.

So, my story whilst living on the edge is also in memory of others whose stories also need to be told to you the reader, to show you what could happen to any one of you if you are brave enough to go out there on your limb, to find more adventure and to then suddenly realise that you are really finding out more about yourself.

The treasure of any journey is not only learning about yourself but also reflecting upon the amazing lessons that others have provided.

Sailing from Norfolk, Virginia to the Azores in the Atlantic Ocean, over 36 days became an intense struggle with all the vagaries of going alone, something I had never done before. And as I reflected later, it was in the silent times, the times beyond friends and family and help that I came to understand more about myself and life on the ocean that made it so memorable.

I hope, with you vicariously sailing along with me day after day and week after week, you also begin to understand more about deep oceaning, its joys and terrors, and perhaps that adventurer in you may reflect on how you would cope in the same circumstances.

So, this is not my journey alone but the journey of us all when we go out there on the edge to peer over any horizon and then finally emerge the better for having left the safe harbour.

Chapter 1

Oceaning Again

I'm going down, sailing sad, rolling heavily, gunnel to gunnel in these crazy confused seas, bare poled, locked down, going down, curled up in foetal warmth, drifting around the universe of my imagination beyond all the uncomfortable challenges of some crazy, wild, angry ocean, beyond caring, just Being, Being still, Being anywhere but here.

I am in my sea-bunk, a tiny capsule of warmth and solitude and safety, locked away and hollow, hiding inside my 23 year old Hunter 34 yacht and the possibility of this lasting for much longer becomes the dichotomy of the whole experience. I want to hit the eject button and cut out of here, hit the road to a beach on a coral atoll, curl up in the sun somewhere and sleep forever. But I'm here trapped, because after days of fighting with Hurricane Barry I've nothing left to give. The arrow of events has refused to follow a steady course. I'm overwhelmed with fatigue and desperately need a rest from the relentless, brutal pounding that I'm taking. I'm in a title fight with "Barry" Muhammad Ali and he's pummelling me to bits in the red corner. He's huffing and puffing and throwing wild bare-knuckled punches and all I can do is feint and duck and hide whilst running scared..

I'm aching all over as I'm going down. I haven't eaten for days and even my ears ache from the continuous roar of this loud brutal ocean, just two feet from my head, whipped into a frenzy by a howling south-westerly wind that seems to go on forever.

Then I remember the old sailing wisdom, "he that would go to sea for pleasure, would go to hell for a pastime" (A.J. Boyd Shellback, 1899), and maybe this is hell, never knowing what could possibly happen next.

Then it all changes in an instant!

There's a very loud long hollow bang and an icy dollop of hard cold sea water hits me in the face and as the boat slams sideways, I'm thrown across the cabin, skidding under the table in one big crumpled cold wet mess. My stomach is thrust up into my throat in one solid lump and I feel doom invading my whole being. Not that I can see it, but I can feel the hard, cold stainless saloon pole pressing deep into my back, giving me some grounding in these moments of despair. My thoughts are focused on the bastard ship that has run us down, how deep we are down in the water and will it tear our guts out as it rolls over us? I'm resigned to my fate, no need to fight anymore as I sink slowly, going down, without a struggle, but it's too quiet for a collision, too quiet and steady for a ship to be pushing us further under. Maybe I've drowned and time has stopped and this stillness is a cold death, as I sink into oblivion.

This is chess now, not checkers. That thought flashes through my mind as another wrong move like lying a-hull in a hurricane, because I am absolutely buggered, could land me in deeper, more dangerous waters. On land if things are not going well the response is to say "will this matter in five years?" but on the ocean that principle is reduced to about five hours, while right now the brutality of this hurricane has condensed it to just five minutes.

In a trance I begin feeling for my sea-boots and find them mixed in with the galley dishes and seat cushions, waiting like pilgrims for retrieval. I drag them on slowly and in a daze, I crawl back into the galley, feeling for my safety harness that hangs below the companionway hatch.

It's there, waiting patiently as I drag it on meticulously, talking myself through the well-practised safety procedure, taking my time as if I have hours, while outside, the seas roar loudly. I know what I am going to meet has to be full of all the demons I could possibly imagine.

There are the demons of the bush when I felt dark shapes behind me as I walked alone down bush paths at night as a kid, or the demons of being run over by a bus as I lay there partly under my truck, changing a tyre, or the worst demon of all, being slowly frozen to death in the wilderness. Now I have to go out and exchange pleasantries and make friends with them all, but it's definitely better than staying locked away inside my battered yacht, 400 miles east of the USA coast. Well out into this cold and wild North Atlantic is the unconscious mind protecting me from a slow death, while Hurricane Barry pounds us to bits.

Time has stopped and I feel above my head for the hatch boards and they are still there. The wave that pooped us has smashed into the cockpit and water is still pouring below but it fortunately hasn't broken the companionway boards. Water had squeezed through the two-inch gap at the top and squirted me in the face. It clearly said "get up and get into action and cease laying there in a daze avoiding what's going on up here." I slide the hatch back and crawl over the wash boards, slamming the hatch behind me and fall into a cockpit still half full of cold frothy sea water.

Henry my self-steerer is crying inconsolably and making loud warring noises without any of the usual gear clack. He is definitely severely injured. We are drifting beam-on to these wild winds which seem to be back over 60 knots. My only anchor in life's ocean is this worn Hunter and I'm putting all my faith in its buoyancy.

This is a very dangerous place to be, riding beam on, trusting to luck to survive, just waiting for another rogue wave to play havoc with us again, as it slams brutally into our sides.

The passing waves are foaming and hissing and dark with menace where there's little visibility so I jam myself into the cockpit seat, disengaging Henry who happily goes comatose as I quietly empty the freezing waters out of my sea-boots.

They say that confronting a storm at sea is like fighting god. All the powers in the universe seem to be against you and in some extraordinary way your irrelevance at that time is deeply humbling. I definitely feel small, overwhelmed and lost.

I look up at the compass and it is still glowing in the dark, reading a heading of 130 degrees, but the GPS has gone, leaving behind a broken power cable as a lasting memory of its bones. I can feel the dodger canvas flapping wildly around the cockpit coaming, hitting me occasionally with loose pieces of material, and I can see that there is a big split in the rail dodger where the last big wave has smashed into us. But the essential water containers are still there, quietly hanging on for dear life and that is a big bonus. Apart from that the steering feels just fine and my obvious next task is to get *Millefleurs* sailing again, downwind and away from these dangerous seas. I have done this before by waiting till her head swings away from the breeze and a random wave pushes us along as it strikes the stern quarter.

There is no starting the motor or hoisting a sail. I'm not up to that, it's too complicated for my mind. I'll have to wait patiently till we have some movement through the water and then work the rudder to get us around but unfortunately there's a real urgency for this manoeuvre.

I hook my harness to the starboard rail and reluctantly crawl aft to see if any sheet lines or others ropes are in the water. I find the Jesus rope looped over the side rail dragging down the leeward side, snaking out aft ready to wash under the boat and foul either the rudder or the propeller.

This is the classic of experiences where it gives the test first and the lesson afterwards, as I've had ropes around the propeller before. I slowly pull it in and re-lash it to the aft push-pit, finding some of the longer lashings I have on it broken, but they're still long enough to secure it well. It is wild up here with the stern regularly being buried in the swell and the cold, cold spray repeatedly taking my breath away.

It's awfully dark as well and I'm not sure what to do when I get back to the cockpit as I'm having a mental freeze. I need a plan, a get out of jail card, an escape from hell battling around this wild crazy deck all alone. Then there's a sudden realisation that pours forth with anguish and pain and gut-wrenching feelings of pure failure. This sailing trail that I've followed so fondly for the last forty years has led me to the edge of this dark cliff.

I'm on my hands and knees, cold wet and dog tired, staring into the abyss with warm tears of failure flooding my cheeks where all those years of experience have come to nought. All I can feel in my innards is sadness and despair and loss as it all comes down to this, a sudden knowing that this ocean is too big for me and haven't others who have followed the same trail, said that too?

I have to step up or step out, there's no excuses left, no bunker to hide in, no more going to sleep. I'm the mouse that once roared, but now I've gone silent and I have to get smart. Some say wisdom gets closer when we stop than when we soar, and I'm hanging on with both hands and the only way I'm going to get a leg up, is to get smart. This is really life or death now and there is no way I can imagine getting out of this dilemma easily as everything about this blow is flashing code orange to bright red and now it's also flashing force 12 on the Beaufort scale.

Then I instinctively realise that if I do start the motor even with the gate valves closed and power for 20 seconds or so, the worst I could do is destroy the rubber impeller. It's safety over machinery now, the despairing angel has spoken wisely and I crawl back to the cockpit, centre the rudder and fire up the motor. I can't hear any motor noise above the roar around me, but I feel continuous vibrations in my feet and the whiff of sweet diesel, so I engage the gearbox and power up.

We begin moving forward and I desperately swing the bow downwind, and immediately stop the motor, breathe a sigh of relief, engage reverse to hold the propeller still and begin steering. We are off again at just 2 knots with the rudder in control and me hoping to keep it that way for the rest of the night.

I know these familiar dance moves now, I've practised them before and I've dodged another deep ocean bullet where fate was definitely giving me a warning.

Most storms at sea are frustrating, annoying and discordant but this one is a bad assed super loud rock song and now it is up to me to keep alert and run before the seas, otherwise I could be pooped again, as these seas are definitely getting steeper and nastier and louder.

My grandma used to say "when in doubt ride the horse in the direction it is going" and I have no choice here. Lying a-hull and drifting before the wind was definitely not a wise survival strategy, particularly when the weather was getting severe and I'd been very lucky as I lay comatose below, hoping it would all go away and leave me becalmed.

It is 0300 hrs according to my mental clock. There's a long, long time before the arrival of dawn when I will clearly see what state the ocean is in and what damage we have sustained. My stomach is still thrust into my mouth through fear, and I hang on hiding low in the cold, wet cockpit hoping for some relief.

These are the worst conditions I've ever been in at sea as Hurricane Barry pounds out his fury in all directions. This is survival through a badly stained looking glass and I clip myself in and wriggle tighter into the cockpit combing, thanking my lucky stars I wasn't in the cockpit when we were pooped.

It was no idle blow and these monstrous seas are still breaking wildly around us as we surge away from them with the biggest scary waves running wildly through us, rather than slamming into our sides and bursting like star shells, as if we were in some fierce battle.

Henry, my self-steerer, is useless, gonzo, gone and as an exercise I start him and try to engage the clutch during a lull, but there is only a whirring noise and some grinding, without any action. I'll have to wait till dawn to check the deck gear and see if there is any damage forward, but all seems well on the helm at present and we are on track, two step dancing with a bear slowly to the east at 2 knots, rolling wickedly like a drunken sailor, with me firmly locked to the helm, steering as delicately as I can straight downwind, with the world crashing all around.

Chapter 2

Arriving USA

I collected my bags in LA International, cleared customs and immigration and headed for the transit lounge for an overnight sleep, as I was catching the early morning flight to Washington. I certainly felt the last 8 years in the bush alone had stretched my dreams a little further, and this new adventure would help me reassess my priorities in life. I felt somewhat overwhelmed by the huge size of the airport, the mass of passengers, the baggage and the craziness of finding one's way around. This was like Disneyland after the simplicity of the bush - all immensely exciting ...life was beginning to roll.

I slept soundly in the airport lounge overnight to save some dollars and reinvigorate my independent spirit, washing in the public bathroom naked, like a poor man saving his money for more important things, putting on the best of my crumpled clothes for the next leg.

I boarded the flight to Washington, hoping for a good American breakfast and some bonhomie from fellow travellers. The plane was full and thankfully I was given a window seat, which allowed me to enjoy the views of the desert landscape of the USA's west coast spread out below me.

After breakfast I discovered that sitting next to me was Mike, one of those fascinating characters you may meet serendipitously on any journey. That's one of the great joys of travelling, the interesting people that you often meet. It reminded me of the saying "every stranger is a friend you haven't met yet", and Mike was like that. He was from Washington and was the owner of Orion Films. Over the years he had made commercial films on a variety of different subjects, which he considered to be his contribution to world culture. Mike shared many fascinating stories of his experiences with well-known actors as well as some of his more unusual storylines.

We talked about the similarities between Australia and the US with both being the big immigrant countries of the world. We discussed the different perspectives which we experienced from living in different hemispheres. We shared humour and discussed our favourite foods. I told him about my travels in South Africa and living in London and he shared his experiences of walking the Appalachian Trail and living in Las Vegas. We talked about our families. He had a Vietnamese wife and I had had a Chinese wife, and we both had two children, a boy and girl, except his were older than mine. He then talked about his new venture in making educational films for various interest groups with his next film in Washington being about educating men in treating and avoiding prostate cancer. Apparently, more men get prostate cancer than women experience breast cancer, and his brief was to somehow address that issue.

His research had shown that one of the paradoxes of gay life is that these men have less prostrate problems because it is assumed that the prostate is being massaged. Apparently, a sect of men in India who massage their prostate regularly, called milking the prostate, also don't experience the problems that western men do. So Mike's new film would attempt to encourage men to regularly massage their prostate when they were in the shower, when exercising or when making love. We laughed at the scenarios one could put into a 10 minute film that would be acceptable to the homophobic men of the largely Christian lobby in the USA, as well as all the other interest groups who would want to put forward their points of view, probably calling this newer practise of massaging your prostate disgusting, a sin or just dirty.

"Making the film isn't hard," said Mike, "but getting through the bullshit is." Isn't that so true in life? We then shared the idea that where there is conflict between parties there paradoxically must be common ground, and the art of any deal was making that common ground bigger.

He hoped he could do just that and I wished him well.

We discussed my proposed sail across the Atlantic and then back across the Pacific to Australia and he shared his passion for making a documentary in south America on the Sandinistas and the contras in Nicaragua. I knew nothing about filming and Mike knew nothing about sailing, but we clicked as mavericks in our own way, each making separate forays into curious human endeavours, possibly in order to understand ourselves and our own particular passions.

At the airport in Washington Mike introduced me to the now elderly crooner Pat Boone, who seemed to know him well. This was a good indication of my new friend's credibility. Pat talked about his only visit to Tasmania when he saw what he considered to be the savage Tasmania devils for the first time. He marvelled at how Walt Disney, by highlighting their peculiar ugliness was able to make them into such an iconic animal, which in the end has made the small island of Tasmania such an interesting destination for many travellers.

Mike and I shared a cab into Washington and I continued on to north Washington with snow still on the March ground, to my pre-booked youth hostel. It was 2200 hrs and the doors were locked, not a good sign. Following my persistent and very loud knocking, the door opened slightly and the night manager sleepily showed me to a room where 12 others were sleeping, some very noisily. I collapsed into my allotted bunk by the door, with my bags close by my side, excited to be in Washington for the first time in my life, ready to launch off into "being that stranger in a strange land" again.

The next day I had much to organise so I headed for the local shopping centre where I opened a bank account with the Bank of America who were very happy for me to transfer $30,000 into my new account. The next item on the list, and a very important one, was a mobile phone. Not one to care about such things as colour, particularly when cost is involved, I bought an inexpensive, pink Virgin phone putting money into my "pay as you go" account.

I discovered from the accounts clerk, much to my delight, that not too far away was a car auction house where I hoped I would be able to buy a van to live in, while I searched for my boat.

I went directly to the auction house and searched through the inventory of cars available until I met a "black hustler" who thought me peculiar but who happily showed me around, explaining all the rules, after I had bought him a cup of coffee and hamburger. Then, realising how green I must be, he casually sold me his dodge van, which was coincidently parked on the street just outside the auction house. I paid $1,000 for it and later discovered that it was worth about a third of that price.

He even came with me to help with the process of changing registration details and arranging the insurance that I needed in order to drive legally in the US. The van wasn't in the best condition, but with some tint on the windows, some new wiper blades, a couple of new tires and the removal of all the four back seats, I had invested in my own travelling motel.

I found a camping store and bought a small gas stove and then it was off to a Goodwill store, where I scored a blow-up mattress, some bedding, plates, cutlery and cooking gear. In the space of three days I was "good to go".

I left Washington early on Saturday morning and headed south to Annapolis, Maryland, and within a few hours I had quickly adjusted to driving on the right-hand side of the road. I soon discovered that the van had a peculiar carburettor problem, whereby I had to keep power on to stop it from cutting out. I guess my dark friend had found a sucker to buy his van, but it was fine as long as I accepted that it was like its previous owner - erratic and promising more than it could deliver. Together we agreed to share our journey south.

It probably was an omen for the boat I was looking for, seemingly fine on the surface but full of hidden problems, as all boats and people are.

Chapter 3

The Dream

I suppose I should explain where this all began and why I'd leave the solid stone castle I had built in southern Australia and take on ocean passaging again, after I had sworn off it all 12 years before.

Well, in 2007 I decided to sail alone across the Atlantic Ocean, from Norfolk, Virginia, USA to Lisbon, Portugal, a distance of about 3400 nautical miles in a straight line, but much longer in a sail boat, to test my ability to sail single handed. I'd come to the east coast of the USA to get myself another sail-boat, my fourth, and going to Europe seemed a nice option, before I returned to Australia.

Deep oceaning that I knew so well is not an exercise in escaping the land and going out there into the deep blue where you leave all your troubles behind. Rather deep oceaning is a clear relationship between rigorous discipline and utter freedom, where your success is always held within your own hands as you softly challenge one of the last great forces of nature. Deep oceaning is like free climbing where the cliffs are usually wet and very cold.

And this long painful ocean journey also changed me in ways I never realised or expected because I went out there hoping to feel my inner lion roar again, whilst in reality it just whimpered and hung on for dear life.

So, this is a personal story of challenge, adventure and the mystical, mixed with fate, and in the end is a conversation we often have with ourselves as we grow older and wiser, believing we have nailed down all the things that could happen and then suddenly realise one's fate is really in the hands of the hunter.

Life is said to always be an amazing journey without a destination, full of highs and lows, triumphs and failures and sometimes joys and then pains that are so deep, they seem to swallow you up. In the end one's discoveries from all those experiences, are the real currencies of life and to get rich one has to go out there and really mix it up with nature.

These are the paradoxes of life that light up any seeker's journey as we search for things that are somehow deep within us that we can't nail down in the bars, or in lovers or the dance halls of life.

I've always found that all long ocean voyages are really searches for things too hard to define, feelings too nefarious to grasp and about things too far away. They seem to involve leaving the familiar and going beyond and they invariably involve establishing a new harmony with oneself. It calls for the challenges of overcoming fears often not known, along with the rewards of constant reassurances that we all can survive and even flourish through almost anything.

There is a wisdom that says the best medicine for oneself is very close to where the poison lurks and for me that was loneliness but there's a sense of healing around the ocean that I really needed after those long hard lonely years back in the bushlands of Australia. Stand on a cliff sometime and look out to sea and you know in your being that you came from out there, somewhere beyond that horizon.

That's the real reward for the oceaner, knowing that you are reaching down into something deep, personal, and utterly mysterious. Usually though, the impetus for major changes and the subsequent discomfort that arises from that search is to eventually intuit we are much more than we can imagine, and I hope that the adventurer in you can vicariously share those same feelings with me, as we voyage together across the Atlantic alone.

What emerges hopefully as we stretch ourselves to the limit is that bigger person, the other warrior, that superhero we'd all like to grow, usually through adversity, becomes the prime catalyst in any growth process, causing us to discover more and more about who we really are.

This is the real reward for any traveller when you drill down into their motives for taking any arduous journey. It is the search for that deep treasure of self-identity and when properly understood it means the discovery of who we really are and the end of those illusions of who we are not, which is the source of all our self-doubts.

The nature of life then seems to be that all travellers are constantly asking questions that can't be answered and going on treks that have no maps. All travellers I discovered are scholars of mobility, writing another chapter in the journals of migrating humans and another line to our nomadic beginnings that we thought were all over. I have heard it said that life is like a strange restaurant where the waiter brings you things you never ordered, nor usually want, but when eaten with gusto makes all the difference, and it often explains a lot when things are not going as well as you'd like.

I soon realised that home for my inner journeyman, that place where I could lay down my burdens and just relax to find my inner lion, was never a piece of soil but a piece of soul, a place where I could be still and feel safe within, secure in what I was becoming and not what I had. For me that was on the ocean.

In the past our country, our food, our music and our companions were all chosen for us through locality, but in this newer, ever-changing world where the walls are getting softer we can now decide on our music or food and even our foreign companions. In fact, there are now over 250 million people on the move around the world, making them the fifth biggest nation - World Global Travellers.

As a world sailor I belonged to this mob, but I had been away from the ocean for the past 12 years, having been land bound and forested in the thick bushlands of southern Australia. I was a lost bona fide oceaner having logged over 150,000 ocean miles across all the oceans of the world and I wanted that rhythm back, I wanted that tug of fate that you only get when you're at least 100 miles offshore and beyond the shackles of conformity. Now I was back, ready to hopefully roar again, feeling reborn, where movement and continual change becomes that newer long sought-after exhilaration, that the land never provides.

My journey across the Atlantic is the beginnings of this new chapter and I am excited and bouncing with anticipation for what the waiters of life will bring this time. The past is never as exciting as the present and I am ready for more of anything. The land has emptied me out, worn me down and those far away horizons have called again. I wanted more, I wanted out of the bush and the heavily forested valley and those things of land like livestock and gardens and buildings that needed my constant daily attention.

I'd finally learnt the strange wisdom of life where almost everyone says they want to be content and settled, but when we are unsettled and empty that's when we grow the most, and that's what I wanted now. I want my inner tired lion to roar again while I was still fit and healthy and able to battle with the uncertainties of it all, on my own terms.

Maybe I was having a late male menopause, needing to unfold my wings and soar again, as my familiar love of deep oceaning was calling me back. I knew that this proposed Atlantic Ocean crossing alone, my own personal epic after the last 8-year retreat into the bush, would be a struggle between me and the elements, between me and my search for some deeper meanings to life.

And I really want the challenge, want to own it and mark it off and call the Atlantic 'done'. In my own "struggle street" mentality I expected that the challenge would be a stretch, but ultimately a kind and caring exercise where the shaking of my foundations would improve who I was when it was all over. This was my last chance I figured, that would help me throw off that dependency persona feeling that didn't fit well with me.

I wanted for a time to be beyond the support of caring arms or familiar faces or even prying eyes, where one's life could be just laid bare and exposed. This was also one of my last chances for "deep adventure" as I was still fit and able to compete with mother nature on an equal footing, searching within my own inner democracy for the struggle between my counting of "beads and the cracking of heads" that comes with menopause.

Perhaps it was my journey of hard truths that we all take at some time, the hard truths about ourselves and our journeys through life so we can be truly authentic. It was perhaps my last foray into one's own garden where the undergrowth must be removed so that those struggling saplings could grow tall.

The sailing in this story then is not so much the subject for safely crossing the Atlantic between the new world of the Americas and the old world of Europe, but rather a lens for seeing beyond, so that I could safely delve into my emptiness, my loneliness and make it more palatable for my old age. Sailing for me was always about that romantic artist whose medium is just the wind and the waves and freedom, who goes down to the ocean to paint what is possible within his soul. That often means drilling down to seeing what is possible when there's nothing more to find.

I often say we go to the theatre to see a man framed in the microcosm of life, battling with his Achilles heel ready to rise above those common frailties we all share, and so I went on this voyage alone, to do the same with my life. At least that's what I believe I set out to do.

So, on 1st March 2007 I took the Qantas metal tube to Los Angeles on a long-haul flight from Melbourne, Australia, tired, worn but ready for another newer long-haul adventure. It was something I had no experience in doing, sailing alone across the Atlantic Ocean, from the East Coast of the USA to Portugal in Europe, via the Azores.

I cleared Customs and Immigration, gaining a tourist visa that allowed me 90 days to get from the West Coast to the East Coast, organise some accommodation and transport, buy a seaworthy yacht on a shoestring budget, get it sailing, load my gear and leave the country in a hasty wake. It was a tall order and awfully unsettling, but that's the nature of any adventure when you always have little money and not much time, but are full of enthusiasm, which is an even bigger currency.

For the last three years I had a hunger gnawing at my insides, waking me at 0300 hrs, tapping my doors of perception, encouraging me to buy another yacht, my fourth, and sail alone across that big wide cold Atlantic.

The last time I was in Los Angeles was in December 2004 when I had flown in to buy another small yacht to sail back to Australia across the Pacific, but it had turned out to be so worn that it couldn't have sailed safely around the bay; I flew home feeling defeated. Now I am back with a longer list of boats to look over on the East Coast, as this part of America gives me access to a bigger string of boats that should be suitable to sail to Lisbon and on to Gibraltar, then down to the Caribbean and on across the Pacific.

I am also attempting to stretch myself further by sailing alone, which I haven't done before, aiming to find parts of me I had never previously explored, aiming to capture the spirit of the ocean that those old revered single-handed sailors had done.

The Herman Melvilles, the Joshua Slocums or the Bernard Moitessiers. Bernard Moitessier in particular, one of the finest single-handed sailors yet said of single handed oceaning, "I am a citizen of the most beautiful nation on earth, a nation whose laws are harsh yet simple, a nation that never cheats, which is immense and without borders, where life is lived in the present. In this limitless nation, this nation of wind, light and peace, there is no other ruler besides the sea."

Herman Melville gave special reasons for my own previous 15 years of oceaning, when he said "there never was a great man yet who spent all his life on land" and the wide Atlantic far ahead of me was going to tell me things about myself and handling loneliness that I had never yet considered, and that's something one can never buy.

On land back in Australia after I had sold *Sundancer* my third yacht in 1995, I had built a 400 tonne stone castle, which I named Waterstone Castle, in Brogo, NSW (more information available on the internet). I built it over eight years with my bare hands, breaking up stone, mixing cement, welding framework, plumbing, wiring and working on a very different adventure of building an esoteric and healing centre in the bushland of southern Australia. That replaced *Sundancer* and ocean expeditions as my prime focus, as I intended to create a community of healers and consciousness seekers to grow myself inwards as well as outwards.

Giving up the freedom of the ocean and the ability to go anywhere around that liquid world, replacing it with this hard, solid fixed abode mired in the politics and permanency of the Brogo Valley in NSW, became my entire focus for eight long lonely years.

During my time in Brogo I financed much of my building with teaching at the local high school. I had started a teaching career back in Hobart, Tasmania, in the 1970s where I taught mainly the serious disciplines of mathematics and science.

I had taught in London as well and even though I loved teaching and sharing my enthusiasm for solving mysteries, I wanted to create my own mystery school of consciousness and healing in the castle which I hoped would help expand my vision of independence and an alternative lifestyle that urban living had long swallowed up. There I could share philosophies and experiences with the seekers of the world, hopefully creating a community of shared enthusiasm, where we could all grow together.

But gradually this newer castle dream also withered on the vine and freedom called loudly again. What had been another possible horizon became too hard without a partner, so I sold the castle in 2004, gave away all my gear and surfed the East Coast of Australia in a van, wandering the shorelines of the country, meeting old sailing friends, travelling old song lines and catching up with the nomad in me that found life on land too rigid, but unsure of where to next.

When I returned to Tasmania in 2004 at the age of 56, to visit my mother who was getting old and grumpy, partly because I hadn't chosen a more stable lifestyle, I suddenly realised I wasn't ready to settle down just yet. She taunted me that I'd never sail again as I was too scared and perhaps she was right, but I knew I had to give oceaning one last bash before I could really decide what I wanted most out of life.

I had to go alone this time, to grow that self-sufficiency I craved, to placate my demons and insecurities. I had to get really unsettled and go out there, possibly throw everything away, invest in another yacht and sail away to freedom on another ocean of possibility, where I could expand that oceanic person, that international citizen, I wanted to become.

I had no qualms about surfing off into the unknown, beginning something anew, particularly after I'd seen a tee-shirt on a guy down the Grand Canyon on an earlier trip through the USA which said "you can do anything except ski through a revolving turnstile" and I thought why not give the revolving turnstile a bash as well?

Fortunately, my plans of getting another boat were very vague and I liked it that way. Life happens when you are making plans and the best travellers I'd shared time with were those who always enjoyed a detour on any journey, as much as I did. Now I have started a new ball rolling and the rest will take care of itself. I have escaped the rigidity of the castle, the daily routine of building and organising, the steady grind of being a dedicated classroom teacher and here I am in the USA, a stranger in a strange land, riding that wonderful "traveller's wave" of spontaneity and freedom, surfing through places one has never been, sleeping in places no one goes and messing with the joys of being wild and on the edge again. In the words of Willie Nelson, I was "on the road again."

Chapter 4

Finding Millefleurs

In Annapolis I found many marinas with huge numbers of boats for sail in the 30-40 ft category, but they were all too expensive for me and would also require much work and money to make them ocean-ready.

They looked pretty and were loaded with toys, but few had decent anchoring gear or cruising sails or strong ocean rigging and none had done any ocean miles. There I met a know-all broker who specialised in power boats and after he found out that I was headed for Europe he offered his special advice: "sailing is for girlies.... get a decent power boat, fill her up with fuel and head east...you can't fail" he said, with a straight face. He obviously had lots of sales experience and plenty of big "diesel suckers" to offer me.

I travelled further south, sleeping in the National forests at night, enjoying the freedom of the big open American vistas which reminded me so much of Australia. The food and fuel were very cheap, as also was the secondhand sailing gear that I continued to source for that elusive boat.

I collected "goodies" from all sorts of goodwill stores. I purchased a 12v drill, a grinder, a small welder, socket sets, fishing jigs, wet weather gear (two sets for $180) and lots more. The van was getting full and my sleeping space was shrinking, but all the bits and pieces I collected made me feel that progress was being made.

In the Solomon Island area on the north side of the Patuxent river in Maryland, I found a 1984 Hunter fibreglass sloop called *Indulgence*, which had a new Yanmar diesel motor, a nice stern lip and heavy rigging as well as a spirit stove and a tiny aft cabin It was genuinely solid as the early Hunters were traditionally heavily "hand- laid" fibreglass hulls. I searched the internet for anyone who had been oceaning in the Hunters but found none.

It didn't seem part of the American psyche to go sailing offshore, much as they seemed to love "gunkholing" from one bay to the next in their thousands, and it appeared that this Hunter was no different. It had never been out of the bay in all of its 20 years. However, it showed promise, with the price being in the low $20,000 and it felt welcoming. I was hooked. It was well cared for and the owners were very pleasant people who had used the boat principally for diving around the Chesapeake area. I walked its deck, checking the minimal offshore gear, going over the rigging and realising that by spending another $5,000 I could get this boat ocean ready. I was excited but decided I needed to look at more boats. I made a low offer and left, heading further south to Virginia and North Carolina.

Within a few days my offer on the Hunter had been accepted and I could feel fate beginning to become involved in the search. (The waiter had brought me something I had vaguely ordered and maybe something I didn't need, but the timing was perfect).

The travelling was encouraging me to reconnect to the nomad within and the thought of this small sloop taking me halfway across the world was helping me connect to that older more adventurous version of myself.

This Hunter 34 seemed to be becoming part of that idea and my bigger plans were finally rolling. I was finally flying over the valleys again, rather than counting the bark on the trees. I back-tracked to Maryland and the Solomons, took *Indulgence* out for a sail and motor and in the space of 3 days I had bought the boat, signed all the papers, secured a month's marina usage and had settled into my new oceaning home.

I didn't want a marine survey done as I could do all the checking myself, secure in my own judgements about the strength of the hull and the deck gear. After two weeks in the States I now had the boat to ready for the long cold Atlantic crossing to Portugal.

I dived on the hull after borrowing diving gear from Mike, who lived on his boat next door to my marina berth. I carefully checked the hull for osmotic bubbles, rudder slop and worn zinc blocks on the propeller shaft. They were good which indicated to me the boat had been well cared for. Slipping the boat was expensive and I'd have to wait at least a month, so I decided it could wait until I reached Australia the following year and threw all my eggs into one basket. It was *Indulgence* or bust, the momentum was building.

The topsides were in good condition but the anti-foul was tired and would have to wait. In fact, there is no anti-foul that stands up to long ocean passages, particularly in the tropics, where the goose barnacles grow long and wild on any surface. The only treatment is regular underwater scrapings when becalmed. It would give me a good reason to welcome being becalmed as I could happily get over the side and swim around my floating home, wiping out the barnacles while enjoying the fact that I owned a floating palace in the realms of another universe.

I moved onboard and set up the forward cabin as my sanctuary, collecting colourful fabric from the local goodwill store and some cosy pillows and a nice doona. I put pictures of my Tasmanian kids on the wall and even added a bold Tasmanian devil which I'd found in an old travel brochure. A man's cave is his sanctuary and his castle, and there's no better spot than a cosy cabin bunk in your own yacht.

In the saloon I installed a large map of the world with all my voyages marked in pencil with more purple dotted lines that I hoped this voyage would take. Looking at the big world in which we live puts the Atlantic into perspective.

I realised that in the next 70 days or so I'd get this girl together, register her with the Australian marine regulations, get her an Aussie passport (ship's papers) and change the name from *Indulgence*, which seemed too prim, to *Millefleurs*, a happier and more expansive choice.

I also needed to register my EPIRB (emergency position indicating radio beacon), buy a life raft in case things really went pear shaped out there, and buy the other 500 things I needed to go offshore.

The preference for name *Millefleurs* originates from a racehorse that I saw in Australia when I was gambling on the horses, and it won…reminding me that the name may be lucky. It means "a thousand flowers" in French and it's choice made me feel that I had become an international citizen again with a USA boat, a French boat name and an Australian flag. I felt good about the universalism - the waiter had been kind.

Boat names are fascinating and I don't enjoy sailing on a boat with a name that I dislike. I've changed the names of all the yachts I've owned to suit me, except for *Sundancer* which I would have liked to have called *Gunbarrel*, because she was long and thin, but I never did start the process. I've owned *Privateer*, the 37 ft boat that was my first and which I built in 1973, to *Marina*, a 44 ft yawl, to 104 ft *Sundancer* and now 34 ft *Millefleurs*. Once as I was sailing on Sydney harbour I even saw a boat called" *She got the house"* and I dipped my flag to him.

For some reason names of boats say much more about the owners than their houses or cars or other possessions can. Some of those which I found to be particularly humorous are *"Tide the knot"*, *"Cat's meow"*, *"I-o-nit"*, *"Vitamin C"*, *"Seas the day"*, *"Lots of knots"*, *"True blew"* Perhaps the act of buying a yacht that can possibly take a sailor out onto the ocean with an alternative lifestyle, means yacht owners are somehow recalibrating who they are, redefining who they want to be, saying "hello look at me!" They're changing their image and seeking new answers to old questions that drive them to get a boat with all its problems, hoping it'll change their life. But the act of renaming a boat, even though its supposed to bring bad luck, is a way of flying a new flag for everyone else to see. Probably a bit like getting a body tattoo.

In the marina I meet the locals, Mike and Glenn, and they become my "go-to men" when I need maritime gear or advice. Mike is a marine electronics engineer who loves a drink and a game of chess and Glenn is a happy entrepreneur who enjoys sailing and delivering boats around Chesapeake Bay. Both have great senses of humour which I very much relate to.

In the same boatyard lives Leo who has trained as a doctor but lives on the hard (permanently slipped) in his little boat, doing yard work and earning enough money to buy himself opium as a regular monthly hit, to relieve the pain of his lost ambitions. Leo says to me early on in our meetings "my life feels like a test I never studied for!" and I'm sure he was right. On another occasion, coming down his boat ladder he sang out, "hey I just drank some boiling water because I wanted to whistle!" I laughed loudly at his wild imagination.

Leo wears unusual t-shirts with phrases like "who knows enough to be a pessimist?" or "I was an atheist till I realised I was god" or his best, "is this the earliest I've been late?" I enjoyed bouncing my odd Australian humour off him. He took up the challenge of sharing the oddities of his crazy lifestyle, whilst living in a boat on the hard with lots of friends, wild humour and odd personal idiosyncrasies.

As an indication of how eccentric Leo was, he kept three rats on his boat as friends – big, black sleek-coated rats, that had wicked eyes, prick ears and shiny, wild whiskers and exhibiting loads of curiosity. They all had names and different personalities and Leo enjoyed nothing better than being asked how Toby or Frederick or Daisy were doing. They spent lots of time tearing up paper or chewing minties that Leo stocked up on regularly for their pleasure, to distract them from eating his boat. When one visited Leo there was the unusual but formal protocol of being re-introduced to his rats, and then making timely and genuine comments about their complexions, health and sleek coats. This made Leo purr like a big old cat.

I enjoyed teasing him about dying on board and being slowly eaten. The rats' sleek coats came from him feeding them a special diet of sunflower seeds, marijuana heads and cold pressed olive oil with warm pistachio nuts. I was never bad mannered enough to tell him I'd like to feed them on bread and water while eating their tucker, but Leo's world was great for his rats, he loved them dearly and who was I to cast doubt on his most unusual pleasures?

The three vagabonds of the boatyard, Mick, Glenn and Leo genuinely entertained me for months and they became my special family. We shared food and stories and they played chess with me while I told them about the world that they'd love to see but never would. They were caught up in the 50-hour weeks that regular work entails in the USA, with low wages and few holidays and no accommodation other than on their boats.

I installed a Raymarine self-steering unit and with Mike's electronic skills he had it humming like a baby. We took it out for runs and with various adjustments had the self-steering working beautifully so it would keep a straight course in strong winds and when coaxed carefully, could even tack the boat while I worked the cockpit winches. It was so efficient looking and I loved it. It was my first self-steering device and I could see myself happily sailing across the Atlantic hardly touching the helm, reading books and writing along the way, as all other round the world single handers do.

I named the self steerer 'Henry' and I could see a rare bond developing between us. At the end of the voyage I even promised to take Henry off the boat and install him in a place of honour in my shed, to talk to in my old age!

I installed a radar reflector that I had bought at a second-hand marine shop in Annapolis and I also bought a heavy-duty sewing machine that could handle heavy sails, along with a 12-120-volt inverter which worked off the boat batteries to power the beast.

I acquired a new storm jib and a no 2 headsail with big blue stripes and I also installed two more reef points in the mainsail and more blocks along the boom. I put in a dive compressor connected to the motor with an adjustable fan belt, and 100ft of dive hose with regulator attached so that I could do any underwater cleaning and repairs, plus retrieve my anchor if it was fouled in dodgy anchorages.

I changed the rubbers in the hatches, replaced all the sheet lines, serviced all the winches and did much, much, more. I collected 200ft of 3/8 bb tested chain and found a 45lb Bruce anchor that had such a good reputation for digging in and holding well in strong blows.

On *Sundancer* I carried a 120lb Bruce anchor and was so pleased with its performance after always relying on CQR anchors, that I had a hankering for the Bruce. The secret to yacht cruising is one's anchoring gear where anchoring well depends upon the length and weight of chain. Even in a strong blow I've been very comfortable, relying on solid anchoring gear.

I built a stern arch out of plywood and fibreglass on which to install the solar panels and radio antenna. I found a nice 8 ft fibreglass dinghy that I could strap to the deck in front of the mast which I was able to easily lift on and off the deck, with just the low powered winches that I had inherited. There were so many more tasks, like building side and stern covers with my trusty sewing machine and writing our name and port of Hobart in bold letters on them.

I set up steps on the stern lip to make entry to the water much easier, renewed the batteries with an extra bank of two, plus I installed shut-off valves to the motor, renewed the fenders, built heavy duty harnesses with double clips, installed a Dan-buoy, life ring holders, new lee sheets on the bunks and replaced all the halyards and sheet lines with heavier gear. The list was endless.

As my day for departure in early June came around, I was beginning to realise that the excitement of another bold adventure was edging closer.

I was almost on the way again, new horizons, bigger vistas, more exciting chapters to my life.

In the last few weeks of harbour life, Richard, an English sailor, came into the marina with his Hunter 34. He was headed for England via Bermuda and I discovered that we had virtually the same boats, except that his was a little older and more worn. We compared notes, did work for each other when more hands were required, such as going up the mast and re-reeving new halyards.

In mid-may Richard finally sailed for Bermuda telling me he'd send me an email describing the ocean-going ability of his Hunter on this offshore passage, and any other details that would be valuable. I liked the idea of him being my pioneer, checking out the performance of these little used Hunters on the big wide ocean.

The day before he set sail he fortunately took pity on me with my one paper chart of the Atlantic and decided I needed world electronic charts that he could install on my computer, if we could get a Wi-Fi connection. We decided to make it as pleasant an experience as possible, so I suggested that I treat him to a coffee and biscuits at Panera Bread across the river. I also promised to call into Walmart to get him some goodies (chocolates, biscuits, minties etc for his departure).

Just before we left Leo discovered our plans and asked if he could join us for Richard's last party ashore. He climbed in the back amongst the loose boating gear, finding some space to rest his long legs and off we headed to Panera Bread, which was one of our favourite haunts for good value soup and coffee after a hard day's work on the boats.

Leo wasn't actually interested in the coffee or the soup or even the party as on arrival he took off to visit the local pet shop while Richard and I used the store's Wi-Fi code to download the world ocean charts onto my computer.

This was an incredible revelation to me and a real eye opener, showing how cruising navigation had changed since I was last sailing using all those old clumsy paper charts. I had actually cruised the world on one chart once, with smaller charts picked up along the way from other cruisers who would trade their charts for supplies, spare deck gear and rum that we always carried as special treats for folks we met along the way.

As Richard and I were downloading and enjoying our treats, Leo returned and asked for the car keys so he could put his new pet rat purchase in the back. We carried on, having finally finished the download, and were sharing our last good times together. We pored over the electronic charts and Richard gave me lessons in how to set up way points and alarm features that really stretched my abilities with this new electronics chart mode of cruising.

Then the busy world of Panera Bread took a huge turn for the worse and we were in a rising storm so to speak, perplexed and battling for understanding. There was a sudden and almighty loud woman's scream which got our attention immediately, and then we were at the local circus without tickets. A very large African-American lady at the table opposite us and much closer to the door, was frantically screaming as she climbed onto her flimsy plastic table wearing high stiletto heels, reaching high for a trapeze that wasn't there. Her husband cowered in his chair in amazement as her high wire act developed, saying repeatedly "you ok honey buns?" Other women and children also began screaming and instead of climbing onto the tables (which was highly entertaining to us), they began heading for the doors, all fanning out from that one table near the door through the exits, in seemingly slow motion, with upbeat Panera music playing gently in the background.

Pandemonium was breaking out, a hurricane was going through the place and chairs were being thrown left, right and centre.

My innocent gaze was suddenly directed to the floor where the trouble had first started and there I spotted Leo on his hands and knees, desperately trying to grab a big, black, furry runaway rat that had suddenly leapt out of his hands onto the lady's table, causing that huge meltdown. He finally headed for our table with a bright red face, explaining that his new friend Herbert wasn't happy in the van all alone. Leo had been so kind as to bring him in to keep the peace and the little bugger had wriggled out of his hands.

All eyes were on us, we had become terrorists by association and before Leo could even sit down with his precious Herbert clutched tightly in his hands, the security detail arrived and we were bundled out without even paying – bonus!!

I guess in the end we were in front, but following that disaster I didn't return to Panera Bread just in case my face was on one of their blacklists as a possible rioter.

The next day Richard sailed and I patiently waited for news.

Two weeks later when he reached Bermuda he sent me an email saying how well his Hunter had handled the challenging weather. He had copped one severe storm and she had ridden it well. I was really pleased to have been assured that I had also randomly chosen such a strong little boat in which to cross the Atlantic.

The mechanics of sailing and crossing oceans weren't any real concern to me now that Richard had given his blessing to my enterprise, and I felt quite relieved that fate had treated me gently so far.

I'd done enough oceaning, although not of late, where the bigger picture was of more interest than the day-to-day mechanics of sailing and navigating.

The relationship between me and the Atlantic, between me and the big ships, between me and the fickle weather and all those things that can't be measured, like the beauty of the ocean, the speed of weather changes, the prevailing breezes, the cold water and how that would reflect off me, was embedded in all the turmoil that was about to begin.

This was the part I needed to explore, acknowledging that we don't so much have experiences but rather, experiences "have us", and how we react to those small moments of intense change, is how we are in all aspects of our life. I was here to do a little stretching, to let go of the last 8 years of rock-solid land and castle building and to reach out for the numinous parts of myself, hopefully experiencing the wisdom of another of Leo's t-shirts that said "regular exposure to awe transforms us."

All the preparations for crossing the Atlantic alone were now done. Mike said to me in those last few days "what if you found a lover in this town who was fantastic and everything you could imagine, would you still leave?" and I said truthfully," if I had to choose between love and freedom then freedom would win hands down." He understood.

The biggest dangers out there on the ocean weren't getting lost or swamped by rogue waves or sharks but by "big blind ships" that regularly rage across the ocean on auto pilot, oblivious to any small sail boat without crew, who can't keep watch 24 hours per day. Size counts especially on the ocean and I would have to sleep a few hours a day without any aids except the puny radar reflector. I'd have to put my faith in the lap of the gods as well as place my security and well-being within myself, regardless of the circumstances.

This is where I trusted that "bigger fella" within to show his hand and I had to happily deal with the cards of fate as they were played.

I was like that old classic cowboy, riding out of town with a packhorse, ready to cross the wide-open desert where "bulldozer ships" raged, sleeping out along the way, avoiding dangers and lack of fresh water, till I finally rode into a new town, with the only compensation being that I was slightly richer for the experience.

The last few weeks in the Solomons were especially hectic, getting in supplies, changing fuel filters, looking at the weather charts and repairing Hal's dodger cover. He often visited to wish me well and swap some of the stories of his long, adventurous military life. After surviving the wars of Korea and Vietnam whilst in the air force, and then getting a plum job in industry, he'd retired onto his smart cruiser, travelling alone all around the Chesapeake Bay area fishing and being free.

His "plum job" came from industry that apparently owed the air force special favours after the UFO Roswell incident. Roswell occurred when a UFO was apparently brought down by radar within the Roswell, New Mexico, military area in 1947, with some saying it was a conspiracy and others saying it was real.

After leaving Las Vegas in 1995 I visited Roswell through sheer curiosity, whilst crossing the States from Boston to Los Angeles, and saw the monument there that said, "we don't know who they were, we don't know why they came, we only know they changed our universe." I was intrigued as I had never placed much faith in conspiracy theories and Hal was about to give me a story that was hard to fit into reality.

After the Roswell incident Hal said that captains of industry apparently had access to the materials that had been recovered, which they reverse-engineered and patented without costs. He said that many aspects of the American economy boomed in the 1960's and 1970's from this extraordinary hand-up technological event, that some say occurred and others say was a hoax.

I was curious as Hal seemed a well-balanced and straight guy with lots of wisdom and concern about the environment and political issues. I asked him to explain as I'd never met anyone who had direct evidence of Roswell and this was his story.

Hal said that he was at an air force base, one down the line from Roswell and the things that were found at the crash site were split between the army and the air force with the recovered material then sent to be inventoried and stored.

One object that drew his interest was a burnt-out junction box with many wires emerging from a central core that, on closer inspection did not use wires as expected, but glass as light filaments. This was apparently reverse-engineered to produce what we now know as high-speed glass data cables (optical fibre). Hal talked for an hour or more about Roswell and there was no doubt he was an observer and a true believer.

Sometimes fact is stranger than fiction and I came away with a new-found belief that Roswell probably did occur and has been covered up ever since. Hal was given that fine job in industry that had set him up for the rest of his life. After all, he had that expensive cruiser and a lifestyle to prove it.

He had a lovely old classic cruiser that needed some specialised work on the dodger top so we did an interesting swap - my labour for free and his story. I'm not sure who gained the most from that friendship.

Chapter 5

Leaving the Chesapeake

It's Saturday morning and tomorrow I'm leaving for Norfolk, Virginia where I can clear the country as my 90-day visa expires in a few days. Norfolk is about 50 miles south of the Solomons at the bottom of Chesapeake Bay and will take a couple of day sails to get there.

Mike comes around to help me clean the hull along with the old owners of the boat. We finish at midday and they take me out for my last meal before I head off. I don't eat much as I like to begin a voyage on an empty stomach. It helps me to adjust to the changing rhythms of life on the ocean and frankly I hate throwing up as it's the closest feeling to dying that I know, and I've been close to dying a few times.

I sleep well on Saturday night knowing that those long lists have been reduced down and there's not a lot I can do now. I would have liked to have replaced the roller furling gear but it's a luxury that I'll do without and since I've never had furling gear before, I'll just make do.

Sunday morning dawns and I'm up early sorting out the sail bags, stowing the gear I won't be needing for a long while and washing down the decks. Mike and Glenn arrive in their runabout and Mike gives me some boxes of food that he says he doesn't need, which includes cans of potatoes, tuna, pork and beans - it's a very kind gesture. I stow them below thinking I won't be needing these as I intend to eat little on the trip across to the Azores, beginning with a 10 day fast that will clean me out and get me in the mood for some of the challenges I know I will face.

Mike also brings me some whisky and a couple of joints but I politely decline explaining that I need to be totally focussed and these so-called 'goodies' could be a fatal distraction. The boys help me untie my lines, and I wave goodbye to Leo and the yard staff and head out of the harbour turning south for Norfolk where I'll finally clear land.

I set the self-steering, increase my motor revs and motor south with Mike and Glenn waving wildly from their boat. They then head back to the harbour. I'm finally alone, apprehensive and nervous, but excited to be off. Hooray!!

I've completed those 3 months of preparations, they're behind me and I can get on with the bigger task of getting this Hunter across the Atlantic. It's a hot and sultry Sunday and there are a few indications of a later westerly breeze running out of the Patuxent river. The Chesapeake Bay is huge and Norfolk, which is home to a huge American naval fleet, is 50 miles further down the bottom of the bay. I doubt whether I'll get there before tomorrow, particularly as I get an early adverse southerly breeze that means I'm doing little more than 3 knots over the ground. I set the self-steerer to clear another point ahead and decide to go below and have a quick tidy up.

After 15 minutes things don't feel quite right so I come back on deck to find I'm heading straight for a runabout with the owner sitting in a deck chair fishing, completely unaware that I'm about to cut him down. I quickly release the self-steering arm and steer around him reminding myself that the self-steerer could be a real danger in this crowded waterway.

I continue to head south and at early evening I anchor in the mouth of the Potomac river, eager to make a cup of tea, have a light sandwich snack and take a long sleep, after feeling that wonderful freedom of escaping from suburbia.

Early Monday morning I'm cautiously off again with a light westerly running out of the river. I soon realise that there are shoals all the way along the western shore and I need to take care to stay in the marked channels. The flies are bad as the day heats up and they do something I've never encountered before - the ferocious buggers bite and come back for more and more. I kill 100, and 200 replace them so I have to cover up to escape their wrath as they leave blood spots all over my exposed skin.

I'm motor-sailing slowly, carefully, chasing channel markers and then I unexpectedly run aground on a corner shoal, that's well outside the markers. I have to run out the anchor abeam after launching the dinghy, and then attach the halyard to the anchor chain and heel *Millefleurs* over to get off. I retrieve the anchoring gear which is covered in sticky black mud and spend another 20 minutes washing down the deck whilst towing the dinghy behind and fighting off those pesky flies. I realise I may not even make Norfolk by this evening as the tide is falling fast, pushing me further out into the main channel, while I attempt to sail on a light westerly southward.

I finally start the motor and chug along but it overheats and I'm forced to return to sailing. The motor obviously needs attention and I pray that I don't have to do any serious repairs before I leave the USA. I sail on and eventually at 2100 hrs find an anchorage outside the main Norfolk harbour where I can rest for the night. There are lights all around and plenty of craft moving about but I sleep well with the anchor light on and the dinghy trailing astern.

The sun rises and I begin searching for the cause of the motor overheating and discover a blocked water trap that has filled with Chesapeake weed. Thank goodness the remedy was easy and I motor slowly into the small boat anchorage on the north side of Norfolk where other cruising boats are anchored and I drop the pick. It's my first 2 day sail for years and I feel relieved that I've ironed out a few bugs, discovered more about the self-steering and practised a little sailing, realising *Millefleurs* needs more breeze than expected to get her to roll along sweetly.

Tomorrow will be another busy day trying to find a replacement for the GPS that doesn't seem to work and is currently giving me positions that are up to 40 miles out. I wish I had Mike's electronics skills available to check out why this GPS is so out of whack.

I go into the coastal town of Newport News and walk what seems to be about 5 miles to a marine store where I buy myself a new GPS and another gallon of methylated spirits that I definitely need for the trip, to feed the hungry spirit stove.

The whole exercise takes most of the day and on my return, I chat to the other cruisers around who seem to favour this anchorage before they enter the inter-coastal waterway that runs all the way south to Florida. None of them are going offshore, although a few are heading for the Bahamas when they get far enough south in Florida to bolt across the gulf stream. They all advise me to stay in the gulf stream until I get level with New York if the breeze is southerly, and then head east, but none have ever heard of anyone going to the Azores, way out in the middle of the north Atlantic. They wish me luck and I head back to tidy up, have a light snack, clear customs via radio, install the new GPS and get ready for the big day, Tuesday 4th June when I'm heading offshore - hell that's tomorrow!!

Chapter 6

Joining the gulf stream North

It's early morning, 5th June, 2007 and I am setting off from Norfolk, Virginia to sail east across the Atlantic to Europe. I am excited, apprehensive and even a little scared to be heading out into the big wide, cold North Atlantic Ocean alone. I've hardly slept with the worries of this new adventure, and I've been wide awake since 0300hrs waiting for first morning light to get me up and going. I want to get out into the ocean, want to figure out the peculiarities of my newly acquired 23-year-old 34ft Hunter yacht, *Millefleurs*, and more importantly, I want to get some sea miles under my belt and settle into a steady ocean rhythm, while the weather is still settled. The day is bright and sunny and there is a light southerly breeze with a clear blue sky.

I call the kids back in Australia with the last of my phone credit and tell them that I am finally off after 90 days in the USA, getting this yacht show on the road and that I'd be out of contact for at least a month, till I arrive in the Azores, a group of Portuguese Islands, three quarters of the way across the Atlantic.

They wish me well as they are used to me heading off into the wild blue yonder with few plans. It's nice to say goodbye to them somehow, showing I still have the adventurer in me, but I shed a few tears for the lost years they've had with me away ocean sailing, particularly when they were young, with absences of up to two years.

Both are at university in Melbourne, Australia. Caroline is just beginning her Psychology degree and Cameron has completed his Medical degree.

I hope the greys of adulthood will gradually replace the black and white judgements of their youth when I left their mum for more crazy adventures. I ask them to pass on my departure details to my mother and other close friends, as my phone credit is almost gone.

My last few dollars are spent on calling Kaye, my partner back in Tasmania, and arranging to meet her in Lisbon in three months' time.

Then an unexpected call comes in. It's Hal, one of those intriguing characters who live around waterfronts, and he's claiming to be from the Inland Revenue Office, wanting to know whether I have paid my US boat tax!! I recognise his mischievous voice and we laugh along until we run out of things to say. I turn off the phone and put it away. I guess I won't be needing it for quite a while.

I pass some huge warships at the entrance to the Norfolk Bay and the gigantic size of US Naval forces becomes obvious. They seem to have vessels of all sizes with helicopters and fast boats anchored everywhere on my starboard side while filling the airwaves with military chatter. As I exit the bay and head out into the gulf stream I see two yachts ahead of me who are also heading north.

Now is the moment of reality, keep going or turn back and find an excuse for calling it quits. They say a man can pretend to be lots of things in this world but he can only pretend to be a sailor for as long as it takes to clear that lonely harbour entrance.

Now I have to stop pretending and get out into the real world of being an oceaner again, letting go of all the conveniences of the familiar shore, cutting those ties that bind us all to solid earth, for the insecure turbulence of an ever-changing ocean.

I radio those yachties ahead who are also "not pretending" and discover they are two Canadians sailing in company and heading north, going home after a season's cruising in the Bahamas. They advise me to keep in the gulf stream while the southerly breeze is blowing and roll north with them, but to cross it if a northerly breeze flows down, as it'll kick up into a wind against current situation, and possibly get really nasty.

We chat about our journeys and match each other's speed - three yachts going north. It feels good having others for company, particularly as I'm just beginning to feel my sea legs and am full of excitement, bravado and bonhomie. And then the unusual happens, which quickly settles any butterflies that I had in my stomach.

The US Navy puts out a radio warning that all vessels within a certain radius seaward of Norfolk Harbour must clear the area within the next hour, as there will be live firing practise. I check the chart and discover that that's where we all are. I call the Canadians on the radio and they are just as outraged as I am. I call the US Navy back and tell them the bad news, but they ignore my call and continue to issue a live firing warning in our area - and we're right in the middle of it now.

I again warn them of the impending drama and add menace to it by threatening them with the wrath of Crocodile Dundee, telling them that he'll come and "piss in their gumboots and bury them in cocky shit" if they continue being stupid, and then I add that if they're about to create an international incident, their commander will be going to Guantanamo Bay, in an orange jumpsuit with no lifejacket! Then I tell them to stick that in their "pipe and smoke it", all in good Aussie humour, of course. I may sound crazy but it helps when dealing with authorities as Paul Hogan showed.

That seems to get their attention. No point risking an international incident with a crazy Oz, so wisely they change their co-ordinates. I'm relieved and make a cup of tea, with Henry my new self-steering device holding a steady course as we roll happily northwards.

The Canadians cheer my bravado and we sail in company steadily heading northwards at 4 knots. With the current we are doing 5.5 knots over the ground…yes, we're really moving and it adds lustre to an already fine day.

We laugh on the radio as the US navy changes its co-ordinates further to the east. I feel kind of powerful after sticking it to the US Navy and it bolsters my confidence in my ability to come out here and deal with whatever emerges. It can't be as troublesome as a band of naval personnel who live in big ships with macho images, but have never sailed a real boat before and then threatening to chase us out of their chosen territory. David has just slain Goliath and the Canadians are impressed.

My new GPS works well with constant speed readouts in either knots or miles per hour which amuses me. Henry steers happily away as I sit in the cockpit surveying my world and declaring there is no place I'd rather be than right here, with these great Canadian mates.

After hoisting a bigger headsail I've been slowly overtaking them and we cover lots of miles of friendship and fun as we roll together up the US east coast, talking regularly about the types of boat we have had and their peculiarities and the joys of the cruising lifestyle. I'm just learning about this Hunter so I take a backseat and they feed me hometown advice about the Hunter yachts, as there are many in the Canadian lakes.

That night I slip ahead of them and soon their masthead lights dip behind me as I turn off my navigation lights and keep watch to save power, contentedly rolling up the USA east coast and gradually working offshore, listening to the quiet murmur of the ocean and the splash of waves on the stern till I lose sight of all land lights.

This is the offshore sailor's boilerplate, go wide at night, increase the rig forward while sailing downhill and steer by the stars. The water is warm in the gulf stream and I sit on watch enjoying all the stars, logging my position regularly on my one paper chart and letting Henry my self-steerer whirr away, making at least 40 corrections every minute. That's either his coded tactics or else *Millefleurs* needs lots of attention on the helm. Her underwater profile with her rudder so far aft allows her to alter direction quickly, meaning she is very flighty on the helm, just like any racing yacht. That's not really what I wanted, but it's what I have, and I'm sure that running down seas means constant helming, but she won't broach easily, which is the real bonus.

Over the next three days I settle into a rhythm where I sleep a few hours during the day and doze in the cockpit at night. There's something about oceaning that strikes my tuning fork, making me hum within, going places, on the move, heading out, feeling vital with self-acceptance and deeper meanings.

They say that sailing alone around the world is the largest non-religious pilgrimage, far bigger than those who want to climb Mount Everest and I concur.

Henry my new helmsman steers much better when I shorten back the rig and stay near 4 knots. The best rig seems to be a reefed main and a bigger jib with the main acting more as a fin, while the jib does the real work. If I sail with a bigger main any gusts of wind cause immediate weather helm and she begins to round up and then Henry cannot hold course. I'm finding Henry may be good in the harbour but he's not really suited to ocean sailing as he doesn't have the muscle.

I worry about the amount of power that he uses, as the batteries seem to go down to less than 12 volts overnight, even though the solar panels are topping them up throughout the day. To counteract this, I begin turning him off and helming manually through half the night, just to ease the load on his little motor and keep the batteries loaded.

I see lots of ships and at night turn my lights on as we pass. I radio a few to check on the weather but none respond, which means they are not listening on channel 16, or they're ignoring a puny yacht that is just a nuisance to their importance and size. One ship does answer as the radio operator, who is from New Zealand, recognises my accent.

He tells me he can't see me on the radar and he's only about 3 miles away, which effectively means the radar reflector is fairly useless where it is set up on the backstay. He also tells me a blow is coming from the south as there is a deep low pressure building near the Bahamas, and strangely it cheers me as a blow will send me north east and further out along the gulf stream, which is just great for my early progress.

During the day I "sail short" to keep Henry happy as the wind slowly increases to 15 knots and I read a book on quantum physics that seems to be a better explanation for our mental reality. It explains collective reality and how you can take a cheek cell from one country to the other side of the world and connect it to a resistance meter.

The owner of that cheek cell has an emotional reaction back home and the cheek cell, 15,000 miles away, responds instantly. The spookiness of it all introduces the mystery of how we are all connected to each other, somehow explaining the old idea of being each other's keepers. I feel the connection to my kids in the same way and it gives me encouragement that I'm not really out here all alone.

My big failure before setting out is now obvious. I should have replaced the roller furling gear as it won't roll at all and the sails do not seem to enjoy sliding up and down the furl. Maybe the furl is too small for the sail guides and as they get wet and salty the challenges increase for a quick sail change, even with lots of lubricant on the furl.

The other problem is that the drum won't roll properly and the furl doesn't furl at all, meaning I have to hoist and drop sails manually rather than wind them in and out. That means I have to exit the cockpit, leave the helm unattended, hoist the sails and then run back to adjust them while keeping *Millefleurs* balanced at the same time. It's a constant challenge that's not going away easily.

It's the one thing I can't fix and something that I couldn't predict, and reminds me that I am never in control of all possibilities. Its working around the unforeseen that makes life interesting, its the mystery of how I'm going to have to cope with the head sail dilemma, that could turn this journey into a difficult life's saga, particularly in any blow.

I'm beginning to flow with the wind and the current and dance to the ocean's music while life ashore now seems so far away. I'm beginning to feel the deeper blue ocean finally breathe through me. I'm averaging 130 miles per day which is great for this little sail boat. Of course, the gulf stream is adding an extra 40 miles per day and I'm rolling north east into the stronger westerlies that will hopefully get me across the Atlantic at around 40 degrees north. Well, that's the plan and the advice from those who've never been out here before.

I guess that after I fall out of the gulf stream current I'll just plod slowly eastwards trying to find a sweet spot that is out of the shipping lanes, balanced between the warmer summer winds south and the colder westerlies up north. The rig I have with the bigger head sails suits that warmer southerly route, but who knows what the weather patterns will bring this year?

I'm loving the early morning hours with the light south westerly breeze and slight swell and the sun booming in from the east, directly off the bow. With Henry steering on medium adjustment I'm able to sit on the bow naked in the sun and the fresh air, practising stopping all that inner mental talk that takes up so much bandwidth, feeling like a free man again moving away from a constantly chattering world.

There's no one out here to talk to so my mind talks to me, sometimes out loud, as it knows no one is listening. It's only when I stop pottering around and take stock of my situation do I realise my talkative-self wants to chatter all day and even long into the night. There seems to be two of us jammed together and then others as well, and sometimes I feel like I have to slip out to the restroom to avoid the noisiness around the table.

Sometimes I'm not sure who I am anymore in some peculiar way as my boundaries are getting softer. The singular has become plural then multiples and sometimes I feel I'm bursting apart at the seams with possibilities. I'm secure within the two dominant faces of Eve though, as there's the one that stands back and observes and the other that gets busy, running around trying to be ahead of time, wanting to be fed, needing someone to talk to and complaining about the things I am missing.

Sometimes I ponder whether I should pass myself a note for which day I'll be me and which day I'll be the other. I've talked to others who have also gone into isolation and they report the same phenomena, where the same quirkiness emerges.

They say travelling alone often becomes a pilgrimage where we pass through the me to find the I which has all of the substance we seek. I don't feel disorientated or schizophrenic or lost, but rather challenged as I seek a newer perspective to the changes that are occurring daily, as more lost personas want to emerge and offer their advice.

My stomach seems to be attached to my well-being in particular, and since I've decided as usual to not eat for the first few days of the trip (so I don't get sea-sick and can settle into the rhythm of the ocean easier), I'm constantly considering all the food I'm missing and all the delights I could be having. Occasionally I even get the smell of fried bacon and buttered toast and even freshly brewed coffee in the gulf stream breeze that must come from my longing for cafes and bars that I've left behind, and I salivate long and hard and question the journey!

Another discovery is the lucidity of my dreams. Without food there is a lightness to my body and mind that is palpable, and I literally seem to float around the deck and have amazingly vivid dreams on quite bizarre themes. This morning for example I awoke from a dream where I was sailing *Sundancer*, one of my previous boats, across a big grassy paddock without any water underneath us. I came alongside a road with power lines and fences, but we sailed on beside them for a time, with me wondering how the ground kept opening up for the keel, while I constantly adjusted sails to keep us from sagging into the power lines.

I was concerned as I gazed skywards what could happen if the wind died and we fell into those threatening lines. It was a genuinely perplexing situation. I was inside the dream as well as watching from the outside, and recognising both states of awareness.

Then we were in a large shed with the keel of *Sundancer* lying on its side next to the boat and I was repairing a leak. I knew I needed a welder and just then the farmer who owned the shed appeared and casually said he'd get me a welder and some welding rods, and off he went. Then I realised that I was still in the dream and the shed was just part of the sideshow, even if it looked old fashioned with all sorts of old farming gear hanging on the walls, familiar to my youth.

I realised too that if I told the farmer this was a dream, he wouldn't bring the welder, and I had to hold that secret from him, had to keep him in the dark so he'd continue to help me.

It didn't seem quite right but then I shot out of the shed, waking up in my bunk, relieved to be away from a keel that needed careful repairing. These are apparently called hypogenic dreams where you suddenly realise you are dreaming and then wake up. They're another level of dreaming where some people report receiving formulae like Einstein's amazing E=MC squared, or you get the phone number of someone you need to contact.

I'd had these before and wondered at their meaning or perhaps it was just elevated awareness, due to my being on the food fast and away from normal reality. Often on previous sailing trips I'd go on fasts for a few days to get me used to the ocean and the benefits that brought were invaluable as they turned each voyage into another level of living where I rarely felt sick and where I lived a little outside normal reality. Of course, I never said anything, lest the new crew think I was a little odd.

I remember on one occasion when we were becalmed a few days out of port I was able to dive under the boat and stay down for at least 4 minutes, which I had never been able to do before. The fasting gave me that extra energy which obviously came from somehow connecting to bigger forces around. I was tempted to put out the new fishing lure, but then remembered I didn't need any fish and it would involve bringing in the Jesus rope that I trailed behind the boat as my lifeline in case I fell overboard. The Jesus rope was 100 feet long with 13 knots in it - the first 12 were for all the apostles and the last for 'by Jesus that was lucky'. It came from old habits where I always streamed a Jesus rope on all of my past voyages.

I am again finding that ocean sailing is definitely the one thing that brings me closest to myself and I find that when one is immersed in the gentleness of the mother ocean and the mentality of navigating and running a sailing vessel, one has to balance those two natures we all hold within. It is an environment filled with full-on Doing, quietly balanced with the timeless qualities of just Being, which makes ocean passaging quite addictive.

Sailing across oceans was also my personal lesson in learning to be comfortable within my own turbulence as a deeper source of contentment and creativity, where the wholeness of a completed voyage became an amazing experience in sheer wild, carefree living that you never found on shore. As Mark Twain said "a man cannot be comfortable without his own approval" and here I am standing on the deck of *Millefleurs* 12 years after I had last sailed, re-remembering all those things I had long practised.

And then I somehow realised I may not be out here to discover more about sailing and the things I know, but rather to learn more about the things I don't know…the workings of a man's mind when he is devoid of conversational inputs, when he is cut off from humanity as his source and when he is on a hard fast. Does he open up to the infinite? Does he embrace the bigger picture of life or does he continue to ask questions when there is no one to answer? Is he like a writer without a dictionary, without reference points, that connects him to some other cleaner reality? And do those 40 days and nights in the desert really send us deeper into ourselves, searching for our own infinity that has surely been with us forever? And is loneliness our greatest enemy or best friend? Does it help us appreciate what we still have in becoming more self-reliant, in battling our insecurities and growing into ourselves?

These are the answers I seem to be here to find, as I sail on the edge across this wide Atlantic.

In the evening I sleep from 1600 to 1700 hrs and then stand watch from 1700 to 2400 hrs, after which I again sleep for an hour. Henry is steering beautifully and the various ships that pass all seemed to be heading west, going from Europe to the States.

Obviously, I am nearing the northerly shipping lanes as ships pass port to port as they go west, so there has to be another shipping lane south of me.

I am getting comfortable with the light south westerly breeze now that has driven me up the gulf stream and I am still in that same gulf stream heading east at about 5 knots over the ground. I have just come on deck after my midnight sleep and am quite shocked to see a ship not more than a quarter of a mile away, crossing my bow.

I've always believed that I'd hear a ship's propeller noise before it could run me down, and even further, I believed I had an inner sixth sense for dangers at sea, yet here I am confronted with the brutal truth, I wasn't as intuitive as I believed. Another 10 minutes of sailing would have put me in front of that ship and it would have all been over. This trip is definitely a solid springboard to get me back into oceaning again and that was definitely a rude shock.

I call the ship on the radio and the operator answers immediately, saying he is heading for Canada. I discover that I am invisible to his radar as well. I turn on my masthead lights but he can't see them either, even with binoculars. He motors on and I gingerly head north-east feeling particularly vulnerable and if I could call someone, anyone, right now and have them join me for the next few weeks after that surprise, then I'd take that "security option" in a heartbeat. This sailing alone in shipping lanes is a real recipe for disaster and my senses aren't anywhere nearly as sharp as I had believed. I go below and log my position.

The GPS puts me 180 miles east of the coast and 400 miles out of Norfolk Va. I am level with New York and am holding the gulf stream that is obviously heading north easterly by now as it curls eastward to head further out into the Atlantic.

I intend to sail on this angle till the gulf stream runs out and then probably head south east to get down to warmer climates with steadier winds. Now I am at 39 degrees 20 north latitude and 73 degrees 50 west.

I put on track pants and a jumper, fit the wet weather gear over the top and sit in the cockpit with a cup of tea to keep watch. I'd like to have changed headsails for the bigger no. 2 jib, but that can wait till morning as this breeze promises to stay light.

During the night I see 5 ships all going westwards but well north of me and I figure I will probably be between shipping lanes for a few days yet. As the sun rises on a greyish day with lots of heavy clouds south of me and the sky streaked with orange and red coloured higher clouds, I can feel something odd in the air.

There is a definite change of weather somewhere, and I hope it isn't a northerly breeze that will soon kick up a lot of sea action, as it begins running against the equatorial gulf current. I place a tuck in the mainsail just in case any change comes through quickly and Henry becomes overpowered.

My boat speed drops to 3.7 knots through the water but 4.5 knots over the ground which seems prudent. I certainly have plenty of sea room out here and any dangers will come from ships, till I get out far enough to clear the shipping lanes.

I'm not sure that coming up the gulf stream was so smart now as it has embedded me in these packed ship's lanes, whereas heading directly out of Norfolk VA and crossing the gulf stream, would have had me on a free run to the Azores and that would have been slightly shorter, but with no help from the gulf stream.

Perhaps I shouldn't have listened to those Canadians following the gulf stream this far north, as the free ride north has turned into one of constant vigilance and worry, which is not the ideal start for any long voyage.

Chapter 7

Settling in to the Atlantic

I've been vanging the main boom with two preventers to stop it from banging about in the lighter breezes. The cockpit dodger, where I've sewn extra flaps down the aft side, blocks the colder breezes now, but will be a great asset later, providing much needed shade when the hot summer rolls in. With Henry steering I can stand in the lee of the stern archway and keep watch - out of the cold breezes and I can even sit on the spare water container aft and relax as we roll along.

For the whole day the weather is heavy and ominous but we seem to be in our own little breeze, with lots of sea birds wheeling around chasing fish, splashing into the water in a frenzy. I check the voltage on the batteries and find that it's above 12.9 indicating that the solar panel is working well, even in overcast conditions. I sleep from 1600 till 1700 hrs and arise without any ships around, realising that I'm very hungry.

Even though it is only 4 days into the voyage I still have to shake off those "sugar blues" that are hitting me regularly, particularly near meal times.

I sail into the night keeping watch and slowly settling into this newer ocean rhythm. I listen to the wind, there's music in it too that I've missed these past years. It's a slower beat to living on land, softer, quieter, deeper, way down in the soul somewhere, hiding down there below the whale's song, below the wave's song, deep and low, resonating only to the universe above.

A ship passes at 2300 hours, no more than 2 miles north of me. When I call him on the radio on high power he answers almost immediately, perhaps indicating that the low power setting isn't working. I discover that he is from the Philippines and the ship is registered in the Cayman Islands, carrying containers from Holland to the USA - now that's a complicated arrangement.

He tells me that there is a deep low pressure in the Bahamas heading back towards the US coast and there are Hurricane Barry warnings out for Florida. That's a worry but I decide we are too far north, at least 400 miles away so it shouldn't worry us for the next few days. Hopefully the skies will clear and Barry will go inland and dissipate. We close contact, wishing each other bon voyage and contact is lost.

I'm alone again ready to keep watch and head eastwards at my lazy 4 knots while the ship motors away at 16 knots. His bright stern lights soon disappear over the horizon reminding me of my aloneness.

It's unusual to get a hurricane this early in the summer season which means that there must be a lot of very warm water down in the Caribbean and perhaps I don't need to go below 36 degrees to keep warm on this trip.

I sail on, musing on my youth when my family was very poor living back in the bush in Tasmania. I guess the complexity of our youth is hard to underestimate as its effects echo throughout our lifetime. For me it was freedom and the desire to explore the mysteries that the old guys talked about experiencing during their war service overseas. When I think back on my past I know that I was fortunate in being allowed to enjoy a great deal of freedom, spending my time fishing, hunting and wandering wild around the Roger River valley in north western Tasmania. My stepfather was a bushman who really enjoyed his fishing and we hunted twice a week with a spotlight after dark to catch wallabies or rabbits for meat to supplement the vegetables which we grew. Once a month my mother, stepfather and I went to town which seemed to be such a long way away, but, in reality was only 12 miles on the bus.

I only met my birth father, Peter when I was 37 years of age. He was a retired police prosecutor from Melbourne who had had an affair with mum who was working in the city at the time.

The relationship ended and mum boldly refused to live in Melbourne, so we went back to Tasmania where I lived with my grandmother in the bush until I was 5 years of age. Mum continued to work as a reluctant domestic for various families in the district. She never talked about Peter or offered any suggestions for us to connect, even though he had paid maintenance for me until I was 16.

When we met for the first time in 1987 at the Melbourne docks, there was no emotion, just a friendly handshake and the words "follow me home and we'll have a cuppa!" I remarked to Peter after the few days we spent together that I had had a great life, with no regrets and I was pleased that I'd lived in the bush rather than the city, when I was growing up. He understood and we shared 12 years of constant happy communications until he died in 2000.

In Roger River we grew most of our own food and milked cows, with my favourite treat being scones with raspberry jam and clotted cream. The cream was skimmed off the top of the milk and was thick and sweet. Whenever I travel I now look for Devonshire teas with cappuccino. Scones are hard to find in most countries but if I ever set up a business it'll be Devonshire teas served in a coffee house. I may not do well, moneywise, but I'll always enjoy my work.

In Roger River our entertainment was generally provided by the neighbours who came to visit often, bringing their stories with them. The adults were all storytellers and since we lived very simply with no radio, refrigerator or stove we valued the simple tales that were told of going to war, being regularly flooded out or travelling across Bass Strait to visit the big city of Melbourne in the state of Victoria,

The most exciting event of the year was when the circus came to town. We would all travel in, enjoy the carnival with the usual colourful clowns and the performing animals and wonder at the amazing things out there in the big wide world.

We'd take the tent and sleep overnight on the riverbank under a tarpaulin, before heading home the next day.

The river itself was our lifeblood as it flowed through the valley and provided life for all the dairy farms and fishing adventures and the forests. My friends and I made rafts to float down the river and in summer we swam in its cold waters and had picnics on the sandy banks. We searched for freshwater crayfish, climbed the big old gum trees and stayed up there for hours, imagining living amongst the trees like monkeys. When the river flooded in winter the waters lapped the houses and we stayed home from school for days, while the native hens would howl all night in delight.

Life was great for me living in the bush in Tasmania in the 1950s. I felt that I was living in the safest place in the world.

Chapter 8

Hurricane Barry

I have plenty of sea room now and I've settled in for the long haul, so the thought of severe weather possibly arriving doesn't seem to worry me a great deal. The major problem will be sailing in reduced visibility whilst trying to spot ships in time. To improve my chances, I begin to angle more to the south-east to get a better angle on the south-west winds and to move away from those northerly shipping lanes. Thoughts of land and friends have diminished and it seems ages since I left, but I wouldn't trade positions with anyone, I'm enjoying the journey.

Sailing, like surfing is self-expression, a release from land-locked pressures, a chance to be fully flexible again. The ocean is our strongest natural force on the planet and affects us all, with a large percentage of people wanting to live close by the sea. We have evolved from the ocean as our blood is similar in concentration to sea water and we develop flippers before fingers in utero. On the ocean we're recharging our solar batteries and taking on another more primal rhythm that is intensely satisfying. We're all solar powered, so when we put ourselves back in that mix we feel strangely alive and energised and connected to the earth spirit again, much like the Aboriginal tribes of the world.

My biggest test now is my growing impatience with the headsail raising problems so I carry some Vaseline in my wet weather gear pocket. Each time I go forward to raise the jib I apply more lubricant to the track and it seems to help. As the sun rises and I'm well clear of land I can see heavy cloud banks around us and I ponder that this may be the spoils coming off Barry even though he is well south. The wind begins to gust through and as the day gets longer I decide to reef down the main and clip on the storm jib, leaving it in its bag, tied to the bow of the upturned dinghy ready for immediate use.

I increase the lashings on the dinghy and stuff rags into the anchor chain pipe after removing the chain from the anchor and taking it aft to strap to the push-pit. That makes the bow free of any gear that could cause trouble and I feel comfortable knowing I'm prepared for any sudden deterioration in the weather.

The wind slowly gusts to 20 knots and I reef the main down to less than half size. We're still rolling along at a steady 4 knots to the south east and appear to have left the gulf stream as our speed over the ground becomes the same as the logged speed. The swells are increasing from the south-west and there is no doubt that things are going to get worse. Rain showers come through regularly and I lose visibility for longer periods of time, as the heavy rain lashes *Millefleurs* and it's really cold as well. The sky is gun metal grey and it warns me of what is about to come.

This change in the weather is becoming a serious concern and I worry about losing visibility and approaching ships. I put on two sets of wet weather gear and tie the hoods tightly together and put some sail tie lashings around my wrists to keep the water from running up my arms, as I helm along. Henry has reached his limits and refuses to keep us tracking without loud screaming and clacking noises as the clutch begins to slip. It's disconcerting but I'm sure there must be some adjustment to the clutch that I can make as there isn't much rudder pressure as I can easily steer with just two fingers. There's nowhere to hide out here if it does blow up. I'm not measuring waves in size anymore but I'm seriously concerned.

I'm on my own and I am imagining having a new idea for sailors - an inflatable cliff to hide behind. I could let it float in the water to windward so that I could tie my bow on to it and hide in the lee till the storm is over. The idea is fun, but the logistics are difficult and it reflects on my rising concern about where this blow is going.

This is the biggest difference between the land and he sea. On land there is always a tree or a cliff or a building to hide behind when the wind gusts and the spray flies, but here it's like sitting in a plastic chair, naked, in the middle of an empty roadway trying to stay dry.

"When the sea roars like a pack of hungry lions, and the wind howls like the sound of the living dead who amongst us are warriors?" said the English writer of the 1800s, William Hazlett.

I'm certainly not a warrior at this moment, I'm just a survivor doing my best to stay strong and I feel the apprehension rising about what I should do to get ready for the next few days. Sitting here in my precarious prison with the cold seeping into my bones I realise my thoughts could become my worst enemy as I've suffered wild storms many times around Cape Horn or in Bass Strait or the Bay of Biscay, but never a hurricane, where the winds could get well over 80 knots for long periods of time.

Being tropical heat driven, rather than by the cold of higher latitudes, means that this blow could flow right up the warm gulf stream and even though I'll miss the eye of the storm, as it heads back towards land, I'll still get the tail of it as it swirls anti-clockwise throwing out long nasty lashings.

I can't let my thoughts begin to imagine the worst that can happen. I have to put my faith in my ability to cope with whatever arises, and further I have to somehow enjoy the turmoil and feel privileged to be out here experiencing something that rarely occurs, especially as I'm on a boat I hardly know and in an ocean that has a long dark history. So, it's really a deadly game of uncertainty.

I remember well my worst storm at sea which was on Christmas Day in 1987 on *Sundancer* as we sailed south from Sydney to Hobart, to join the Tall Ships race for Australia's Bicentennial celebrations in 1988.

I had a full round-the-world crew, ready to tackle the journey from Sydney to Hobart and then sail on to England around Cape Horn. They were excited to be finally living their dreams looking forward to their first genuine sea gale.

We were sailing south with a 2 knot current sweeping us along and were 2 days out of Sydney slowly getting into the routine of sail changing, watch keeping and sharing stories as the 12 crewmen from all corners of the world were bonding into a dedicated sailing team. We were 40 miles off the Australian coast chasing this east coast current, running hard south with it, much like the gulf stream off the US coast. We were under a full rig of 3 headsails and a full mainsail when the north easterly wind swiftly died and immediately a southerly buster came in underneath it at 50 knots, as it sometimes does on this Australian south coast. This is known as the dangerous "southerly buster".

We immediately reduced sail down to storm jibs and a deep reefed mainsail. I was proud of a crew who acted fast with enthusiasm and good humour. We were left heading south east, hard on a strong south westerly wind which soon kicked up a huge sea as the wind whipped up into the strong current. We were soon down to 2 storm jibs, then just one, with a deep reefed main which was our customary practise against adverse winds. The seas became shorter and steeper as the south westerly blast howled and soon we were pounding and leaping off waves and burying the bow while the crew were getting sicker.

We continued holding our course and slowly sailing towards Bass Strait making steady progress into the dark night giving the crew a taste of a fine sailing boat handling very adverse conditions. Chaos was everywhere below with hatches leaking and loose gear creating wider circles of mayhem, while the crew were being thrown out of their bunks as their fears mounted.

Then a rogue wave came through and catapulted Steve, one of our most experienced crewmen, out of the cockpit, throwing him against the rails and giving him a massive haematoma as well as broken ribs, while fortunately still attached to the boat by his harness. John, the American helmsman, was smashed into the wheel, breaking his teeth and I could see that some of the crew were reconsidering their pending around the world adventure.

At this stage it was near 2300 hours and very dark, cold and rough. After getting the injured crew off the deck, we turned away between waves as our practised safety retreat began, sailing slowly northwards under one storm jib and then down to no rig at all, easing that wickedly southerly motion into a more languid northerly flow. We were under bare poles and running slowly at 3 knots and losing ground to the south when another rogue wave came barrelling through and pooped us.

Crashing heavily on the stern deck it totally overwhelmed us, breaking the next helmsman's ribs and bending the heavy-duty stainless wheel out of shape. Tonnes of water poured below after filling the cockpit, and for the next 6 hours we sailed north as the winds slowly eased, the swell went down and we dried the boat out and calmed the crew.

That was the crew's first storm at sea, a frightening experience and one never to be forgotten. That southerly buster had roared through hard and it went quickly, but the wind against the current created a dangerous seaway that caused us more damage in 6 hours than *Sundancer* had ever experienced on any of her three circumnavigations. This is the very condition that occurs about every 7 years, decimating the Sydney-Hobart yacht race fleet as it races south into Bass Strait after leaving Sydney on Boxing Day.

It was at this moment that I lost half of my around the world crew. Their spirits were broken, they were devastated after seeing how one blow could turn heaven into hell, and they figured that if this pounding could happen off southern Australia, then how much worse would it be off Cape Horn?

It's part and parcel of sea life of course that any approaching storm, given the right circumstances, can develop into a fierce hiding, where the power of the storm can overwhelm any small yacht. Now all I can do if this blow develops is to ride it out keeping the bicycle upright and acting like the proverbial cork in a bottle, particularly as I have plenty of sea room and no time limits.

I prepare *Millefleurs* by locking down all the hatches, double lashing the deck gear, emptying out the cockpit lockers and tying up the covers around the rails so that the crashing wave action won't bend the rails in. I go below and stow all the movable gear, putting the trusty kettle in a locker, turning off all the hull valves and rigging double lee-sheets on my saloon bunk.

This front is developing quickly which is annoying but damn it, I'll just practise being a coward, save the boat, save the gear, blend into the turmoil and ride it out. This is definitely a moody sea and soon I'll be caught up in its tempestuousness and its pain, its darkness and its malevolence. I'm not just an observer but am an unwilling combatant battling with the changes, dancing to its thrusts and facing its reality. It has been said that we mustn't argue with reality as we'll lose every time.

It feels to me as if there's quicksand here and there's nowhere to find solid ground, but at least it's rhythmic and all I need to do is to fit into that groove and slide along with it. The sunlight is bleak as the blow develops and now I can see the ocean is white in all directions with a 40 knot blow from the south-west turning the ocean into a maelstrom.

There's a thrilling collective dance of scudding clouds congregating and then forcefully separating as another line squall rips them apart. There's torture and turmoil as they dance and rip like lace curtains creating a sombre backdrop to a wholly dangerous day. I am surfing down dark waves, chiselling out rough edges that could get me killed, sliding through the frothy turbulence created by these tortuous winds, driving *Millefleurs* on like a crazy surfboard.

Courage just stands and cheers from the sidelines, while hope and trust are my only sensible companions. I hang onto the cold wet helm tightly with ever whitened knuckles. Rain squalls are coming through regularly and Henry seems unable to cope, even with this tiny storm jib, as the surges seem to continually overpower the clutch.

I turn him off, saving him for another day and take over the helm full-time. Visibility is getting critical and there is no way I can avoid a ship if it suddenly appears on my track. Fate kicks in as my fragile mind takes a back seat. Thinking is over, it's autopilot now for me, blending my sailing skills with the ferocious ocean, fitting in with a crazy motion that's developing, going up and down and sideways all at the same time.

I snap the self steerer on, more in hope than anything and rush forward to get the storm jib down and lashed to the forestay with the wildly swinging halyard dragged back to the mast and cleated up hard.

I rush back to the cockpit as Henry screams out his displeasure and I turn him off as we slide sideways down another monster swell with little forward motion. I grab the helm and use what little forward motion there is to get *Millefleurs* stern to the waves, where the wind on the bare rigging can push me forward again. It takes all of 5 minutes to finally get her out of her death roll between raging swells and get her sailing away from each wave, bare poled at two knots.

Phew, that was a timely warning, don't let this boat go into lying beam-on with these rising swells or you're asking for real kick-ass.

At times I thought I'd have to start the motor or get some jib up to get forward drive to escape lying beam-on to the swells, but I hang on in the craziness, willing water to flow over the rudder so it can steer us away and, more by chance than skill we are off again, when another monster wave slams into our stern, driving us forward at 6 knots like a flighty surfboard. Fortunately, we quickly settle down to the dull 2 knots, where life becomes ever more dependable.

I sail all day like this on pure instinct, wedged in the cockpit, feeling the wind rise and fall but never falling below 60 knots which soon begins to feel mildly enjoyable. I think of Richard emailing me about how his Hunter handled the rough weather that he endured on the way to Bermuda and I appreciate the comfort he gives from that simple sharing act.

I wasn't alone, Richard's experience is with me as a talisman and my position out here in the craziness of it all feels a whole lot better with him. Sailing is now getting like the greasy pig competition where the pig only gets stronger and you eventually have to make friends with him or let him go. I can't let him go, we are in this paddock together and I have to somehow make friends. I have to admit to a feeling of powerlessness in this situation and I remember the Alcoholics Anonymous metaphor where they admit defeat in order to win, and I sure want to win.

As the daylight dies and the sky darkens my night vision develops and I begin sourcing the comforting idea that it will be easier to spot ship's lights at night, rather than their murky silhouette in the day and even this small bit of wisdom warms my heart. I am a spider hanging on a thin web hoping for that elusive message to blow through, that one day this will be over and the sun will shine as usual and all will be well in the Atlantic.

I am taking the wind and seas on the starboard quarter humming with the local Atlantic frequency, plunging down breakers but not with the gay abandon of a surfer - that's too reckless, too wild. I'm going down with caution like a man who is hungry but only has $5 in his pocket, going down each breaker with gentle awareness and fingertip control of the helm. Taking care to only correct the rudder when I am deep down in the water, where it will have the most effect. Praying that it is strong enough for the loads imposed on it, steering with my stomach, using feelings rather than thought, getting into pure survival mode as there's no alternative now.

My sense of survival is concentrated into each tiny moment where time has no meaning and no amount of thought can reshape this reality. This is not a novel as I'm a genuine refugee, echoing these Atlantic colours of deep blue and solid grey that are squeezing me through their pores. I'm frozen in time, trapped in my version of Auschwitz with a melancholic awareness of the dark narrow chasm between heaven and hell, between survival and death, between hope and despair.

I'm firmly wedged in the port cockpit seat, gum-booted feet pushed up hard against the pedestal and my wet weather gear pulled tight around my forehead, slowly heading eastward into a very dark night with the loud roar of an angry sea all around. Time stands still when another monster wave comes barrelling through. It's like free falling for the first time with a brand new untried parachute, unsure if there is a time when the ripcord should be safely pulled or just falling until I feel something solid beneath my feet.

The wind finally eases around midnight and drops to 35 knots and I genuinely feel that it's all over. The seas grudgingly go down, almost as if they can sense the change and I engage Henry to see if he can steer bare poled and he does as I push his steering protocols to the highest settings. I need a sleep, to warm up, to escape from the maelstrom and the bunk is my best choice way beyond keeping watch or making miles.

I watch Henry for 10 minutes and he seems ok as I talk to him quietly, reminding him of my need for rest. I take a quick look around and dive below, jamming the hatch tight and taking off my wet weather gear. I dress myself in all the warm clothes I have and then wriggle the wet weather gear back on over the top and then fall into the bunk with feelings of pure relief.

I know I'll get hot and sweaty but that is far better than being cold. In fact, I have a deep aversion to being cold, with my worst fear being slowly freezing to death with the life force being sucked out of me as I go rigid and hang onto what little heat there is left inside. That's my hell, way beyond falling out of a plane or crashing in a car, being shot or even being swamped by a monster wave.

I lay down, dozing for half an hour, trying to shut out the noise, but I can't sleep as I feel the winds are increasing again and our motion is either getting wilder or I'm beginning to get more afraid just hiding below.

I can hear Henry battling along and his "talk" becomes my mantra as I will him lots of power and future sunny days. I sing out to him to keep things together up there and then laugh at my stupidity. The truth is at this stage of the blow there's no way I'm game to swear at Henry or even offer criticism, in case he goes on strike and I'm forced to confront those angry seas again. Then my mind hits me with the dark thought that a rogue wave will come roaring through and bury me under a crushed boat and the damn thought gets bigger and more real the harder I try to avoid it. I imagine saying goodbye to all those I love without them knowing how I died. I imagine there will be no wreckage as everything will disintegrate as the boat goes down with me in it, hopefully without too much pain and struggle.

I'm definitely living on the edge where the quiet pool of life seems a long way away and all is movement and change and the gamble of living on in uncertainty pounds loudly at my door.

I'm comforted by the risk taker's mantra "If you're not living on the edge, then you're taking up too much room" while at this moment in time I'd prefer to be sitting in a warm cosy movie theatre enjoying someone else's Struggle Street.

I know some of us live long lives and some short ones, and usually there is no choice in the matter. A base jumping friend told me he had lost 3 friends in the previous year and still he wasn't ready to give up, knowing that each time he dived free, may be his last. After 500 base jumps his numbers were about up. In these circumstances I am better off - if I just lie in my bunk and let life take its course. There is no easy death when we cling desperately to life, making deals with the higher powers that if we are allowed to live we'll agree to work for charities for the rest of our days. That's being a beggar on the altar of discontent and turning ourselves into a lie. The acceptance of our passing with honour and integrity, with love for others and dignity is the best I can imagine that we can do for ourselves and, strangely, it's a satisfying thought in all this craziness.

I make a pledge though that if I get through this blow I'm going to choose all the things that I can about my final demise. I'm going to choose the music, write the words, organise the entertainment and hopefully have a party beforehand that will send me off as I want. It'll be my own wake where I'll sit with friends, have them exchange tales, good and bad, share some wonderful bonhomie and a few drinks. That way I'll get to enjoy it all. My will will be set in place, all my goodbyes written and if I can choose the time of passing all the better, hopefully with a glass of rum and some Irish music belting out.

Life surely is not about arriving at death in good health, well preserved with great blood pressure and fine lungs, but rather sliding in sideways totally used up with a big smile and a happy wave saying w-t-f was that all about?

In times of desperation these pleasant thoughts are wildly entertaining and I laugh at the madness of life as I bury myself deeper in my bunk. We are all searching for peace and harmony I tell myself and the acceptance of a "good death" is one of those important things in life. I realise that dying out here alone and far away from land may be one of the best deaths I could imagine.

The fears leave me and I float away in harmony feeling happy and contented that if I go now, I will still live on in the memories of those I loved, as a decent, happy bloke. I drift in harmony as I achieve some long-lost oneness with this sea as an art form, as it provides a sense of permanency in the midst of all the chaos. I even imagine being in a Canberra (Australia) art gallery looking at all the paintings, particularly the works of Albert Namatjira, an Australian Aboriginal artist, who was able to finally capture the true serenity of the eucalyptus trees, even though they are the most chaotic of all the earth's great forest trees, without any regularity at all to their shape. They're a lot like this crazy ocean slowly being torn apart.

My mind is definitely getting stronger even though it's obviously been getting wilder outside, as *Millefleurs* is constantly being thrown around like a rag doll and Henry provides the only stability with his constant whirrs and clacks. If one wants to be brave here then I have to reset my thinking, accepting that change and stability have to be composites and not opposites.

I realise that I'm not in the least bit hungry. All my senses are focused on surviving and willing myself to stay strong and using my mind to stay calm, even though I am desperately tired. I'm trying to transport myself elsewhere as a flickering light at the end of my own tunnel.

The gambler within feels like he has worn out his welcome and I feel empathic to my own base jumper who wants to sneak off into another quieter pool of living where dealing a hand is not going to be your last.

It is said that at the end of your life all your stories go through your mind and that is what is happening to me now. I am experiencing my triumphs like they were yesterday and my tragedies similarly, and I wonder if this is the end of it all as my spirit is realising it will soon be over. Did my psyche know more than my present level of life, was I doomed or was I refusing to acknowledge the reality of my position as the wind howls banshee-like in the rigging and we are being tossed around viciously and randomly? I am too warm and afraid to get out of my bunk, I just want to lay here and let it all happen, I have lost the will to fight when the odds seem too big to challenge, avoidance being the better part of valour.

I wish I had some of Mike's whisky or even a sleeping pill or something that would put me to sleep and I could either wake up or just die without knowing which way the pendulum was swinging.

Somehow, I am achieving an acceptance of it all that is pleasurable, I'm high on survival dopamines and nothing else exists except the warmth around me and the "big fella" inside who is living on one-time, rubbing my forehead and telling me fairy tales, while the little scared me goes on holiday.

I've been close to death a few times before and the same things happen. You go quiet, the mind goes easy and all one's struggles drift away to be replaced by a sense of floating outside the body, in a warm bath with no cares in the world, oblivious to all the drama taking place. I even begin to laugh and then to cry for no apparent reason, except for the joy of life, for the fun of living, for all the great people I have known.

There is no blackness in my mood swings now and I feel comforted. Life is over, the boat has been smashed and I am probably going down with it and have gone to sleep. I have decided somehow that this is one of those hypnagogic dreams and maybe I'll wake up back on land and get up out of bed and have breakfast and smile at all the drama. Those adversities early in my life were surely vaccinating me from the stresses of the moment as I am feeling emotionally resilient in some powerful and wise way. I stop struggling and let peaceful feelings sweep over me.

It is a reality in life that sometimes we have to submit to something bigger than ourselves and that's what's happening now. I'm out here like a man trapped in a room full of mirrors as the ocean wakes me up to my vulnerabilities and fears. I feel naked, cold, scared and yet intensely curious about where this is all heading. I am even smiling sad, curled up in foetal warmth, drifting around the universe of imagination beyond all the uncomfortable challenges of some crazy ocean, beyond caring, just Being, Being still, Being anywhere. I am in my sea-bunk, a capsule of content and the impossibility of this lasting for much longer becomes the dichotomy of the whole experience.

"Anyone who says they're not afraid at the time of a hurricane is either a fool, a liar or a bit of both." **Anderson Cooper.**

Then it all changes in an instant!!

There's a very loud and resounding bang and a stream of water hits me in the face and in shock I am thrown bodily across the cabin skidding under the table in one big crumpled mess. Not that I can see it, but I can feel the hard stainless mounting pole pressing down hard onto my back.

My thoughts are focused on the mongrel ship that has run us down and how deep we are down in the water, but it is too quiet for that, too still and calm for a ship to be pushing me further under. This is chess not checkers now and another wrong move could land me in deeper waters. On land if things are going bad then the response is to say "will this matter in 5 years?" but on the ocean that principle is reduced to 5 hours, while right now the brutality of the hurricane has condensed it to just 5 minutes or less.

In a trance I begin feeling for my sea boots and find them mixed in with the galley dishes and seat cushions waiting like pilgrims for retrieval. I drag them on and crawl back into the galley feeling for my harness that hangs below the hatch. It's there patiently waiting and I drag it on slowly and meticulously, taking my time while the seas roar outside and I know what I am going out to meet has to be full of all the demons I could possibly imagine. There were the demons of the bush when I felt something behind me as I walked alone at night as a kid, or the demons of being run over by a bus as

I lay there partly under my vehicle, changing a tyre, or the worst demon of all, for me, being frozen to death in the snow.

Now I have to go out and exchange pleasantries and make friends with them all, and strangely it is better than staying locked away here inside.

Time has stopped and I feel above my head for the hatch boards and they are still there. The wave that pooped us has smashed into the cockpit and water is still pouring below but it fortunately hasn't broken the companionway boards. Water had squeezed through the 2 inch gap at the top and squirted me in the face. It clearly says, "get up and get into action and cease laying there in a daze avoiding what's going on up here."

I slide back the hatch and crawl over the wash boards, slamming the hatch behind me and fall into a cockpit still half full of cold frothy sea water. Henry is crying inconsolably and making loud warring noises without any of the usual gear clack. He is definitely severely injured and we are drifting beam-on to a wild wind which seems to be back over 60 knots. This is a very dangerous place to be, riding beam-on, trusting to luck to survive, just waiting for another rogue wave to play havoc with us again, as it slams brutally into our sides.

The passing waves are foaming, hissing and dark with little visibility at all. I jam myself into the cockpit seat and disengage Henry who goes quiet as I quickly empty the freezing water out of my boots.

I look up at the compass and it is still glowing in the dark, reading a heading of 130 degrees, but the GPS has gone, leaving behind a broken power cable as a lasting memory of its bones. I can feel the dodger pieces flapping wildly around the cockpit, hitting me occasionally with loose pieces of material and I can see that there is a big split in the rail dodger where the wave smashed into us. But the essential water containers are quietly hanging on for dear life and that is a bonus. Apart from that the steering feels fine and my obvious next task is to get *Millefleurs* sailing again downwind away from these dangerous seas. I have done this before by waiting till her head swings away from the breeze and a wave pushes us along as it strikes the stern quarter.

There is no starting the motor or hoisting a sail. I'm not up to that, it's too complicated for my mind. I'll have to wait patiently till we have some movement through the water and then work the rudder to get us around. This manoeuvre is really life and death for us now and there is no way I can imagine doing it easily. Then I realise that if I do start the motor even with the gate valves closed, and power for 20 seconds or so, the worst I could do is destroy the rubber impeller. It's safety over machinery now.

I hook my harness to the starboard rail and reluctantly crawl aft to see if any sheet lines or other lines are in the water, before starting the motor. I find the Jesus rope looped over the side rails dragging down the leeward side, snaking out aft ready to wash under the boat and foul either the rudder or the propeller. This is the classic of experiences where it gives you the test first and the lesson afterwards, as I've had ropes around the propeller before. I slowly pull it in and re-lash it to the aft push-pit, finding some of the longer lashings I have on it broken, but still long enough to secure it well. It is wild up here with the stern regularly being buried in the swell and the cold, cold spray repeatedly taking my breath away.

Even though it's really dark I feel much better now that I have a plan and am taking control of my hell by being up here, battling around this wild crazy deck. I crawl back to the cockpit, centre the rudder and fire up the motor. I can't hear any motor noise above the roar around me, but there are continuous vibrations and as I engage the gearbox and power up we begin moving forward as I desperately swing the bow downwind.

I immediately stop the motor, breathe a sigh of relief, engage reverse to hold the propeller still and begin steering downwind. We are off again with the rudder in control and me hoping to keep it that way for the rest of the night.

Fate has definitely given me a warning and now it is up to me to keep alert and run before the seas, otherwise I could be pooped again, reminding me that these seas are definitely getting steeper and nastier. Lying ahull and drifting before the wind was not a good survival strategy, particularly when the weather was getting severe and I've been lucky as I lay comatose below, hoping it would all go away and leave me becalmed.

It is 0300 hrs according to my mental clock. There's a long, long time before dawn arrives when I will clearly see what state the ocean is in and what damage we have sustained. My stomach is thrust into my mouth through fear and I hang on hiding low in the cockpit hoping for some relief.

These are the worst conditions I've ever been in as Hurricane Barry sends out his fury in all directions. I clip myself in and wriggle tighter into the cockpit seat, thanking my lucky stars that I wasn't in the cockpit when we were pooped. It was no idle blow and these monstrous seas are still breaking wildly around us as we surge away from them with the big scary waves running through us, rather than slamming into our side and bursting like wild star shells, as if we were in some fierce battle.

Henry is useless, gonzo, gone and as an exercise I start him and try to engage the clutch in a lull, but there is only a whirring noise and some grinding, without any action. I'll have to wait till dawn to check the deck gear and see if there is any damage forward but all seems well on the helm at present and we are on track, heading to the east at 2 knots rolling along like a drunken sailor firmly locked to the helm with the world crashing all around me.

Dawn comes slowly, inch by inch and the ocean becomes lighter but no less fierce, with white streaks following big swells where the seas look like a flowing river moving past as we wallow along, extra alert to keep applying minimum helming corrections so as to not use a lot of rudder, which would slow down our progress and maybe cause us to go into another beam-on drift.

I am tired and cold but with the coming of the dawn, and the amazing wild scene occurring all around it makes me feel that it is somehow a real privilege to be here.

Someday I'll tell this crazy story to friends over a beer and a game of chess and hopefully it'll scare them to death, as they comfort me with a nice red wine, telling me what a brave lad I am for working so hard to stay alive!

As I take a look at the rigging I see that the spreaders are cutting wild arcs across the skies and I feel like a painter with only one colour - grey.

I am reminded of going into art galleries in various cities and seeing those classic paintings of the big bad ocean, where ships are always portrayed disappearing into huge swells with tattered rigs and sailors in sou'westers, hanging from the helm two at a time, with their intrepid fearful eyes as big as saucers. Well this is it in real life and if I had a video camera and lots of courage I'm sure I could capture the nightmare on film to show to you! That is if I had someone to steer and another one to get me the camera!

I'm up to my pussy's bow so to speak, stretched out bone on bone without cartilage, being hammered down into the waves, pressed down to the very bottom of each swell with the buoyancy in *Millefleurs* being our only saving grace. Hurricane Barry winds heel us over from gunnel to gunnel as we roll heavily, challenging the very integrity of Mr Hunter and his fibreglass creation, cutting huge swathes of forward vision to tiny pieces. There is a madness and a purity at the same time and I play shouting games with the larger waves, challenging them to leave me alone, telling them we are friends really as they have had to come all this way to say hello and hopefully wish me well, rather than caning my hide. I seem to be pushing sh*t uphill without finding any top.

My hands are sore and salt-water white from holding the kicking wheel and I'm afraid to let go, lest the rudder get damaged. and then I just laugh, laughing out loud as I vividly remember the couple's tale where the wife says to her husband, "honey I have really sore hands from holding the broom so tight" and he replies blandly "well my dear, next time you should drive the car!!"

It's odd how humour forces us to put life into perspective, to get this nightmare into something manageable. There are no stimulants needed here, no nicotine or bundy rum or leafy stuff to elevate this dream and get me beyond the tick-tock of slow time, where living with each minute seems like a long, long hour.

I'm living inside a runaway wind tunnel with an ambivalent terrorist holding the buttons and hopefully we can all share my very real drama as long as my batteries don't run out. I ponder on why our lives are so short. My childhood was gone in a blur, my adolescence was a wild struggle to get to adulthood and my adulthood has been a slow grind to make a living through wild rides of adventure. Hopefully, after this storm I will be reminding myself every day not to let my old age slowly slide into dependency and death, without some solid semblance of resistance. This is my wake-up call to stand beside that childhood when I knew little, and my adolescence when I challenged all, to my adulthood when I repeatedly questioned the status quo about my beliefs, prejudices, wisdoms and happiness and all those elements of life that have been reduced down to just this.

I'm even beginning to appreciate the battlefield before me with loud ums and ahs at the forces of nature mixing and clashing and tearing each other apart, while still realising how fortunate I am. I'm not just a spectator, we're all in this together. I stand here admiring how close the beauty and the suppressed violence of the ocean are, how close the absolute crazy and perfectly sublime forces are, like one's faith in survival and then disaster as just two moments of the same movement. The more I enjoy the show and barrack from the sidelines like an avid spectator, the more the show lights up for me.

We are in a virtuous circle with the ocean and myself inextricably linked, and unlike the tree falling in the forest, I am here to hear all the sounds and enjoy the show. This is survival personified, it's what I came out here to find, albeit in a gentler way.

Just then someone gently whispers in my ear telling me the good news for the whole day, that puts all in perspective. "below 50 degrees south, there is no law and below 60 degrees south there is no god" and I feel I'm below 60 degrees now and fortunately there are no icebergs.

Around midday, from my rough observations, the clouds continue to scud across the sky while the wind has increased to 60-70 knots. I have no way of telling the wind strength but the tell tales on the rigging stand out like solid boards, while the waves have lost all their tops as the wild winds rip any peaks apart, sending them flying in solid foam. I'm definitely thirsty and every time a rain squall comes through I lick the water off my wet weather gear and off the backs of my hand, to stop my lips from stinging. My hands look like they are 100 years old with water wrinkles and white skin and I can see clearly what death looks like.

I am not in the least bit hungry. A hot pie would probably make me puke, while even a tiny Mars bar could be threatening. Fortunately, I am deep into my fast and I'm getting other sources of energy probably from the forces of the wind and the wildness of the ocean's melee or from just plain fear.

The depth of my minimalist philosophy that 'to be happy with a little is difficult, but to be happy with a lot is impossible' is playing itself out in buckets. There is a little and a lot all at the same time here in this blow and when the two opposing forces come together there is enough for all. That's what I tell myself aloud as I remember more of my friend Gerhardt's advice "change the way you look at things and the things you look at change."

I've been doing that all day with some success, although occasionally, when a big wave bursts over me, I shake the cold sea water off my face and point to the sky and tell Hurricane Barry to f*ck off in no uncertain terms, hoping he will hear me and cut the shit.

It also helps me feel more in control of things and even a tiny bit braver, as I brazenly challenge the enormous might of nature.

As the afternoon wears on I feel increasingly like a spectator at the circus. The wind seems to slowly moderate every 20 minutes or so and the screaming 60s are replaced by the howling 50s and sometimes the roaring 40s and then it cycles up again for another round in this big Atlantic boxing ring.

But it is getting back into a 5 hour ocean cycle somewhat. I can feel that there is a real light at the end of the tunnel.

My mind has become one big fog, time has lost all its tick-tock meaning, and even the wild motion is becoming blasé and par for the course. What is remarkable though is the direct relationship between the seas and the wind. As soon as the wind howls the seas roar, and as the wind eases so do the seas, in almost perfect melody synch. They are in a strange orchestra here bound together in symphony, one needing the other, each reflecting the other's face and yet the wind is the master, flattening the swells, beating them regularly into submission so that all I see as the swell disintegrates is spray and foam and relatively flat water. Then it cycles up again.

And then I break through, I'm over the hill of endurance and into the flow of life. I'm now one with the wind and the waves, one with the all of the all, the ocean is no longer out there, it's inside and I can feel it's power, it's rhythm, it's beauty and I begin smiling with the knowing that I am one with it all. I wonder what it's like in 100 knot winds and encourage it to show me what it can do. Perhaps the seas just become a flat river of foam with everything being driven before them and only afterwards as the wind drops will the swells reappear. As this wind begins to lull to 30 knots briefly for a few minutes and then rise again, I can see those swells emerging like sentinels, finding their own voice and rolling through, passing me seemingly without menace, smiling and happy to have their own shape back, as they finally triumph over the cold bully wind.

I feel, as night settles in with the long slow fading of light that the blow is nearly over. Barry has worn himself out and apart from minor damage and a little water below we are back on our feet again. Even though the swells are high and occasionally we slide down the face of some extra-large swells like we are skiing in the alps. My arms are tired, and I wish I just had that broom even while I'm cold, exhilarated and hopeful that this flirtation with disaster is eventually coming to an end, sometime in the next day or so.

Around midnight, according to my body clock, the moon flits through the cloud cover like a low battery torch and that is food for my soul.

I am jammed in the weather side cockpit to starboard with my legs pushed up against the port cockpit wall, steering with one hand and holding the cockpit combing with the other hand and watching the seas abeam in the low moonlight, when one of the most remarkable things in my whole sailing life happens. They say ocean wisdom and your survival on it is a million pieces of life enduring information but this one is out of my scope.

Someone begins to swim past me, starboard side, not more than 10 metres away stroking evenly in what I assume is a dark wet suit and he is making ground on me slowly. The mammalian brain responds to surprise and fear in the same way and I'm not sure whether he's coming as a pirate to plunder, or whether he's just lost and lonely. We're both moving eastwards away from land and I want to inform him he's going the wrong way, but feel embarrassed to tell him anything, as he obviously knows what he's doing. Maybe I shouldn't interrupt his odd behaviour as he may get angry and board me.

Perhaps he fell off a boat close by, perhaps we are near the shore somewhere and we've been driven off course and he's out for an evening's training session. There's no sense in it at all, but I do shout out to this poor bugger some incomprehensible sounds like "hey…. mate" and he props in the water, so he is real.

As I slide alongside him I can see his face and I shout out above the melee, "how long have you been doing that for?" and he answers "36 hours" in a strong Australian accent, which shocks me. I shout back "you want to come up for a drink?" Immediately feeling rather selfish as it's me that wants him to steer, while I'll make us both a hot drink. I feel embarrassed that I'm thinking about taking advantage of this newly discovered friend, even though we have just met by some weird accident, I'm pleased we can't see each other's faces too clearly. They say a stranger may be a friend you've never met yet and I could be in luck. It's amazing how fast the mind thinks, when a car crash is impending, and all normality has drained out the window.

But he doesn't seem to indicate any concerns or desire to join me as he shouts back "no thanks, I'll keep going" in that same broad Aussie bush accent, as he swims off slowly, moving away from me, leaving me behind, swimming off with long fluid unhurried strokes. I want to call out, I want to offer him some peanut butter and a towel, I desperately want him to come back, but there's nothing I can say but "w-t-f was that all about?"

Then I ponder, was that me getting out of here? We spoke the same language, we resonated. Was I deserting the ship, leaving the scene, off to better places? Had I really gone down with my boat and wouldn't accept that it was all over? Can you ever know when reality shifts under the eye of the survivor and becomes fluid again? Surprise or fear. "Hell, what's going on here…I must be losing my marbles!!"

And then I slowly twig, I'm hallucinating and that's not good. I'm surely out of my tree, but I'm confident I'm not about to join him for an evening dip. I've been a long time in this contest and I desperately need some sleep, but who the hell's going to steer? I'd have even offered the helm to my swimming mate, but he has graciously declined and probably was a lousy helmsman and fortunately, there was some moon, otherwise I wouldn't have seen him swimming by.

Then I realise with a jolt that the wind has eased to 25 knots and somehow the seas are going down. Was there a lapse in my concentration, did I just dream all that, where has the time gone since the wind was much fiercer just a few minutes ago, or was that swimmer an angel swinging by? I'm definitely on the other side of the storm now, still moving eastwards at one knot, and life's a whole lot better. My slow progress explains how that Aussie could overtake me and yet I still seem to have steerage, with my stern lifting to the swell, slowly ploughing eastwards.

"Lock the helm" my inner voice says, "and curl up for a while, maybe sleep till dawn" and I needed no better advice. I lock the helm, swing beam-on to the swell and I curl up into the cockpit seat with my warm wet-weather gear tight around me, pulling the hood over my face and drifting off into the sleep of angels, challenging fate to make friends. *Millefleurs* drifts safely in the arms of a dying breeze, occasionally crashed by passing waves, but safe in the knowing that we have survived the worst of the blow. On the other side of this sleep is also a genuine understanding that *Millefleurs*, this puny 34 ft Hunter glass yacht that I barely know, is a damn good sea boat and equal to any other boat I've sailed before in severe weather. Her strength is that she can float high, move easily and track at the lowest speeds, even though she rolls wickedly. I guess you can't have everything.

It is said that the basic principle of life is that the deepest things are learned in unknown territory and I awake a few hours later with the sun rising, intermittently shining through thick scudding clouds that are moving faster up there than down here. It's dawn and we have survived the hurricane and the mystery of that guy swimming past is the same kind of mystery that has synchronicity written all over it. It's moved me around the ocean before, avoiding fierce waves and blind ships, with my *Millefleurs* bobbing along albatross-like to the east.

If there is an independent fate or someone is watching over us then I've been blessed knowing that my life could have taken one of two directions yesterday. Either I was that swimmer heading for exhaustion or a worn sailor heading east, with the latter offering me first prize in the local sea lottery.

There is still uncertainty here and there's definitely fear of the unknown as my imagination runs wild. I remember the old ocean maps in the unexplored regions of the world that said "here there be dragons" and maybe that says I'm crossing my own unexplored region, maybe it's my own psyche's deep dark ocean causing me trouble. It's a dilemma that will linger but I'm not going to knock on wood or pour libations into the waves to negate any bad magic.

In fact, I'm secretly hoping for another swimmer tonight, who may deliver a bag of fresh croissants!! I sit up slowly stretching my cold worn-out body and survey the deck for damage. The dinghy is not in its chocks, having been twisted sideways, where it has been forced end-on by a crashing wave. The sail bags are all tied down and all sheets are still around the cockpit cleats. My trusty cockpit buckets are gone though and the dodger cover has been torn off its eyelets in two places. The starboard stern cover has a full length split in it. All are repairable later when I have the energy. I'll make good the mayhem, but the GPS is gone which will make navigation interesting and Henry looks ok superficially, but he has haemorrhaged inside somewhere, and he is surely my biggest loss.

I leave the deck and go below and find water sloshing around the cabin floor. It's not a lot, but it's a nuisance as we roll, with noisy, gurgling momentum that offends my seamanship rules, reminding me warily that we could be slowly sinking. The water either came through the hatch, or the keel bolts have worked loose in the struggle for survival, and I need to deal with this now.

I painfully collect a bucket from the aft cabin, pull up the floor panels and slowly bail out the bilge in sheer exhaustion. I'm so tired I even pee in the bilge rather than risk getting back in the cockpit. This task takes half an hour and 20 buckets of water which warms me up, particularly as I am trying to balance the bucket, scoop up water from the narrow space below with a plastic cup and throw it in the bucket and then out into the cockpit. I'm absolutely buggered, jaded and "Aussie shagged", but the bilge water is getting shallower. I check the keel bolts with the large universal wrench and find a couple slightly loose and crank them up to at least 100 lbs of pressure. Then I watch to see if any more water comes in. Thankfully all seems ok, so I replace the floor covers and proceed to make a hot cup of tea which is probably the worst thing I can do, as everything moves and rolls and boiling water could be my worst enemy.

I wisely change my mind, turn off the stove, put the kettle away and go upstairs to get some fresh air as I'm feeling slightly sick and very, very heady.

Sitting in the cockpit, restoring my sense of well-being after all that struggle below with the wind around 25 knots and the tell tales flapping idly as we drift beam-on to the south-west swell that has also lost its menace, is strangely a real joy. I take one last look around for ships and go below, sliding the hatch to, and dive into my damp bunk still in my wet weather gear, but it's no concern.

Frankly I'd love to get the heavy gear off and put on some dry clothes but I don't have the energy. I fall asleep instantly for the second time today and hope to sleep forever, waking up to find we're in the Azores with warm breezes and bright sunlight.

I slowly awake later, stiff, sore and hungry and resolve that today is the day I'm definitely going to start eating again. It's not so much the food I need for energy, but the comfort of sweet things like muesli bars and honey in my tea and the taste of fried rice.

I slowly climb out of my damp bunk and emerge gingerly onto deck into a cold grey day with the winds still gusting to 25 knots, into what one could say is a lousy day, but after yesterday's weather, it's magic. The sun is up there somewhere, the wind has nearly blown itself out and the seas are going down. What more could I want apart from a nice hot shower, warm clothes and much more sleep? I'm on a high because *Millefleurs* has come through with flying colours and we're a real team through sheer adversity.

Chapter 9

Recovering after Barry

I'm conscious now that this tiny sailboat could possibly take me around the world, even through the wild Southern Ocean, but I would definitely remove the stern lip, as the swells slap it so hard that the whole boat shakes, when battered from astern. The rig is strong and the design is fine for any ocean crossing so I'm sure we'll get back to Australia safely in the next few years.

My navigation tools are gone but I do have the plastic sextant as well as the nautical almanac that was difficult to secure in this post-sextant era and that one paper chart that I discovered in the Solomons. I also know that with a little practise, even though I don't have the sea tables, I can figure out my position at noon. At least I can become a latitude sailor which is what they did in the old days before accurate clocks were available. Surely the Azores can't be too hard to find, since I'm near it's latitude and it's only 3,000 miles to the east. One advantage is that I do have an electronic clock on the bulkhead and by using it I'll be able to work out my longitude from the maximum height of the sun at noon, called altitude by time, so I'm really in luck. I have all I need for the next leg so, no turning back.

I decide to eat a spoonful of honey and wait for a while before eating anything else. The honey tastes like love which is what I could use right now and that love feeling spreads from my tongue to my whole body, as I sit rolling drunkenly, going nowhere, while in the throes of that amazing feeling of love, love, love.

I'm only 6 days out, just 400 miles offshore and a long way from Horta, but I have been through one of the worst experiences of my life alone and I didn't crack up, apart from watching Mr Mystery swim by. He's not going to play on my mind for too long.

In fact, I quite enjoyed his antics and laugh to myself as I imagine telling my friends somewhere late at night the vision that I beheld. Not of angels or UFOs but a guy swimming past me in the Atlantic with his "underpants on his head." that'll get them in!.

I laugh to myself as I remember one of the strangest guys that I met in my travels while in South Africa at the Durban yacht club, where we cruising folk were having our Christmas barbecue in 1991. I imagine this same sort of guy swimming past me, except that this little guy had a big ring in his left ear. I remarked to him that that ring must give him trouble when he is sailing, as it could get hooked up on a cleat and he could hang there for days!! He laughed at the prospect and said the ring had been forced upon him in Haiti, and it sure did give him trouble when he worked the deck of his boat, but he was reluctant to take it out. Now here was a story I relished, in the vein of some pirate with a big ring in his ear leaping from boat to boat, plundering and causing mayhem around Haiti.

Tony though, was a quiet 25-year-old Englishman, not given to exaggeration, who had left home in his 27 ft folk boat with his dog Felix in 1988, deciding to sail as far and for as long as he could upon the oceans of his dreams. He had beautiful dreams of seeing the world from the level of a heaving deck, catching flying fish and whispering to the dolphins. He was a gentle, softly-spoken guy, and I couldn't imagine him doing harm to anyone, let alone being a pirate. His story goes: "I was heading for Panama after sailing up through the West Indies and on passing west of Haiti I decided to pull into a sweet looking bay and anchor for the night. After anchoring and relaxing in the cockpit" he said, "I heard music on the shore and a party happening, so I decided to launch my dinghy and illegally go ashore and join the party."

"There I met Elsie who was the life of the party and she seemed to really like me, calling me her 'long lost sailor, soul mate' and introducing me to all her friends.

But when invited back to my floating palace in the bay she politely declined, saying that she never slept with a man on the first night. At 0300 hrs Tony rowed back to his boat without Elsie, but with fantastic memories of lots of rum, good dakka, bonhomie and lots of kisses from Elsie, deciding to sleep and then sail at first light. However, life intervened as it often does, because at first light he awoke to find Elsie crawling into his bunk, naked and wet from having swum out. He said, "she filled up my life for the next

30 days, being the most aggressive lover any man could imagine. Nothing was a bother to her and nothing was off the table. We were both deeply in love with lust and life, with me totally neglecting my poor dog who I couldn't risk taking ashore." Tony said, "I had finally found my south seas' maiden, the girl of my dreams but I had to eventually leave because the hurricane season was coming and I had to get to Panama to cross the Pacific in time for the cruising season. So I broke the sad news to her after a month telling her that I was leaving the next day. Elsie, as expected, had a total meltdown. I implored her to come with me but she had no passport. Between tears she said she'd wait for my return, vehemently promising she'd love me forever. We were fated to be together as in her mind I was her ideal man, her soulmate, even with my funny British accent but she was adamant she wouldn't sail on a little boat like mine across any ocean. That convinced me that it was time to leave, otherwise my bigger dream was gone - it was either love or freedom, and I chose freedom.

That last night together Tony said, "Elsie and I made wild love till the early hours of the morning and then she, in deep passion, bit me right through the ear whilst giving me the most amazing "white flash" orgasm that could turn any naked man into a jellyfish. It was then that she put this big ring in my ear, saying, 'you'll come back to me or die cause if you take this ring out lots of bad luck will come your way.' "I was impressed," said Tony, "by her passion and conviction and my sadomasochistic reactions. She swam ashore and I sailed away, hoping to find love like that somewhere else in the world or perhaps return to Haiti, sometime in the future."

Two hours out of the anchorage Tony said, "I went below, leaving my poorly neglected dog, Felix, in the cockpit, happy to have me back again, no longer having to compete with a lusty maiden," he said, "I logged my position and worked out the best course to Panama. The ring as you can imagine, was causing me so much annoyance and pain that I took it out, admiring its size and how, if left in place, it could turn my cultured English ear into an Irish cauliflower, hanging somewhere well below my knees!"

"I put it under the navigation table for safe storage, but when I went back to the cockpit, Felix was frothing at the mouth and moaning in pain and within 30 minutes he was dead. "He'd not been ashore, he seemed content as we sailed and now he was gone. Then," he said, "I remembered the curse of that ring and I put this great big cleat hanging ring back in my ear as fast as I could, regardless of the pain, and it's been there ever since," he added with a smile. "If I do find another maiden I will finally take it out, maybe after getting a blessing from some Shaman. Otherwise, I'll return to Haiti and live there with Elsie and have a dozen kids and probably another big earring to balance this one, when she puts that long awaited fantastic and passionate Haiti bite on me."

Now that was a story every bit as good as my swimmer and they say we are nothing more than our stories. What I loved about travelling was collecting those stories and using them to make a dull day, like today, into something enjoyable. As an avid social being I do worry about those guys who become hermits. They retreat into themselves and miss out on all the fun stories of others that can brighten their day and those stories can be passed on like buried treasure. Tony literally passed me his "ring story parcel" complete with the mystery of whether he would go back to Haiti. Wouldn't it be a good day, as I wallow alone out here, if I could call Tony these 16 years later, from where I am now and ask him if he is still sailing and did he make it back to England?

I would then surprise him with my location and make arrangements to meet him in the Azores. I'd also ask him to bring me another spare self steerer. Wouldn't that be absolutely great?

I just sit here smiling crazily at the absurdity of life and how, given our new technology maybe we'll all be able to fill in those gaps that would make any chosen reality possible.

There are no islands between me and the Azores, with the only dangers being ships and wild storms. I decide to make a cup of tea somehow, even though the roll is unsettling, and treat myself to a muesli bar or two as I ponder that thought of somehow meeting Tony in the future with his big earring.

I take off my wet weather gear and change into some dry clothes with a fresh t-shirt, some jeans and a thick top. I wipe the wet weather gear dry before putting it on again. The cup of tea takes a long while to make as I try to hold myself still in the galley and keep all the parts of the exercise separate, until I can pour the boiling water. I put the cup delicately in its holder in the cockpit and emerge with two muesli bars that are going to be the centre of my focus for the next few hours.

Then carefully, between rolls, I go forward and untie the storm jib and gingerly hoist it with the sheets cleated both sides, to keep it from flogging.

It's a tiny sail and reaches just halfway to the spreaders, but it gives us stability and direction. I then scamper back to the cockpit and coax *Millefleurs* around onto an easterly course with the fresh breeze coming over the starboard quarter taking me just south of east, an excellent course at a graceful 3 knots. I crank in the storm jib, flattening it up hard and we're off, storm nearly over with a new day beginning.

I sink contentedly into the cockpit seat, dry as a bone and happy as a turtle as I sip my tea, sample the muesli bar that tastes like the best Devonshire tea ever made, and savour the moment, telling myself with some persuasion that this is really living and like Willie Nelson, "we're on the road again, going places we've never been."

Thornton Wilder says, "we are only alive in those moments when our hearts are conscious of our treasures" and the treasures I now have make my heart soar and my gratitude is something to be savoured. I have a good solid boat that can stand up to any Atlantic pounding, I have warm clothes and dry gear and plenty of food and no ring in my ear. I imagine that that ring would be more than a nuisance and laugh along with Tony hoping he can hear me wherever he is on that future "connecting line".

Maybe I'll sail down to Haiti and find Elsie, but bugger getting a ring in my ear, I'll take circumcision any day! I turn my imagination instead to just being a poor old cowboy who has loaded his packhorse and ridden out into the desert with all his food and water, hoping to cross the wide expanse of sand, singing quietly in the saddle, as I follow the stars into the night, hankering to reach the Los Alamos of my dreams, where maidens stand in the bars giving out free drinks and big wet kisses. Life and imagination are truly an amazing experience, I wouldn't be dead for quids. I feel that if I approach life from the gratitude side then there is a pure feeling of nobility in my soul for having survived unscathed, even amongst all the chaos that was out here yesterday.

When it comes to the important things of life like freedom and love, health and choice, the valuable response is I guess whether you take those treasures for granted or whether you take them with gratitude. and it's with a profound sense of gratitude that I'm still here, floating high and probably a little crazy, which allows me to turn this very ordinary day into an extraordinary experience.

Cicero said, according to my philosophy professor of the sixties, that "gratitude is not only the greatest virtue, but the parent of all others" and I raise my cup of Earl Grey tea to him and thank the Romans for contributing much to our world culture.

Now the second stage of this journey is about to unfold. The first week has been ships and getting off the coast safely and now the big journey is about to unfold further and I'm excited, if a little apprehensive. I came out here to settle in and learn how to cope with rough weather and the uncertainty of *Millefleurs*, while at the same time avoiding something about myself that I didn't understand.

There is a sudden realisation that there are two people inside me competing for my attention. The two of us have been together for years and when the chips are down and I'm in serious trouble the second persona emerges and takes the 'me' by the hand and we cruise off safely together to another adventure. The 'me' complains and swears and loves causing a bit of chaos while the other guy is more interested in analysing, standing back and dissecting the consciousness of it all. I love both and both wanted to go on this voyage.

The 'me', the Peter, didn't want to fast or sail alone or cross the cold north Atlantic. In fact, the Peter kept saying "let's go to the Bahamas and hang out there eating bananas and drinking rum before going on to Panama" and in the height of the storm I really wish I had listened to him.

The other guy grudgingly admits that the Bahamas were probably the better choice adding with a counter from the maxim that says, "adversity introduces a man to himself." This is the trip we both planned as something we had to do, before we both gave up sailing, so I guess he wins.

The strange thing about these two characters that co-exist inside me, is that the real person, 'I' is totally separate from these two characters and yet we seem to co-exist in a trinity that can get quite crowded at times.

There's the student, the teacher and the headmaster, or in more universal terms, the Einstein, the Groucho and Harpo Marx.

No matter how the three of us present ourselves to the world we are all secretly limping along trying to figure out how much of ourselves can be exchanged with the outer world and each other, when really there's something bigger inside that's being fused steadily together.

As Margaret Meade, the American cultural anthropologist says, "the distance to our centre is short, but the road getting there is long" and in the last few days there have been lots of potholes as well. And then I remember line for line my son, Cameron's creative writing piece which he wrote about me all those years ago, when he was just 14 years of age. He had sailed many ocean miles with me, far away from schooling and the pains of adolescence and grew from the experiences.

He kept the poem a secret but his sister Caroline fortunately gave me a copy one day when I was feeling nostalgic about leaving my kids behind for more adventures.

This is his poem:

DAD

"He sat on the rail, impervious to the breeze, unmoving, strong, impenetrable
The chiselled features of his weather-beaten face ran continuously with the rusty rigging
And in the shadowy dusk his immobile form and the yacht beneath become one
Everything about him seemed to tell a story, an encounter with a hurricane, a narrow
Escape from a coral reef, a lifetime of sailing the ocean currents
His hands were rough and knotted from constantly trimming the sails,
His torso deep and powerful complementing his lengthy but curiously stocky legs
His sharp profile was like the outline of a coastal map of the world
But it was his eyes that struck me, even after all these years. like cobalt gems they glistened,
deeply recessed under his thick brow
The blue was indescribable, in fact I often wondered whether he carried all the earth's ocean within them
They shone light and dark at the same instant, radiating intensity, wisdom and knowledge. Mirrors of the sea and yet much more than mirrors because his engaging stare communicated something deep, something primal, a closeness to nature, salt of the earth
Then all at once the mood changed, his jaw dropped, the creases in his face began to tighten and his forehead lifted
He grinned knowingly at me, laughing heartily, his chest heaving, his eyes sparkling
I grinned back and began to laugh myself, lost in the moment
I seemed to laugh forever,
That's what I like about my dad, I thought to myself
that salty laugh, that knowing presence, yeah, that's what I like

***

I think about my kids often and wonder where their journeys will lead.

Cameron sailed with me from an early age and lived with many international crews, honing his reality of being an international citizen.

Hopefully his unusual education in life will help him to appreciate the joys of living and travelling and acknowledge that each person all around the world is uniquely different. Cameron is like his mum - conservative, hard-working and reliable while Caroline is more like me with a mercurial temperament, loves change, new places and new ideas. I imagine her being a traveller all her life, while Cameron will settle somewhere and put down deep roots.

It's amazing how each child reflects something deeply personal in us, their parents, and maybe they're just old friends returning as children to tell us a lot more about ourselves and vice versa of course.

Mary, my first wife and I parted after 25 years of a happy marriage, not because we had serious relationship problems but because we had differing journeys. What I had to become to stay in that relationship was too difficult to accept and I sadly sailed away, appreciating freedom more than love. The two children were the beautiful bonus and we gave each other freedom to be more of ourselves without all those binding strings.

We are still, as they say in Australia, mates, friends on another level of being, sharing something we created, that we have set free.

Chapter 10

Sam

What is going on as hurricane Barry dies I'm not sure, but the wind is down around 18 knots with a large swell from the south-west and still lots of white caps, but all seems well with us.

The seas are now much more gentle and to add to the calmer surroundings 3 dolphins swing by and, although they only stay briefly, sizing us up as being too slow for their ideas of mutual fun, they bring a sense of order and joy to an otherwise dull day. We sail on, making good miles to the east while the cloud cover is slowly thinning out in all directions. A bright sun peeps through occasionally, just for a few seconds now and then, promising brighter sunny days ahead. The time after a storm is not as many people think, a brief respite, sandwiched between another inevitable storm but rather it is the long gap between storms at sea that rarely occur with such ferocity as Barry that gives me confidence that the rest of the trip to Horta will probably be storm free.

I do know though from experience that the demons of my imagination are more dangerous and subversive than those that could possibly walk through my daily ocean's door within the next month. At midday the sun is again shining through patchy cloud banks and I drop the headsail, drag out my sextant and take sights of the sun as it peaks. I feel a strong loyalty to the sextant, almost as if it's a magical instrument, and I've had many over the years. At one stage I used to collect, restore and sell them.

I enjoy the magic of sighting the sun, adjusting the shading till the sun can be seen clearly against the horizon and then rocking the sun on the moving horizon till I've captured that magical vertical reading.

There is an art form to it and I am enjoying reconnecting to the rhythm of this newer sextant, even though it's just a cheap plastic one. And according to the almanac at 12.15 local time for the sun's zenith and from the sights, I'm able to deduce that we're at latitude 39 degrees 11 minutes north. I'm slightly south of New York and I log it on the chart, estimating from dead reckoning my longitude position as 70 degrees west longitude which puts me only about 250 miles east of the US coast and certainly not as far out as I thought. To get a more accurate longitude I'll need more time with a steadier sun and with the readings taken over a period of at least half an hour, to find the exact time at which the sun passes overhead. That can wait for later. I can also take a shot of the pole star in the evening or in the early morning, and with a few minor corrections I'll get my latitude as well.

The wind is still too strong to safely hoist the mainsail on my own particularly when I have to hurry back to the helm, so that we don't get flattened or gybe away dangerously. What's more I realise I don't have the energy or the nerve to do it, so I cautiously re-hoist the storm jib and we set off for another afternoon's run to the south east at 3 knots, with lots of swell and some brilliant white-caps. I'm hoping the calming effect of the evening will provide us with a smoother ride and maybe more sail later.

I glance behind me just in time to see a whale surfacing a boat length away and I'm so surprised that I do a "double take." I'm not sure what kind of whale he is, but he's big, black and shiny and slightly worrying, being so close to the boat and obviously interested in my presence. He dives and I wish him bon voyage, but he surfaces beside me to windward, blowing oily fumes in my direction. I can see his eye, every bit as big as my head, surveying this strange creature that's wallowing along minding its own business as well, without any motor noise.

He stays on the surface choofing loudly, sending a steamy cloud into the chilly air and I say to him as I hesitantly stand to attention, boldly expressing my Groucho Marx personality, "fancy a quick game of checkers?" His eye rolls around as he focuses on this moving thing on the deck of this weird object and I swear he smiles, blows another puff of oily steam and dives again softly and decisively, appearing a few minutes later in front of us while moving steadily away to the south-east. He seems to be travelling at a lazy 4 knots and enjoying the bigger swells as they lift him high out of the water, while he rhythmically fins in the hollows and breathes on the crest. With that much evolution I'm sure storms at sea have little influence on whales and dolphins and their only dangers out here are fast moving ships. In that regard we're in the same boat and that game of checkers doesn't seem so out of order.

Today I feel a real sense of the freedom of life which, after the last few confined wet and windy days gives me permission to just 'Be'. I'm pleased I didn't hoist the main as the breeze is still heavy, chilly and fresh and I didn't want to cope with more spray and bashing through lumpy waves. I love 'doing' but sometimes 'being' is more fun and a lot wiser. The Italians have a saying that the secret to living well is "doing nothing better" and even though their economy is rat-shit and the black market runs the country, I applaud the behaviour of the old guys who seem to sit on every available seat each morning in their market squares, in tight huddled groups, contemplating life and doing absolutely nothing, while everyone else is frantically industrious around them.

When the railroad tracks of the Protestant work ethic were laid down in my youthful mind I learned to be always doing something, anything - that was the only way to be rewarded and, only after 12 hours of 'doing' work per day, was one allowed to just 'be'. Now I can feel comfortable about doing nothing, about sailing 50% efficiently, and feeling totally worthwhile.

I recall that I had worked hard in my youth to get an education and a degree, working long hours driving taxis on the weekends and teaching during the week. I was also building a boat in the backyard, running a small building company and trying, like everyone else, to get a foot in the door of the economy, while I was still young and able. I'd somehow succeeded with two houses and a boat, a hard-working wife and two kids, but it was never enough. That Protestant work ethic was drilled so deeply into my psyche to continually do more. I had practised those hard lessons of 'doing more and more' for success before anything else, and now at the age of 57 I've decided that I have to get off that unhappiness treadmill and practise just 'being'.

Getting rid of the stone castle with its 5 bedrooms, the demanding wood furnace, the cleaning, and much, much more, was finally my big dive back into minimalism. Doing was over, I wanted freedom to just be, even coming out here where I expected to sit back and let Henry take me across the Atlantic, was becoming more of an exercise of another "big long doing". Maybe this was the last big doing before I have those final "changes of life" moments. Women, from my observations, have their change of life at about 48 years of age and men have theirs at about 52. I think mine came a little later when I began to literally practise the art of the Japanese tea ceremony in my odd little way. The ceremony says every little step in making a simple cup of tea is valuable and can be used to focus only on that tiny step, to the exclusion of all other things. In this way one becomes grounded and out of the mind where one's quiet 'being' takes over, being in the here and now, being content and taking time to do the simple things in life well, as if the whole axis of one's life hinges on that one cup of tea. It makes each moment a sacred time for self, rather that hurrying to get more things done.

And in this moment, I remind myself that sitting here in the cockpit, watching the horizon, talking to whales, feeling the breeze beginning to ease below 15 knots is another special moment in time when I can just 'be'.

Perhaps if this is the only lesson I can absorb on this whole journey across the Atlantic, it will all be worthwhile.

As evening approaches, I can feel the breeze easing more and more and I decide that I'll hoist a reefed main somehow without Henry controlling the helm. I practise first, leaving the locked helm for 10 seconds, rushing to the mast, untying one small tie on the sail cover and then being forced to rush back to correct the course. There is no way *Millefleurs* will steer a course on her own, she is the proverbial drunken sailor, diving this way and that without any rhyme or reason. I wait for a lull between waves and rush up to loosen more ties and rush back to re-correct the course. There seems to be only one practical way to get this girl sailing - lock the helm, let her go her own way, hoist the mainsail as quickly as possible and then rush back to correct the course, regardless of whether she gybes or rounds up.

It's riskier, regarding the life of the sails, but there is no other option and I'll try to get Henry on the job again soon, even if it's to hold a brief course while I hoist the rig. I get the double reefed main up with the preventer to port to stop any dangerous gybes and then get us back on course, sailing eastwards at 4 knots. I remind myself I'm at least keeping up with the whale, but I think he is doing it a lot easier.

We sail into the night with the wind down to 12 knots, steadier, with a dying swell and a gentle roll as the waves pass under us heading northeast.

The night is very dark and a moon may emerge much later, but I doubt I'll see it through the heavy cloud cover from west to east. The light of the compass is my only reliable companion and occasionally I get a snatch of some stars to the south, but nothing is in context and I have no idea which name fits which star. I make a wish and play around with the idea that the sky will clear and suddenly it will light up with stars.

It doesn't happen of course and at 2200 hrs I decide to drop the rig and sleep for a while.

I hate the idea of dropping the main as I know the drama in raising it again only increases, but undisturbed sleep is more important now. I sleep for an hour and come on deck at 2300hrs and with the helm still locked, I begin hoisting the storm jib first and then working on the mainsail. I get both up somehow as *Millefleurs* heads up into the breeze, which is better than gybing, and then she stalls as I lock off the main and run back to the helm. She heels over 20 degrees and falls away as I ease the preventer and we're off again to the east south east on 110 degrees compass, slipping along quietly to a 10-knot breeze making 4 knots on a flattening sea, with lots of phosphorescence all around shimmering out the stern like a ghostly trail.

That's how planes were able to spot ships during World War 11. They waited for dark nights and followed the phosphorescent trails which were particularly bright from a fleet of ships steaming together. Maybe if I'm spottable from a plane crossing over the Atlantic he'll drop me some croissants and chocolate!

I've got a couple more muesli bars secreted in my pocket and today I've had some rolled oats, dried fruit and honey with UHT (long-life) milk and I'm feeling great. My hunger is for sweetness and these USA muesli bars I particularly savour as they are chocolate coated with nuts inside and, like the tea ceremony I bite off a tiny piece of bar and put the rest away and see how long I can suck that bar. I refuse to bite it because then it'll be gone in a flash and I'll want more. I'm trying consciously to drag the flavour out of another small piece of muesli bar, when something very strange happens.

A dark figure, an apparition, a stranger, sits down next to me in the cockpit and I smell tobacco smoke and hear rusting. I realise that this is every bit as exotic as a whiff of vanilla, as I can smell that too.

It's dark in the leeward side of the cockpit, but someone is sitting there and I'm not only frightened and perplexed, but curious as hell.

Is this the swimmer who has finally caught up to us and has slid quietly over the stern rails to get into the cockpit? But of course, he wouldn't smell of tobacco or vanilla which seems to calm my nerves considerably. He's only an arm's length away, reminding me of my big fear as a teenager of waking up and finding someone in my bedroom.

I say loudly, in mock anger perhaps, trying to take the initiative before he, whatever he is, overwhelms me, "where the hell did you come from?" and he replies softly in an American deep south drawl, "from anywhere and everywhere, just dropping in to say hi!"

This display of friendship makes me feel a little rude for my initial hostility and fear and I reply, "man, you scared the hell out of me creeping up on me like that" and he says, "sorry, it's the first time I've scared anyone in a long time, I'm Sam."

I say, "these last few days have been pretty hectic and now you appear.' He replies, "well I did appear last night as I swam past to remind you when you needed sleep badly man, and I even changed my accent!" Now I know he is a friend and not an evil spirit who has come to cause me grief, so I say with joy and excitement, "you sound familiar Sam, you're like someone I know but it's a long time ago." Then he says slowly to emphasise his words, "we've been together on sailing ships before and we've crossed this bit of the ocean many times, but always in bigger boats with lots of sails. Always with many crew, but today I thought I'd come to help you for a while, give you a hand up maybe, help hold a course, reconnect when you need a friend." Then he adds "we've had lots of good times and lots of tough times in the past and we always stuck together, and this is one of those times. you need some help man, you need a companion, you've been in a bit of bad shape these past few days."

I say, "you're damn right, I wasn't sure I'd get through the other night when I was flattened by a wave, and now there's still a long way to go and I'm struggling."

Sam suggests we have a sing together and he begins to sing a song I know well. *"Way down upon the Swannee river, far, far away, that's where my heart is yearning ever, home where the old folks stay."*

The chorus follows but it's not familiar to me but Sam obviously has a handle on it, *"all the world is sad and dreary, everywhere I roam, oh darkies, how my heart grows weary far from the old folks home."*

Sam continues on in his beautiful deep voice, singing more verses to the song I'd vaguely heard in the past, but at least I could join in the chorus. We sing on for ages, Sam with his full-throated voice and me with my puny echoes. Then he said "that was fun man" and he quietly hums away for quite a while with songs that I knew and some I'd never heard, but the ambience and fellowship Sam was creating was just beautiful and suddenly I realised I had a mate, a friend a companion who was filling me up with warmth and good cheer that I was surely missing, sailing alone.

I didn't care where he had come from or even how he could possibly appear in my lonely cockpit, but the fabric of my universe is definitely being stretched, perhaps the veil is being torn apart and I am opening up to bigger possibilities. In Stephen Dedalus's book *Ulysses* he says, "we walk through ourselves meeting robbers, ghosts, giants, old men, young men, wives, wisdom and brothers in laws, but always (in some weird way) meeting ourselves."

Curiosity, intrigue and excitement are running wildly through my veins as this newest movie starts to roll in my life. I remember Ralph Waldo Emerson's famous saying, "our life is not so much threatened as our perception" and I'm ready for whatever this is. It's like being given a warm rum by a long-lost friend, then sitting back and savouring it, enjoying the immense essence of it all.

There is no point in calling on my logical self in this situation as Sam is just perfect for the moment and he has brought more than I could ever imagine... the fun of a friend calling in to say hello, when all hell has gone down. I say, "Sam do you know the song *Me and Bobby McGee?*" and he says, "one of my favourites." We begin singing away as we sail along and we rage on with Sam's fantastic voice belting out such a beautiful song that connects us both into a real unity of spirit. We sing the same song 3 times in various ways, adding new words here and there with me making up rhythm by drumming on the deck.

As we sit quietly sailing along, chatting and musing on life, the half-moon flitters across the water giving sparkling life to a quietening scene, showing the swell is finally going down and Sam says, "like to hear a bit of humour about wisdom?" and I say "yes, yes, yes."

He says two old friends, Paddy and Mick, are sitting at the bar drinking and Mick says, "Paddy how come you so wise?" and Paddy says, "cause I just am" and Mick says, "no, Paddy, there's something you have that I don't have" and Paddy says, "you're damn right Mick there is something I have that you don't have!" "What is it Paddy, cause I sure could do with some wisdom, I've been making some foolish mistakes lately and it's wearing on my mind. My Betty is calling me silly and I ain't happy. What is it Paddy... why are you so damn wise?"

And Paddy says with a serious look on his face, "it's because I take wise pills!" to which Mick replies "Paddy, if you could give me some of those wise pills that would sure make me happy."

At this point Paddy pulls out some round black pills from his pocket and puts them on the bar counter and says, "there you go Mick, take one of these, chew it up, sit back and feel wise."

Mick says gratefully, "Paddy you my best friend," and he takes one of the black pills, pops it in his mouth, chews it up, takes a drink, swallows and sits back smiling. After a while he says, "Paddy, I don't feel no wiser!" and Paddy says, "well take two Mick."

Which he does, chews them up, takes a drink, sits back and waits again. After a while, feeling very disappointed, he says, "Paddy I still don't feel no wiser" so Paddy says with a laugh, "well Mick, you sure need lots of wise pills, take the lot."

Mick eagerly swallows them all, sits back chewing away and then green stuff starts coming out of the corners of his mouth and runs down his chin. Finally he says, "Paddy these wise pills taste like sheep shit!"

With a big smile on his face Paddy says, "now Mick you're getting wise!!"

I giggle away with the best gift someone can give me…some humour out here, no matter how trite or silly but just fun, to twist my mind off the rational path and cause me to laugh along with the silliness of life.

We sit in silence for a long time, with me helming along, taking an occasional look around the horizon feeling as if I am in communion with some greater part of myself that accepts all and goes with the flow. No questions spring to mind, no answers are sought, just an appreciation of the magnificence of being somewhere in the universe amongst the stars and the ocean, with a mate, feeling content with my new familiar companion.

I say to Sam somewhere near dawn "you know the wise thing for me is to get some sleep, I'm really tired" and Sam says, "drop the sails man, lock the helm, go below and I'll keep watch."

And I do, thankful that Sam will keep an eye out for ships and wake me if necessary. I'm out like a light.

I wake at dawn and, remembering Sam is on watch, I burst into the cockpit ready for more conversations, but Sam is gone and the cockpit seems very dark and empty. It seems like a close friend has left without saying goodbye and I feel sad. I guess I'm feeling vulnerable again as I'm on my own without the usual support systems around. Being alone was a big part of my childhood and I savoured long periods of time hunting and fishing by myself.

When I went to boarding school which was then a long way from home, at the age of 13, my vulnerability hit me big time, I was an outsider, I didn't belong and I realised I had to fit into another pattern of living. There were 240 boarders sleeping in one big dormitory with just a locker for personal items that had to be guarded jealously. I sought refuge in solitary pursuits like making a crystal radio set and sitting beside the college fence using the wire as an antenna, listening to my own radio world beyond the prison confines.

When the inevitable bullies crossed my boundaries teasing me for sneaking off, I fought with a ferocity they didn't know I had, so they eventually left me alone. Then as I grew older and wiser I learnt that being vulnerable is not a sign of weakness but bravery. Our vulnerability is something more than a weakness, it's a sign, a reflection of the enormous nerve and strength that you can tip quickly into heroism. It's about cathartically owning up to who you really are, which can trigger an empathic murmur of recognition, or a hand reaching out in support, as we are all fragile in some respects.

Now I feel ok about my own cowardice and vulnerability during that storm as those are the demons I've been challenging these last few days and they're slowly losing their potency.

Females do this much better than males because they can accept retreating while losing and so their fears of spiders and mice and storms at sea are somehow for society much easier to accept.

The vulnerability of our shadows eventually have to be faced and stared down. My vulnerability of being alone and lost and particularly cold while confronted with a hugely malevolent storm demon is one of the many reasons I am out here getting ready to continue sailing again, whilst knowing my fears in the uncertainty of it all are shadows that will either disappear or bury me.

I make some breakfast and a cup of Earl Grey tea and sit in the cockpit eating and wondering what this journey is all about. It's getting damn interesting. So far it's produced a hurricane, a swimmer, a whale and Sam. The winds are down to 10 knots swinging more to the west, while the seas are relatively flat with a low swell and no white caps. I'm not sure what day it is and I don't care. I've been out here at least a week, although it seems like a month. I know I could look at the nautical almanac but naming and numbering things has lost its appeal.

Around me is water and sky and as I slowly look up, I see the clouds have parted and the sun is just rising over the horizon. Today looks perfect for making more miles as I have left the thought world behind and all that's important now, is how I feel. There's no need to even consider what rig to put up or when, I'll just know when the time is right.

I eat my breakfast slowly and enjoy the cup of tea with a little dash of honey that has solidified in the jar, probably due to the cold.

I go below to clean up and put on warm gear for the day's run. It is said that if you go at half speed you create twice the enjoyment. So I take my time and soak in the sun, both gifts denied to many. I'm rich out here, I'm King of my new castle. I could be bored watching this ocean but I believe the ocean is a perfect metaphor for the workings of my happiness and vulnerability that I've come out here to explore in some perverse way.

Wise men have said that when you are travelling and insecure you are closest to your home, because what you feel when you are still and lost, is your own home within.

I do hope my inner home begins to form soon into something quite beautiful, and, like the world traveller who through sheer experience begins to see the world without fear and himself without insecurities, that's what I want.

The ocean is definitely magnificent and wild and unstable because the simpleness of the sea provides stark contrast to the many other treasures that interrupt this sameness. The whale swims by, dolphins visit and bring their enthusiasm for living and each wave has a story of its own. These treasures punctuate the sameness, accentuating the many shades of difference.

The Tibetans say you don't choose a life, you live one and I'm deeply into this one. As the face of the ocean changes it's providing me with a richer backdrop to beauty, uncertainty and creativity, more than any home I've ever occupied has ever provided. I should never be bored out here, the subtle changes are constant, and yet tolerating boredom is also a necessary function of this day to day living.

According to researchers in the USA in 1952, 26% of people were regularly bored. In 1978 this had jumped to 38% and in 2007 had increased to 41%. Yes, almost half our population is now bored and that stems from our youth, where the art of tolerating boredom is developed, just like resilience, vulnerability and adversity.

Yet this has been lost in our present youth with all their toys and instant access to stimulating games, while in contrast the Japanese tea ceremony is a real mental counter to that idea of living your life well. It is an exercise in using boredom as a profound way of turning the simple and gentle art of living, similar to oceaning, into a profoundly graceful act of tapping into one's own inner wisdoms. It's taking oneself and practising being content, being complete without anything but oneself, and that could be the most difficult thing we humans face.

Happiness comes directly from being in rhythm with one's whole self, without any need for more. Being alert and still, sailing along quietly, enjoying the solitude, finding those sweet spots in life where all things are in harmony and maybe that's the answer to any boredom.

Boredom doesn't come from being without stimulation, but from being bored with oneself, with losing touch with one's inner potential, with a loss of gratitude for just being alive and healthy. And a lot of my chosen complexity has gone. Henry has collapsed, the GPS has taken a swim and the furler is useless. Now it's just will and wind and water to get me to Horta. I'm free wheeling, meeting the Atlantic head on, eyeball to eyeball, breath to breeze and we're in this tussle together. Without me being here there would be no story to tell, no words to print, just a blurred canvas. Now I'm changing that tune, I whistle to the wind, hum to the horizon, chortle to the swells and we're getting along just fine, and as I bury myself in the mystery of the day it seems to get better and brighter every long hour.

If I delve into my past for things I should have done before I left port and the hundreds of bigger possibilities for the future, it could occupy my whole day. Introspection is fine to some degree but it can get out of hand quickly. My imagination could drive me wild and this genuine simplicity of day to day living while sailing across this vast ocean, would dissolve. My mind is really poorly equipped to make me happy, fulfilled or even content.

I'll leave that to my feelings and just 'being' in the moment. and then I remember another random t-shirt that I saw said, "if I'm not in my right mind, my left mind gets pretty busy!" I know if I finish this voyage content and fulfilled, it won't be because of my active mind, but rather because of my contented 'being'.

With that in mind I decide after breakfast that it's time to have a simple ocean wash. Not with some hot water from the kettle but with numerous buckets of cold sea water, and then I'll get to work on Henry.

I find two more of my remaining spare buckets, attach lanyards to the handles, collect some cheap hair shampoo and stand on the aft deck ready for a bracing wash. The first bucket of sea water is cold, bloody cold and I shiver madly. With vigorous hair rubbing and hollering and more detergent, the next bucket seems friendlier and after another couple of buckets I feel cleansed and energised and the body seems to take on a new zest for life.

I begin a small dance on deck between each ocean swell, imagining I am an Australian Aborigine dancing for sheer joy, circling the earthy rumble of the didgeridoo. I dance away reminding myself that my happiness has a lot to do with rhythmic movement.

The rhythm of the ocean stored in my DNA reconnects me to the lost spirit of this ocean dance and I'm feeling better already. I'm reconnecting to older rhythms, deeper feelings, bigger days. The day is getting warmer and I see a couple of frigate birds wheeling to the south of me, hunting fish shoals. I particularly enjoy their boundless energy as life is returning to normal and I feel completely free of the adversities of the last few days, particularly after that baptism of cold heavy sea water.

I go below and find the tools to take Henry off the wheel and get him below and into a cardboard box, where I can dismantle his innards. Getting him off the wheel is bad enough, as he puts up quite a struggle, while I attempt to undo all the holding alum bolts and then carefully extract the motor from the helm without dropping any of the vital parts into the cockpit.

Gingerly I take him below and put him in a box on the settee and begin the delicate process of delving into the secrets of how it all runs. Maybe I should have done this before, but I didn't have the heart or inclination back in the marina, believing Henry was bullet proof and would work for months without giving up, particularly after the cost and the promises of those salesmen who'd never been out of sight of land.

I separate the inner and outer hub and, alarmingly, many small black ball bearings fall out, fortunately rolling around in the box. I'm glad I didn't just open Henry up in the cockpit and have some fall out into the cockpit drains. As I pull out the gearbox and extract the gears I discover that they're made of black plastic, and, to my dismay I find that the teeth are all chopped out. The plastic empire has sucked me in, longevity and reliability are gone. I try to file out the teeth, even though the warranty says I can't even open up the gearbox without the loss of the warranty.

Obviously the manufacturers never ever considered that there may be a sailor in need who could possibly be a long way from any repair shop. I finally have to accept that the piece of equipment I have accepted as reliable is just useless and it's not up to any ocean crossing.

This is a bit like having a PSA test for prostate cancer and find it's all clear and then realise that this does not guarantee you are free from cancer! I re-examine the manual and begin to realise I should have bought a spare motor, a spare gearbox and spare belts and probably had some limited training in fixing this damn machine.

It's sophisticated but not sturdy. Hardly useful on any long ocean passage without spares. I wonder out loud how many others have been caught out like myself and even without the storm, I doubt whether this Raymarine was up to any ocean voyage with those plastic gears. I silently curse the bastards and grin at being so easily fooled. I guess it also reflects the modern age where product promises are bigger sellers than product reliability.

I go upstairs and refit Henry to the helm and finally I get excited and hopeful that he will be able to steer again, even briefly, with the rejuvenated gears, even if it's only while I hoist the sails. I kind of challenge my luck and have another cup of tea and a muesli bar before I turn Henry on.

I unlock the helm, engage Henry and alter the compass settings, but Henry just cries out loudly, like a lost lamb. He shudders and jerks but seems unable to control the helm. There's a will there, a brain at work, but no results. It's the plastic gears that are buggered and I'll just have to live with the consequences. He's done, gonzo, gone, shot. I swear a little and go forward, hoist the mainsail, return to the helm and begin to steer. I turn Henry on again but no luck and I realise I have to drop the main and go forward to put up the no.3 jib first, without any steering device, before attempting to put up the reefed main. *Millefleurs* drifts till the jib is hoisted and then she dives downwind. I rush back to the helm to steer without the mainsail.

I'm frustrated, realising that I have to balance getting the mainsail up to stop the roll while getting some speed out of the jib to give us steering ability. I wait till we're in a relative lull and run forward to get up the main. I get it half hoisted, cleat it off and rush back to the helm to do some more adjustments between waves. I gradually get the main further up, taut with the preventers still on, and we're raging off to the east in a 10 knot breeze. I begin to shout out Willie Nelson's "On the road again" in a hopelessly broken voice. Hell, I wish I could sing!

Chapter 11

Dolphins and more horizons

I look to the horizon and wonder how many horizons there will be before I'm too tired to steer. I'm definitely not here to invent the wheel but rather to keep it turning. With Henry gone and this Hunter being so flighty there are certainly going to be long, long hours on the helm that will require patience and perseverance and many hours of lost sleep. Up until I dissected Henry I assumed it was the belt slipping as I'd adjusted it often to maintain steerage but now I know for sure that Henry is as useless as his warranty and I consider writing a vicious letter to Raymarine telling them their flashy tool is a toy. I want to shoot from the hip with malice, I want to walk into their offices in my wet weather gear, throw the unit on the floor and jump on it. I even consider asking for my money back and all sorts of malevolent strategies, but I know that letting the injustice of it all colour my journey is surely a useless exercise. It is another lesson learnt. Adjust to the now and get on with it, what is, is.

We sail down one horizon and then another, moving between 4 and 5 knots on a flat sea with the sun building south of me into a full-blown ball of bright joy, charging the ocean and nature all around. Birds are wheeling, there is plenty of energy in the air and we gallop along like a well-tuned horse, kept in check by my solid hand reins. A small pod of dolphins comes from the north, wheels around us and joins for just a short while. I take the winch handle and tap the hull gently as they come alongside and stare up at me, rolling and twisting in sheer delight. I'd like to get into the water with them, but I remembered on *Sundancer* we tried that a number of times. Whenever we lowered a crew member quietly into the water while the dolphins played happily around us, it always caused them to take flight.

The dolphins may play happily around until the person hits the water and then they leave in a hurry, off somewhere else, leaving the uncertainty of our intentions behind. I guess their curiosity is overshadowed by their wariness. Those dolphins that come around humans regularly and can be fed, like at Monkey Mia in Western Australia, are obviously accustomed to strange creatures in the water, but wild dolphins won't have a bar of it. Perhaps they think we are predators and there's a common reflex that keeps them shy and aloof.

I decide to shake out the reef in the main and now the fun begins. Lock the helm, run up to the mast, release the ties, take a look at the course, run back, make a correction, run back to the mast and continue the cycle. It takes 4 or 5 lunges at the mast to finally get it cranked up and sheeted off. Hoisting sail has become my most important task and my most difficult, but it is essential if I'm to cross this ocean. I desperately try to think of a way around it. If I could hoist the mainsail from the cockpit that'd make life a lot easier and I plan to give it a try later, maybe, even putting a block at the base of the mast and reaving a halyard through it back to the cockpit.

The thought encourages me to consider how I can improve this delicate situation that I am in, without a helmsman to help me out, because desperation often brings creativity from somewhere within, reducing the complexity of survival down to some simplicity of action. To dispel the disappointment of the self-steering failure I deliberately try to ignore the reality of the situation and sail along, trying to remember weird signs I have seen, for no particular reason than they tickle my fancy. I remember one on the fence of a roadside apple orchard in Tasmania's Derwent Valley, where I was teaching in the 1970's. The sign was displayed during one summer but it didn't last long. It seemed to attract stray bullet holes as it said "is there life after death? trespass and find out!" I do love signs, particularly peculiar ones that often say a lot more about the owner of the sign than the message.

This sign was on an old garage wall in South Dakota, USA and it read, "if we can't fix your brakes, we can make your horn louder" and I laughed all the way up the road. Those signs definitely express the creativity of humorous minds.

I watch a ship passing north of me close to the horizon. I stare at him for a while, not sure whether it is a small dark cloud that is disappearing over the horizon or a fishing vessel closer to my position. Either way he represents civilisation passing me by, but I have no desire to call him on the radio. He is heading west, obviously going to the USA from somewhere in

Europe, and then I see containers on deck through my binoculars as he rises and falls against the skyline. That indicates that the shipping lane going west to America is north of me and if I continue east south east, I'll stay between the south and north lanes for at least another 2 days.

We roll on to the east and midday passes without me wanting to get a sight. I guess I'm quieting the curious thinking mind and letting reality take charge for a while. It's not my usual behaviour though as I always want to interrogate those mysteries around me, breaking them down into understandable units and then synthesising the results.

The calculations of getting a position fix from the sextant is the constant challenge now as it helps me to feel in charge of the situation but that's a bit unsettling here where I'm really in charge of nothing. Uncertainty rules the waves, chance and the unusual and the spontaneous are the valued men on this chessboard. In chess terms it's like having a board full of horses and no Queen to protect me and I'd better get used to that for the next month or so.

In the same vein of uncertainty, I've always tended to avoid lawyers, clergymen and bankers who expect the world to behave in a regular fashion. Logic is their prince and analysis is their forte as they are easily fazed by the irregularities that life inevitably throws up.

They're always so sure of themselves and yet in reality are often more vulnerable to the vagaries of life than the average taxi driver. I well remember John, a Queen's Counsel lawyer, who sailed twice with us in the Sydney to Hobart yearly cruise on board *Sundancer* in the mid-1980s. There we ran ahead of the fleet to be in Hobart as spectators when the race fleet arrived. Normally the crew members were young and adventurous, finding another way to experience the famous race without all the drama and months of training and the pain of being wet, tired and cold for days at a time. I was never sure why John came, as he only stood watch if he didn't have to helm. He also never wanted to cook or do sail changes, and he showed no interest in the race fleet. He was an enigma and I was curious, hoping to discover more about him. He intrigued me and the rest of the crew, as he never initiated a conversation, nor offered to help out in any way.

One morning we were on watch together and I attempted to get into his mind, to hopefully understand what made him tick.

"John," I said, "how long have you been in the law?" he replied "38 years, the last 5 as a Queen's Counsel."

"Do you enjoy it?" I inquired. He reflected on my question long after lighting a cigarette and taking another drink of coffee. "Law has its moments, particularly when you represent horrible crooks who should be shot twice, just in case you missed them the first time!" I laughed long and hard at the stories he told of well-known crooks he had represented, lost the cases and then sent them a huge bill for a failed endeavour that equalised the trouble they caused others. He said it was society's ways of getting even, that having incompetent lawyers representing crooks, evened out the odds for the whole of society. He said it was on a par with clergymen who society bred and fed, to keep the honest citizens calm, while putting up with all the injustices in the system.

I said "John, is there a wisdom you'd give to a conscientious young lawyer just starting out in the field?" he pondered a while, smoked another cigarette, took a pee over the side and said "yeah there are one of two rules that I would like to tell aspiring lawyers." I was hooked, I thought I'd found his secret, got down to his core, engaged him in some deep wisdom that I would be able to share with others. "Tell me John, if I become a lawyer what would be your first bit of sage advice?" and he said slowly and reverently, almost as if he was delivering a sermon, "in God we trust and all else cash!", somehow marrying the clergyman and the lawyer into a common bond of practice. Then he went silent and disappeared below.

I left it at that, figuring I had become just a little wiser. He came back up on deck in a rush soon after, sat down and giggled a bit. I could see that a possible breakdown had figured in his career somewhere, and we were really taking him on the ocean so that he could get away from his office and be out of contact with that mean world of law. Then I got really bold as I continued our first bit of shared momentum by saying "John, my good man, any more words of advice?" and he sat for a bit longer, lit another cigarette and went into a deep reflective mode that had me worrying how much he was charging for advice. Finally he continued, "the second rule in law is like life, 'a friend in need is a bloody nuisance!'"

Now I wasn't sure if that was meant for me or if it was some exotic rule for Queen's Counsels. Even if he could just hold the helm while I am sail changing, I'm glad that John is not out here with me now, as he could turn a good day into real bloody misery, and I'd probably be desperately calling that freighter by now, imploring the captain to take him home.

At 1700hrs I realise I need some more sleep so I drop the main and leave the jib backed, heave-to with a locked helm, and go below. The jib does stop the roll a little and I'm asleep in a flash, enjoying the comfort of a dry bed and a quiet ocean.

This is paradise after the misery of survival and it's like when one stops banging his head against the wall.

I awake at 1800 hours and climb on deck to take a look around. All is quiet, there are no ships and the breeze is calling for more sail. The clouds billow softly on the south west horizon and steam towards me doing pirouettes and silent shape shifting and then pass overhead slowly vanishing over the north eastern horizon like lazy jet vapour trails as I sit quietly deciding what to do.

We are hove-to, drifting northeast at half a knot creating a wake that flattens the swell and *Millefleurs* seems comfortable as she slowly rolls up to the wind, picks up some momentum and then falls away to repeat the pattern. This will be my new sleep mode when the wind is light as that one sail up also makes it much easier to be seen from a passing ship's deck. I finally go forward and hoist the main and come back to the helm, release the steering brake, ease the jib and we begin sailing away. I swing us onto an easterly course and sheet hard on the jib. With the approaching evening I'll be able to make good miles in this lighter breeze and hopefully, after another short sleep, I'll be able to sail well into the night and maybe through until morning.

The sun is still strong from the west and I sit wearing just a t-shirt and shorts enjoying the dream of living like a King without the responsibility.

I see a white object in the water ahead and as I sail up to it, it glints in the sun and something breaks the surface of the water around it. As I get closer and closer I see what I have found in this trackless wasteland. It's a lost fishing buoy, with a dulled metal tag attached and a line beneath that is harbouring a school of dark hand sized fish. Around the line are metres of seaweed, mussels and algae growth that indicate that this buoy has been out here a long time.

I know there'll be small crabs and hundreds of tiny bits of life floating along on this lost island heading nowhere in particular, just living in the moment and I'm arriving from nowhere just to check out its progress. I leave it there as a monument to nature and its powerful web of life and sail on. No treasure found.

I wonder one day after passing that buoy if humans will develop immersion capsules that could house 2 or 3 people and drift around the ocean for years maybe collecting all their food from the colonies of fish and mussels and other life that attaches to them, giving them a better alternative than Mars. The people on board would be able to express self-sufficiency and other amazing real life experiments and begin to practise living in the moment, instead of doing military service and practising shooting others.

They'd be able to practise minimalism with strong connection to mother ocean and be students of a whole new movement where humanity begins to move back to the sea for survival. Perhaps we could send volunteers out for a year to start off the program and they could practise the mental and spiritual art of just 'being'. If I volunteered I'd like to do it in the tropics and maybe have a floating island with palm trees and thatched huts and a colony of dolphins around me as we floated lazily around. And that's the rub! We humans are forever creative and ambitious and adventurous and soon we would have the whole ocean full of huge life rafts with musicians on one raft and painters on another and hopefully Jehovah Witnesses on blue rafts, so that we could see them coming.

Now that's what I liked about Leo back in the boatyard in the Solomons. Regardless of his circumstances he brought his own sunshine, along with his rats. When I told him how many signs I'd seen around the streets of America saying, "will work for food" he reminded me that he knew that so well, having been out of work for 5 years.

He's been doing odd jobs in order to survive and was forced to live on his donated boat on the hard, because it was cheaper. He said, "I've got a medical degree and certificates of all kinds but no one wants to employ me. I guess at the age of 50 I'm out of the race."

Then he shared a story about his friend's experience. "You know, my friend Bert up north, he's also got a medical degree plus other trauma certificates and he's been out of work for 3 years, but just last year he finally hit the jackpot. He got a job, would you believe, selling toothbrushes of all things!" I say, "no way, there can't be any money in doing that."

Leo says, "you're damn right. After three months of just making petrol money Bert was about to turn it in, and then he hit it big time. You know he began selling so many toothbrushes that the boss from New York rang him up.

'Hey Bert you were my worst salesman, now you're my best. You know, I've got 57 guys out there on the road selling toothbrushes, and you've come from bottom to top salesman in the last month, how come? You must have some technique I don't know about, I'd like you to show me so that I can spread it to my boys and I'll give you a fat bonus."

Bert grins. "Yeah, I do boss, I'm onto a winner that'll knock your socks off, make your false teeth rattle and your glass eye squeak, but I'd like a bonus of $500 up front, and 50 free toothbrushes, before I make you wiser."

"Now you're stretching our friendship" says the boss "but ok, I'm coming to visit you and bringing your bonus, where are you?"

"Chicago airport" says Bert.

"I'll be out there on Monday morning and I'll call you when my flight lands," the boss replies.

Monday morning arrives and the boss contacts Bert, who is out the front doors of the airport. He's paid off the security guys to guarantee his spot, and is working his business with the arriving passengers.

When he emerges from the main entrance the boss sees Bert beside a table covered with a gorgeous white tablecloth and on the table are rows of toothbrushes, dip and crackers.

He comes over to Bert and says, "I'd like to see how you do this Bud?" and passes Bert his wad of cash, 50 toothbrushes and some chocolates for good luck.

Bert is impressed and says, "you stand over there, boss, take it easy and just watch me!"

A guy comes out of the airport with his bags and as he strolls past, Bert casually looks him in the eye, smiles and says, "hey Buddy you feel like a French cracker?" and the guy says, "sure do." Bert indicates towards the plate of crackers and then says, "you might find they're a little dry, want to try some dip?" and the guy dips his cracker in the bowl and takes a bite. He then spits out the cracker exclaiming loudly between spits, "that dip tastes like shit."

Bert says with a wink to the boss, "it is shit, wanna buy a toothbrush?"

With that story Leo repaid me for being kicked out of Panera Bread and gave me a wonderful story that I've just shared with you and may be useful if you also get retrenched one day and need a job!

Chapter 12

Starry, starry nights

It's 2100 hrs and I've seen 4 jets passing overhead against the darkening sky tonight, silently heading east with their distinctive strobing lights, reminding me of all those passengers who are about an hour out of New York heading for London, without an inkling that there is someone below watching their progress and hankering for some meaningful conversation.

I wish I had a radio so that I could talk to pilots, but I'm not sure what I'd say, with them travelling near the speed of sound and me sailing along slowly at walking pace. Of course, I'd ask them if they wanted to swap places and tell them how great it is down here and how lonely it must be up there!! Maybe in the future we'll all have phones that can contact anyone anywhere. My mind goes off into another scenario that keeps me amused for another few hours as I continue hand steering and avoid thinking about food or when I'll finally get off the helm and be able to dive into my bunk.

At midnight I decide to turn in and rest up for a while. I lock the helm, drop the main and leave the jib up, winched in hard to stop it chafing and to keep us hove-to. For some reason I wonder whether I should put on the masthead light as I have enough power now that Henry has quit. I go below, press the masthead switch and for the first time in days am feeling more comfortable, totally forgetting about ships running me down (because I have that big bright light to pre-warn them). I crawl into my bunk and am out like a light.

I wake at 0130 hrs, climb into the cockpit and take a look around. I'd like to lie in my bunk for longer but the breeze is still blowing at 8 knots and I feel the call of the sailors advice, "never waste a fair breeze" as I prepare for another all-night vigil.

I make a cup of tea, put a couple of muesli bars in my pocket, put on my wet weather gear for warmth and head back to the cockpit, not forgetting to turn off the masthead light.

I look up at the stars and recognize the pole star, the big dipper, Scorpio and many others. I'm reminded that the stars in the southern hemisphere are even brighter than here as they angle more directly towards the Milky Way, which is full of stars. Wherever you are the stars are a constant reminder that we all share the same night sky and I really enjoy finding twinkling Sirius, the brightest star in the sky in the big dog constellation or the blood red Betelgeuse in the Orion constellation or the tactical pointers in the Southern Cross, that are not visible from here. When the ancients stared at the night sky they didn't see another place, rather another state of being and that thought adds value to my whole panorama. I'd like to take a sextant shot of the pole star north of me to check my latitude, but there's no moon and without any horizon the sextant is redundant. It was a nice idea from my probing mind but has been cancelled out by reality, adding it's quiet and more reasoned voice.

I go forward and hoist the full mainsail and purposely take my time, completely forgetting about keeping on course, ignoring the possibility that we may jibe or turn back to the west. I'm just being content in my present state of being. It's one of those Zen moments when I feel disconnected from the result, just letting the moment fill out to the horizon.

The main rises easily, clearing the rigging and goes high in my sky before I cleat it off. It almost smiles at me and I feel that we are finally becoming a team. We've all got our own personality and we're all here to get safely to Horta. The main begins to pull us up into the breeze as we swing around to head south and I carefully pick my way back to the cockpit, refusing to be a slave to the rig or the helm or time.

I settle down comfortably, release the wheel brake and slowly swing onto a more easterly course. That feels better and it fits in with the beauty of sailing that I have so missed after Henry died. I realise that my desire not to waste a moment off course has become a burden to my own well-being.

If I take more time to hoist the rig and become less concerned about our heading then I can produce more of those Zen moments that I desperately need, which will hopefully lead me to improve my gratitude and appreciation of where I am and how far I've come. My values are definitely being stretched and here they can only be not in what I know but in what I sense.

It's a beautiful night, with the stars shimmering quietly, indicating light breezes up high and as I look up I see another trans-Atlantic flight well to the south of me also heading eastwards, flashing along like a determined firefly, reminding me that the world still rolls on while I sleep. If I could just continue appreciating every moment of life then everything would be beautiful and I'd have no reason to grumble or complain again and that would be like winning the lottery. The night is definitely more for feeling and the day more for thinking, and tonight I feel my spirit soaring with that plane as it barrels eastwards. It's almost like I am feeling my way through the night air rather than pushing along and that's why I've often noted that most cruising yachtsmen love the nights for passage making and the racing crew love the days.

There's much more spirit in the night and it reminds me of Shirley MacLaine's assertion that "spirituality is really the authentic discovery of one's capacity to feel" as sweet loving connections do belong much more to balmy tropical nights than those hot sunny days. Sailing in the night trade winds is what I enjoyed the most about ocean passaging - rolling along through a tropical night is a beautiful, warm, luscious, feeling particularly when one is able to appreciate the mass of stars overhead feeding that ambience below.

Those fresh trade winds blowing through my hair and the steady ocean rhythm cause me now to tap away at the helm and feel as though I'm soaring through the heavens, a long way above the earth in a journey somewhere far distant. It's like being in a spaceship heading for Mars with solar winds at your back. I imagine those astronauts who will eventually fly to Mars in tiny spaceships with their huge solar sails spread to the heavens, could receive their most basic training by going on long ocean passages. There they could absorb the necessary steady rhythm, the longed-for peace of mind and that delightful richness of spirit which should be a vital ingredient in their long 4 year trips to the far planet.

The real beauty of the tropics is that the nights are much better for sailing, being more settled, when the night trades drop down to 10-12 knots, from their usual boisterous 15-18 knot afternoon bursts. The swells also lay down a little more, seemingly taking a nap till dawn when they pick up again.

I am continually reminded that I need to go slower and apply less haste to my deck labours now, as my toes are suffering dreadfully from constant knocks and bangs that sometimes have me bent over in pain and swearing like a trooper. The same sets of cleats, chain plates and pieces of rigging seem to reach out as I rush past and belt me on the toes, just for the hell of it. My toes are now too sore for me to put on sea-boots and perhaps that is a positive thing as I really dislike booting up for a number of reasons. They take time to put on, I tend to slip around in them and during the day I swear they make my feet smell. The bruises I've already taken also refuse to heal. I like sailing in bare feet so the logical solution is to go slower with less haste and watch where I step. That's more easily said than done as I'd received that advice regularly from my mother who said I was always too impulsive, caring little about my safety as I usually reached for things beyond my scope. Changing one's nature sure is a battle, particularly when the deck on this Hunter is a man-made obstacle course set up to fool anyone not wearing steel capped boots.

My feet are made for water and not for solid objects down low and I only wish God had put a spare set of eyes in my ankles somewhere.

We sail on and at around 0500hrs a ship catches up to me from astern, well lit up like a cruise liner, south of my track. It steams past, slowly disappearing over the eastern horizon, leaving that longed-for connection in its wake. It's a love-hate relationship that I have with passing ships and I hope I don't see any more till I'm close to port. However, their passing does tell me things I need to know. They indicate that I'm getting down into the easterly shipping lane and since I haven't seen any west bound ships for a few days that must mean that I'm still within the middle of the lanes but getting to its southern edge. My best plan is to go further south to get below the easterly shipping lane and push down into those warmer waters with their siren's call of gentle trade winds and flying fish. That means heading towards the 35 degree latitude mark which is south of Horta by about 150 miles, and staying down low till it's a few hundred miles away and then sailing northwards again.

Another two planes pass over, heading eastwards over this lonely stretch of water and they seem to be welcoming me to join them as they move from one continent to the other. I am enthralled. Reality says I am just the lonely voyeur trying to make sense of it all, as I slowly crawl along in their wake.

I finally decide, as dawn approaches, to make a cup of tea on the run by rigging lines around the wheel, attaching blocks either side of the cockpit, and leading them below while I work the stove. I hustle around getting the gear together whilst also steering and I note that I'll continually have to adjust course, using the tell-tale flags which indicate the angle of the wind from where I sit anywhere in the cockpit seat to keep on course, as there is no compass in the galley. I set up the lines and eventually get the system working safely.

I note that there is a star in the west over my stern more likely a planet because it is so bright, maybe Jupiter, which I can use instead of the tell tales. If I glance at it every few seconds whilst boiling the water and also holding the reins I can practise steering this horse along the right course from the galley. It does take concentration though, and I'm getting short of it as this boat won't track for more than 5 seconds without a correction. Still, it's nice to be below out of the cold wind within the ambience of the warm stove making a cuppa as I talk to the helm and practise making smaller adjustments to keep that star locked in the companionway.

The star is a better guide than the dark tell-tale flags and I'd love to just hang here and forget about checking the horizon for boats or making any adjustments, but that's just not possible. I make my tea successfully, collect another muesli bar, load some rolled oats into a bowl, add some UHT milk and more sunflower seeds and go back to the cockpit seat, untying the lines from the wheel and setting them aside for later use. That was fun and I'll have to regard that exercise as almost time out from my deck work, even though it takes much more concentration. That could be my Zen practise for each day.

This is going to be a beautiful day. I feel like I'm sitting here folding whipped cream waiting for scones and jam to arrive. We're 10 days out, with little cloud apart from some high cirrus, a flat sea and 10 knot winds from aft. I have the full main and the no.3 jib up and I consider poling out the jib to windward to catch more breeze, but that would be a delicate job, particularly in getting the pole up and trying to steer, and then if the breeze hardens I have the reverse situation with a flying pole maybe causing a lot of damage to my rigging. I really am at the mercy of the helm and will have to adjust my sailing techniques for getting the most miles out of *Millefleurs*.

We are rolling towards the east at 4 knots and in daily sailing that's 100 miles per day, which is what the average cruising boat does on most passages if they don't motor through the lulls.

I'm enjoying rolling along at a good walking pace watching the birds, the flotsam here and there and practising "no thinking" which is one of the hardest things I've attempted. It's easy for a minute or so, but then I find myself thinking about some odd thing from the past and I start again. I look at the clock below and undertake 5 minute sessions of "no think" and then let my mind default to its usual detective roll of assessing the ocean, considering all possibilities and potentials and interrogating each one. My plan over the voyage is to practise "no think" for longer periods of time if it's possible, for no other reason than it being a valuable discipline.

I feel it will come in handy as I'm trying to live entirely in the moment, being happy to just be in this amazing environment enjoying the whole uncertainty of it all. It is said that the only thing certain in life is uncertainty, sandwiched between birth and death, and if I can stop my mind from trying to mentally control all possible chance factors and just let the voyage unroll on its own, then I'll be really ahead of the game. In fact I remember seeing a t-shirt on a lawyer friend that read "hold on now, let me overthink this!" That's exactly what I must avoid at all costs.

At about 0900hrs the breeze begins to fill in from the south west and I'm really pleased with myself for delaying the difficult task of poling out the jib. I try rigging lines to the helm from aft so that I can sit on the water containers at the stern and steer from a better vantage point. I am literally ploughing my own furrow that is rather winding but unlike the land there are few traces left, save a few swirls along a dotted wake. I figure that *Millefleurs*'s unpredictable steering ability is because she has a short keel with a spade rudder well aft, which separates the hull's grip on the water and the rudder's impact. She's like driving a forklift with the steering from behind as the keel and rudder are too far apart to assist each other, making her inherently unstable on the run. That is great for racing around the buoys where you need to tack fast and often, but quite at odds with ocean trekking where you need to hold course for long periods of time just as the old sailing ships did.

That's why those old clippers with the wisdom of experience over hundreds of circumnavigations had long deep keels giving them stability and a good grip on the water. Midday comes and I avoid the idea of taking a sight, not because I'm content with being unsure of where I am, but rather because the drama of dropping the rig and re-hoisting weighs heavily on my mind. The log says we have advanced 22 miles since dawn and that's encouraging. I've crossed 4 horizons and I've kept myself amused by observing all the things I've passed in the water.

There is flotsam every 20 minutes or so and as I get closer to the next piece of junk, I sail over to it for fun, say hello and admire the colony of sea life that has collected around that piece of land that has ended up out here by sheer chance. I imagine the pieces of junk are escapees that have come to help the ocean feed its colonies rather than being the lost residue of human waste. Plastic objects are the most common, particularly fishing floats of all sizes, and plastic bottles of various colours, most of which have been left out here by passing boats. I grab my boat hook and try snagging some as I sail slowly past, sometimes luffing up to get a better grab at it. It's a skill I can practise, imagining that it's treasure left for my passing, requiring me to interpret some personal meaning from each item I spot.

I see a largish white buoy ahead and practise my drill. I've been standing aft steering and looking well ahead steering by the lines. After deciding my angle of approach I quickly step up onto the starboard deck whilst stand-steering with my foot on the helm and holding the boat hook out ready for action. Then as I slowly sweep past I hopefully hook the target with the boat hook and haul it up onto the deck. It's my new "clay target shooting range" and I'm planning on being the best shot in town! Fortunately on this buoy there's a longish broken line and a clip attached to it which I easily hook and haul up onto the deck while I keep on tracking.

All this gear indicates that it's broken loose from some larger fishing device and now here it is on my deck, crawling with sea lice, covered in goose barnacles and trailing bits of long brown slimy weed. It's been out here for a while, judging from the size of the colony around it as every surface is completely covered, apart from the top of the white foam buoy. The buoy even has a number on it, N22, and I wonder what the code means and how by chance it ended up with me.

I sit in the cockpit helming with my left leg and picking over my new acquisition, wondering how good it will be when I find some real treasure.

If I was really creative I could maybe make some soup out of the barnacles, adding some herbs and a little rice and dine like a sea gypsy, but I quickly decide against it. I clean the barnacles off the buoy, casually tossing them overboard and hitch the float and the line to my stern rail. It could come in handy later as an anchor trip buoy and after all that effort I couldn't just toss it back into the ocean. I've even thought of a whole new enterprise in which I could launch a hundred ships with thousands of zealots who would sail the oceans fishing for flotsam. Then every year they would meet somewhere like Gibraltar where they'd have a festival and auction off the loot. Maybe we could have a reality TV show called "Lost and Found" where all sorts of people could connect lost objects with their owners. Maybe we could start a new treasure hunt where people can drop bottles into the ocean with genuine messages of treasure that can only be claimed on the festival day.

At 1600 hours I feel ready for a nap. The wind is steady, the sky is clear and the sun beams down onto a flat ocean and sailing is perfect, but sleep is more important. I look around the horizon in a full and slow 360 sweep and it is all clear. I lock the helm, drop the main, leave the jib up and go below to the land of nod.

At 1750 hours I come back on deck restored and ready to make the best of this breeze. I make a cup of tea and fill my bowl with some oats, nuts and grains and put it beside the helm for later. I put my cup in the cup holder and, noting that we are headed up to the breeze with a backed jib, I hoist a three quarter main and head back to the helm to haul us back on course. The wind is about 12 knots from the south west and we begin to roll off to the east again in a pattern that is getting very regular. I'd like to make another 30 nautical miles before the next sleep and that will put my daily run up to about 70 miles. I look out across the ocean with the sun behind me and it is totally empty. The sky is clear as well and I imagine a landscape with points here and there to garner interest, but here it is almost monotonous and empty.

There's not even a bird or a flying fish, a dolphin or a whale. I've been deserted, left alone, in a space too large to comprehend. This is emptiness personified, and it's what I came out here to comprehend, my own emptiness, whatever that means. As I look towards the horizon I know I'm surrounded by myriads of life forms that are totally comfortable in being out here, all happily co-existing. The growth on the buoy, the weed on the cord, the intensity of life around that small floating universe, show me that potential and possibility are only achieved within ourselves through grasping the powers of emptiness and possibility and making the best of what we have. I'm excited again, I'm on the roll. The sun goes down and I am left sailing along quietly, heading east and slowly working on myself every day in the pursuit of happiness as an art form, rather than it being an accident. It is said that wisdom and happiness are often nearer when we stoop rather than soar, and another 8 hours on the demanding helm will have me stooping a lot further than I can imagine, but hopefully happy in the pain now that I know it won't break me.

As darkness moves in the breeze begins to swing more towards the west and I'm forced to head more to the south east to keep the rig full.

If the breeze continues to back then I'll gybe over and head north east and stay between the shipping lanes rather than cut deeper into the southern lane, even though it'll be a lot warmer down there with probably a degree rise every 100 miles south. This seems to be the best tactic I can employ after considering all the possibilities of going north for more wind or south for more warmth. Stars are out again, bright in the sky but I miss the Southern Cross and the Milky Way where the Aboriginal emu lies, pointing to all the other constellations.

The emu is the spiritual animal of the Australian aborigines and it is so important to their spiritual life that very few tribes eat emus. There is no emu out tonight and the northern stars are a whole new play book for me. Up high there is Ursa Major, Cassiopeia, Canopus and in particular Polaris or the North Star, around which the whole sky rotates during the night.

Stars occupy a big part of my appreciation of the dark night out here and I'm reminded of C.S. Lewis's words, "and men said that the blood of the stars flowed in their veins" from the connections they made to them as they sailed upon unknown waters. I'm more familiar with the southern night sky but recognise that the northern stars are much easier to navigate. Here a sailor can navigate off the one pole star, finding his latitude with how high the pole star is in the sky, and that's a real bonus.

There's a lot of phosphorescence in the water and big blobs as large as car tires light up around the hull, setting off other blobs further out, showing they are all connected in some odd way. All I need now are some dolphins to come swimming by, creating long torpedo trails as they glide through the water forming glowing ribbon trails of wonder and mystery.

At 2200 hours the wind has moved into the north-west and I gybe over, by controlling the main with the preventer and then bringing the jib over to starboard where I settle down to the new north-easterly track.

That was easy as the breeze was no more than 8 knots and we roll along with the southerly swell pushing us gently from behind as we glide downhill to another horizon. The night will be quite dark as the new moon is not ready for a few days yet, while the fun of dark night sailing quietly over a smooth sea is just perfect. The bow can't be seen, the stars reflect across the water like flashing torch beams while the occasional falling star streaks across the sky. Those phosphorescence trails flash up the sails, creating magic in my lifestyle, encouraging me to be content with this unique and amazing lot for tonight.

At 2300 hours I drop the main, lock the helm and sheet in the jib and go below to make a snack of cheese that I've wrapped in vinegar cloth to keep fresh, and crackers. There's a little fur on the cheese, wow my own "blue cheese", so I wipe it off with some more vinegar and cut thin slices that taste so good.

I make a cup of tea and go back to the cockpit to just sit, relax and enjoy the night without helming. After a while I go below as *Millefleurs* lies hove-to, turn on the masthead light and roll into my bunk. I'm getting into the second week of this voyage and settling down to the routine of the ocean, the weather and keeping this boat rolling forward.

Persistence and patience will get me through each day if I just live in the moment, taking each day as it comes, wanting to be nowhere but right where I am. I go to sleep with the thought that I've gathered somewhere from some wise man's quote "that man is poor, not who has little but who hankers for more." I wake a little after midnight and take a quick look around before turning off the masthead light. I dress in warm clothes, wet weather gear and sea boots, make a cup of tea and climb on deck again to begin another round of sailing. The sky is clear, the wind is north-westerly at 7 knots and the sea is smooth. How magnificent as these are ideal conditions for making more miles to the north east.

I hoist the rig and run back to the helm as we go into a gentle gybe and I finally let her go a full 360 degree before we settle on a course of north east. I settle back in the cockpit and head for more horizons somewhere ahead in the dark. I look to the north and see the Pole Star and Ursa Major and Cassiopeia, while overhead is Taurus and Orion the Hunter. They all seem so familiar, along with all the other constellations, creating a language of recognition and greetings and gratitude where all things in my nightly sky are in their place. I particularly like the myth of Orion the Hunter heading out to hunt the big bear, but if he gets tired he turns towards the Pleiades, the 7 little sisters, and goes bedding instead. But I like my version of the Pleiades cluster which is another version that brings that lovely bunch of stars into focus. The Pleiades are a cluster of 7 stars which are almost impossible to see clearly with the naked eye, because they need a really clear sky for observation. They are the mystery of this night sky and in fact if one can see all 7 at once it means there is no wind up there to distort one's vision and the next day will usually be a lovely clear day.

Pleiades is my personal weather forecaster tonight and all seems well with this traveller.

Chapter 13

Me and Bobby McGee

At 0400 hrs I reluctantly drop the jib, leaving the mainsail up to reduce the roll and go below for a sleep. I've not seen any ships' lights tonight but I turn on the masthead light as a precaution, and fall into the arms of sleep as if it is the greatest placebo in the world.

I'm awake at 0600 hrs as the sun peaks above the horizon and I sit quietly in the cockpit with a cup of tea and practise solar gazing for three or four 20 second bursts. I'm a child of the universe again and like everything around me I belong to this ocean as much as it belongs to me. I'm the bee in this beehive and my nectar is the breeze. I have the sun and a cup of tea and I feel at home in my sailing capsule wanting no more than I have.

After resting quietly for half an hour I decide I need to roll on so I hoist the jib and slowly get *Millefleurs* moving to the east noting that there are more dark clouds to the north west shaping into possible thunderheads that may develop into another blow and that's my only worry for the day. The breeze is hard and cold from the north-west and slowly builds to 12 knots as I fumble to get my wet weather gear on and settle down to some more hard sailing. To be ahead of the game I need to reef the main by dropping it entirely, tying in the reef, adjusting the out-haul and re-hoisting. After frequent trips to the helm and back to the boom I'm finally able to re-hoist a double reefed main and then I race back to the helm like a crazed man to find I'm way off course. This steering problem and the reefing systems are getting monotonous but I mustn't let it annoy me. It takes considerable time to put in a simple reef and trying to marry helming and hoisting sail has become a real challenge for my patience while good for my persistence. I feel better about being a coward and reefing early, as I feel another blow creeping up on me from the north-west and hopefully it will roll through quickly.

Those dark cumulus clouds indicate a strengthening disturbance and I'm pleased that I'm not too far north to get the full strength of another cold front barrelling hard through from the west.

I attach lines to the helm and go below to prepare some breakfast of rolled oats, raisins, seeds and nuts, but the strict attention I need to apply to the helming lines means I don't push my luck by cooking the oats. I just add cold milk and get back into the cockpit to see white caps charging across the ocean indicating that the impending change is almost upon us. And then suddenly a 20 knot gust hits us and we surge away to the east at 6 knots with just enough rig to make life interesting. We surge along with me eating my breakfast in bursts whilst standing and helming with one hand and holding the cereal pot in the other. Our wake whitens out behind us and I can't let go of the wheel so I use the pot like a mug and pour breakfast into my mouth enjoying all the tastes, while keeping *Millefleurs* on a broad reach, straight tracking with more and more white caps building up behind us.

This is going to be another hand to hand combat, another test of my resolve to keep rolling out more and more sea miles. The swells are beginning to roll through like soldiers in formation with bright white hats and dark blue tuxedos, each independent, stand-alone sentinels heading out for a day's drill, driven on by an impetuous, ragged wind. Some cold blustery heavy showers come through and I squeeze my wet weather hood on while continuing to empty the food pot and dropping it into the cockpit at my feet. How long will this squall last and will it develop into something more than a passing wind? My mind wants to interrogate the breeze and be ahead of the game, while reality says there's nothing I can do with the uncertainty, just enjoy the ride.

We settle down to a little over 5 knots which is relatively fast for this little girl with the no. 3 jib doing most of the work and the main providing heel and stability.

The breeze is holding steady at 20 knots and after an hour I realise we are in for another long blow, but I am well fed, have warm gear on and have a whole day to enjoy the ride to the east with a north-westerly swell beginning to build. Midday rolls by with the seas building and some gusts touch 25 knots and boy am I glad I double reefed the main and have only the working jib up, which is also on the edge of it's comfortable range. However, I realise there's no way I can change that jib now, other than just dropping it and sailing alone on the main but that'd make the rig too unbalanced for easy helming. So I stick to pounding out mile after mile, being overpowered occasionally, luffing up with the rig cracking loudly like a starter's gun and then falling away to run squarer, blocking the jib with the mainsail and easing back to broad reaching as the breeze eases down to 20 knots again.

It's a challenge that I enjoy and it occupies all my attention and energy, sometimes leaving me panting from the exertion, keeping me quite warm and conscious of paying close attention to every line squall that comes raging through, kicking up white caps as trail blazers, helping me to read the face of the ocean like a warning bell. I am certainly appreciating these miles we are carving out and stand behind the helm riding the gusts like a tennis player, waiting for the next serve. I look up to the horizon and I realise visibility has been reduced considerably with these passing showers and heavy moist air. The sky is heavily overcast while the ocean has taken on a mass of white caps that extend in all directions. Once again, we are prisoners of intemperate weather and all I can do is enjoy the hurly burly all around as we plunge eastwards caught in the maelstroms of nature powers. I begin singing and tapping my feet and imagining that I am putting on a performance for the wind gods, who will eventually feel placated and leave us alone, as they race away to the east.

By 1500 hours I realise this wind is not going to die off so easily and as I slowly tire I decide to drop the jib and jog along on the tiny mainsail alone, until things get easier.

Now I have to consider how I can get the jib down and tied off without going into a gybe in this breeze, which could cause some real damage. There are not many options apart from easing *Millefleurs* up into the breeze while letting the jib sheet fly as it cracks and bangs. I then plan to rush forward to drop the wildly flapping beast, tie it down, re-tension the halyard and work my way back down the windward deck with us heeling over, and then get in behind the helm again to drive her off downwind. Here goes, there's no alternative, as I race forward to begin this planned dowsing of the jib.

I'm back in the cockpit 5 minutes later and it may have taken only about 300 seconds but it seemed like forever, as a loose jib flogging at the end of a released sheet is a sailor's nightmare. I am exhausted and if I had tried to wear the harness, clipping on as I raced forward, the jib would have been going crazy for twice the time. Safety is important but sometimes reality says you have to rely upon your ability to survive regardless of the circumstances, otherwise caution hampers your progress.

Being back behind the helm again running off to the east with the breeze at 25 knots means we are lazily rolling downwind at 4 knots while I ponder why I have kept sailing for so long before reefing down. Now that we are under control, the panic over, the motion is easy and I'll just continue quietly easing away till the blow has passed through.

Then it begins to rain and rain some more, with heavy downpours relieved by gusty breezes. It stops for a brief period and then it starts pouring down again. This is usual as the rain usually comes after the blow heralding the end of the front. There's even an old sailor's wisdom that says, "wind before the rain, soon it will be fine again."

Soon the heavy showers merge into a light sprinkle and by dusk the skies have cleared, the wind is definitely easing and as the sun goes down the wind drops down to 12 knots and I am forced to either hoist the jib again or sleep for a while. I decide to drop the main, lock the helm, make some corn soup with crackers and then turn in for a well-earned rest.

I turn on the masthead light while taking a look around the horizon and then dive into my bunk with the hatch open and the sky clearing to the west. I sleep till 2100 hours and emerge to take a look around and see a ship's steaming lights away to the south of me heading east. He is close to the horizon, so is easily 6 miles away and that indicates that I'm getting down into that east-going shipping channel. I'm happy to receive that warning. I'd rather be south than north.

I make a cup of tea recognising that the swell has eased and the breeze is more westerly at about 10 knots. The sky is clearing with stars pouring through around the horizon, but it's cold out there. I rug up with warm clothes and wet weather gear and go forward to hoist the mainsail and then the no.3 jib and then scramble back to the helm to get back on course. I hook more to the south east with the dying westerly on my starboard quarter and I imagine following that ship that just rolled by as maybe he's the "passing messenger" telling me to head further south towards the warmth. I sail on at 4 knots running downwind on a settling sea and this is the time to make good miles to the south east and get warmer.

There's a lot of phosphorescence around and we create a sparkling silver trail through the darker ocean, rollicking along with me singing away promising myself to fix the broken CD player somehow and get some more rhythm into this voyage.

These nights are awfully long without any moon or music and I'm looking forward to those big bright moonlit nights, where the seas feel friendly and welcoming.

I can then cruise along using the moon as my prime marker, talking quietly to myself, telling stories and jokes to an audience of just one. I suddenly bang into something in the water and the hull reverberates like a drum as a piece of flotsam trundles noisily down the port side and escapes out the stern. I begin imagining that it's a drum or a large log and I thank my lucky stars I didn't hit it head on or cause some damage like a pierced hull.

I guess oceaning is all about taking chances and some unlucky yachtsmen I have personally known have sunk from hitting large objects just like that one adrift in the ocean. Somehow all of life is also like a piece of flotsam on an ocean voyage.

We are born into some strange earth spot, get caught up in the flow, experience many things that shape who we are and then we die. The Buddhists say we keep doing the same things lifetime after lifetime, purposely becoming male or female, black or white and all the colours in between. Sometimes we may be wealthy and other times desperately poor. Each lifetime we add experience after experience that grows us into the image of our own piece of humanity at its best, melding and mixing, watering and seeding, recovering and separating ideas, hunches and thoughts that somehow help us as individuals to grow wiser, more conscious, full of virtues and nobility as we stand on the shoulders of those who have gone before.

The sailing is quiet again and steady with a gentle westerly and a working rig that keeps us heading south east at 4 knots. The night is dark with stars appearing and disappearing through the slowly shifting clouds. Midnight passes and we sail into the most difficult time of the day for me. It's the dog watch between 0200 hrs and 0600 hrs when I really want to sleep but am chained to the wheel of this cantankerous yacht. I try steering without looking, practising using my other senses to keep course and that works well until I realise with a jolt that I've gone to sleep and we are well off course as the jib is shaking and flapping around.

I try singing and that helps, but all I want to do is to sink into my bunk and sleep the night away. I realise that in the last two weeks I've not slept for a period longer than 2 hours and now I just have to forgo miles and have a decent 3-4 hour sleep.

The conditions are perfect for stopping for a rest without feeling guilty. I'd love the world to just stop for a day, to be becalmed, still, upon a painted ocean where I could just sleep all day long. That would be my heaven right now. I drop the rig, take a long look around the horizon, casting a mental spell upon my position, trusting that no ship will come near me as I head for the bunk.

I'm asleep in 5 minutes and when I awake its near dawn and I feel refreshed and ready for a whole day of sailing south-east again, on towards those tropics and sea birds, flying fish and coconut palms, across the southerly shipping channel and into safer waters. When I struggle into the cockpit the dawn is breaking with the promise of a warm bright day. There are light winds and smooth seas and hopefully maybe a becalmment for a few days, where I'll just sleep for hours, maybe take a swim and just do nothing, not even touch the helm once.

As the sun rises I sit in the cockpit with a cup of tea and practise my solar gazing, allowing myself to float off into emptiness, tranquillity and deep peace where there is nothing to disturb my equanimity and well-being. I remain like this for a good 30 minutes, beyond thought, beyond any cares and worries, beyond the thought of any ship sneaking up on me, beyond any concerns for the uncertainty of the ocean.

I'm 58 years old this year and I don't feel old, perhaps a little tired and worn, carrying a few more aches in the shoulder blades from constant helming and sore feet from constantly kicking my toes on deck gear. I believe that we're only getting older when we lose the incentive to learn something new which is fuelled by curiosity.

I feel intensely interested in this day to day sailing roller coaster, as we head east-wards winging each day as if it's the beginning of another whole new adventure.

My dream would be to learn something new every day for the rest of my life, as a happy mind is constantly expanding the possibilities for living well. Curiosity is the wick in the candle of learning and as long as I can keep the candle burning bright I feel like I am contributing a great deal to my own well-being. Today I have an important task to complete and that is to pull the CD player apart and find out why it's not performing.

I reluctantly drop the rig and go below and check the power supply and find that that's fine. I check the fuse and that's OK. Then I check the speaker wires by running a continuity check with my electrical meter. Ah, that's the problem, there's a break in the circuit somewhere so I unscrew the speaker to find that it's badly corroded around the junction box. When I tug on the wires one comes away, completely worn out. I find some spare wire and replace a foot section where the salt water has dripped onto the wire and once completed I fire up the player with a Kris Kristofferson CD. Soon I'm happily listening to one of his classic songs *"Sunday morning coming down."* I turn it up louder and return to the cockpit, proud to have settled the CD player issue and ready to enjoy music again across the Atlantic. I laugh as the next song plays - *"Help me make it through the night"* reminding me of my situation. Soon after raising the rig I'm sitting happily immersed in the lyrics of one of the finest song writers of the last century. What a bonus to have him out here and what fun to have the CD player again on call. It was worth all the effort of finding the problem and sorting it out rather than waiting for another time.

Next time when the dolphins come around I'm going to rock their flippers and see if they enjoy the music as well.

The morning breeze is light from the south west and I decide to hoist a full rig of no.3 jib and full mainsail and track off to the east. If I'd been in a hurry and felt inclined I could have hoisted the no. 2 jib but I realise that getting it down in another hardening breeze such as I experienced yesterday may be difficult. I'll save the bigger jib until later, when I'm full of beans and in more of a hurry. I hoist the jib first on a short sheet line and then get the full mainsail up as well. I deliberately slow my usual rush to the helm, letting fate take its hand as we begin to slide away from the breeze. We slowly gather speed and *Millefleurs* heads south up into the breeze but she doesn't go through the tack and falls away to head east again and gathers more momentum to again head south and then stall.

This is self-steering at its worst, like being hove-to and climbing up to the breeze and falling away in slow motion to constantly repeat the cycle as one slowly reaches across the water. I break the cycle by unlocking the helm and steering east until we reach 3.5 knots in this 8-knot breeze and we idle eastwards into another whole new day ready for whatever eventuates.

Mr Kristofferson does his concert below and I remember the first time that I heard *"Me and Bobby McGee."* I was immediately in love with the hippie ride to freedom from Baton Rouge to New Orleans on the thumb. In 1995 driving across the USA from Boston to Los Angeles, I travelled the same Bobby McGee trail in reverse and had the CD also rocking in the wagon when I passed Salinas. I realised that music is the first time that kids are able to express themselves with something that is not directly related to their parents.

As a child of the swinging sixties, I found that music was something that allowed me to feel that I wasn't missing much of the action over there in San Francisco, even though I was a university student living on bread and sausages in Hobart, Tasmania. That was near the end of the world or at least it felt like it.

Upon climbing Mount Wellington which overlooked the city, I felt that I could possibly see the end of the world from there, but with the music of the world rolling in, I knew I was really in paradise. Music and protests and street marches against the Vietnam War whilst studying kept life interesting and I remembered the truisms of one social commentator who said "If you're not a socialist by the age of 20 you have no feelings, and if you're not a capitalist by the age of 40 then you have no head."

All those eager socialists that I met at university in the 1960s have all become capitalists and careerists. Few like me have dropped out to pursue freedom beyond all the 'isms. However, right now I wouldn't mind being a 'four poster bed capitalist' with an electric blanket and a tray of fine cuisine resting on my chest, rather than rolling along out here, cold and hungry.

Loneliness is not something that worries me now, but it did when I first went to boarding school at the age of 13. There, for the first time in my life, I suffered homesickness and the pain in my guts was horrible. The emptiness of knowing no one, being away from the freedom of wandering the hills and fishing the river, being under the thumb of "black robe" covered priests who had God as their only friend and prime reason for how they lived. The longer that homesickness went on the more despair I suffered, but it forced me to let go of something I loved and live in the moment, where I either adapted or died. The anguish in my heart was through a lack of understanding and self-acceptance and I admire those people who get up and go, leaving all behind. It makes them stronger and explains why immigrants do so well in hostile environments from sheer persistence and hard work and the ability to handle being all alone.

Loneliness is also about losing contact with those beautiful moments of life that have filled you up with joy and the zest for life. The sounds of friendly voices, the smell of familiar foods, the joy of sleeping in your own bed, these I had lost at Marist College in Burnie when I was 13.

I've realised later you can even be lonely in a crowded room, as I was then, as it often highlights your disconnection from others and yourself, illustrating that loneliness may be only a lost connection to the person you really are and that is what creates the despair. That explains why no one can fill that gap except yourself. So, at college at an early age I realised that no one could help me overcome my loneliness except myself.

I was selected in the grade 7 football team as I had been a captain of my local primary school team and I knew I could do well and make many friends, but after being selected I realised again that I couldn't play as I had no jumper. Mum was too poor, so I couldn't ask her to buy me one. I sadly sat out of football until grade 9 when I worked at the timber mill in my area during the school holidays to earn enough money to buy my own jumper. Perhaps there were spare jumpers at the school, but I was too embarrassed to ask. Life is never equal nor is it meant to be.

We all suffer in some way throughout life and loneliness is another human frailty we endure for the very reason that adversity often introduces us to ourselves.

The day is warming so I remove my wet weather gear and sit high on the cockpit coaming, steering with my feet. Nothing is going to change the day and that pleases me as I can be happy with the rig I'm carrying, knowing that it'll carry us for another whole day to the east without any sail changes. Life seems to have lost a lot of the complications with fewer choices to make. I remember a dream I had last night. I was searching for something I'd lost but couldn't find it and was confused, unable to go forward. I felt like an absent-minded cowboy who has lost the horse he was riding and was unable to find any tracks. Perhaps my psyche was telling me that if I was separated from *Millefleurs* as she sailed away I would be left out here to die.

I've heard of boats being found without their occupants and I wonder what pain they must have suffered, being absolutely alone without any hope, seeing their boat sailing away and knowing for sure it's just a matter of time before they drown. That would be an anguish that would be hard to bear and you would hope to die quickly from sheer exhaustion maybe after desperately trying to swim after your haven.

Perhaps Sam swum past that night of the storm to show me that you can never give up, even in the worst circumstances, otherwise you're letting the deep inner core of yourself down.

Chapter 14

Swimming off

My mind returns to the connections that Sam and I must have in this vast universe and I refuse to think that it is just a random act of kindness that brings Sam to talk to me. It is said that nothing is the same as anything, and I feel that there is a huge divide between my limited day to day awareness and the bigger machinations of the cosmos. Perhaps we all have guardian angels who come to us in times of need and maybe that overboard sailor drifting alone out in the ocean as his boat sails away breaks that divide through sheer desperation and angels came to help him die peacefully.

Maybe we all have a desperate need for companionship and when we are under deep stress science now says the pineal gland releases a psychedelic spirit molecule similar chemically to LSD, that allows us to enter Alice in Wonderland's amazing world, where dreams and reality blend into one, shielding us from the pain of life. The ability some people have to alter time, to intuit things unknown, to heal others at a distance or even to interpret their dreams intrigues me. The potential of the psyche, that huge bank of experiences stored there and the amazing ability under stress to access this knowing, is like a mother knowing how to give birth.

Our connection to a larger bank of information that the east calls the akashic, emerges in the most unusual ways, bringing guidance and the capacity to overcome even the direst of circumstances, and that was of special interest to me.

Whilst crossing the USA in 1995 as I passed through Sedona, Arizona I saw a sign for a course in past life hypnosis, which was about to begin. So, I enrolled and spent a week experiencing and practising being under hypnosis while delving into past lives.

Some say it is rubbish and some are frightened by the possibility that we could have lived many lives up until now, with all that information stored in our psyche. I've noticed it is only a few controlling ideologies like Christianity that dismiss past lives. I've seen kids 4 years old who are chess champions and have received no special instruction. I've heard of youth who have become the most amazing musicians without having had years of lessons and I've read of soulmate connections that defy logic.

Each day I ponder who I am and where I am heading particularly as I watch the sun rise and set, imagining the sun is part of me and is filling me with the energy of the universe and yet even that is not enough. Perhaps this strong connection to the sun explains why the Scots have a fascination with watching the sunset and old sailors also watched that same sun set, waiting for that proverbial green flash that somehow seemed to be like discovering gold at the end of the day. I've tried to see the green flash thousands of times at sunset and even at sunrise but have never been lucky enough to see it. Others sailing with me have never seen it either and we often wonder whether the green flash may be a myth perpetrated by some drunk Scot hoping to see the green hills of home!

At midday I heave-to with all sails up and the helm locked to windward as we lie stalled and hove-to. I don't like leaving sails up to chafe like this but I don't need that constant battle with getting them up and down while the breeze is gentle and steady. I make a light meal as I'm getting over the fast slowly, but my hunger is getting insatiable and I want to snack all day. I make a big pot of rice, open up one of Mike's canned chicken breasts and sit in the cockpit and quickly eat the lot. Then I go hunting for something sweet and find a labelled can that says, "chocolate sauced pudding." Yum. I punch a hole in it and boil the can in the rice pot for 10 minutes. There's cake inside mixed with caramel sauce and I can't stop eating the lot. No way can I leave some for later.

My stomach has become a tyrant and it demands food, food and more food after the long fast I have been through, and it's my new addiction that I've fallen in love with. All addictions are your first love and this one currently outshines all other pleasurable things that I have at my disposal. Now I am over-full and decide that sleep is the best medicine after that huge meal, my first feast for a long time. I know if I had beers I'd be into them as well, and after a quick look around the horizon I retire and am soon into my bunk sleeping soundly.

Two hours later I'm suddenly nightmarishly awake and frightened. I dash up on deck fully expecting a ship to be bearing down on me, but the horizon is ship-less and I put it down to too much food and a bad dream. My body was over-full and my mind was agitated and insecure and uncomfortable with my slow progress. My thoughts were no longer my best friends. I could feel the growing pressure of being on the alert every moment of the day, waiting for that "terrorist ship" to come roaring over the horizon, heading directly for me.

Negativity was creeping in and I felt the need to test the EPIRB beacon to see if it was still ok. I well remember the trouble that beacon had caused immediately after I had purchased it on Mike's prompting. That simple EPIRB has to be registered with an international rescue body but something had gone wrong in the registration process, as Tasmania, Australia became Tanzania, Africa, and I doubt whether Tanzania was going to coordinate a search for some unknown citizen who had become lost in the Atlantic!

Over some weeks I finally succeeded in changing the registration back to Tasmania, Australia, but it involved cancelling one registration and taking up another, making me wonder if the expense was worth all the effort. As I told Mike, the truth is that no one is coming way out here to rescue me, and I don't blame them. That simple attitude seems to satisfy all my negative thoughts and settle me down to reality.

However, to satisfy Mike I did spend lots of energy and money in getting that new beacon before I sailed. Now I know I definitely should have spent that money on a new furler and I would have been immensely richer for the effort. Bouts of worry were definitely coming more often now and I guess they were the expected "black dog blues" that confront any adventurer testing the unknown and I was no exception. That last rush into the cockpit to avoid the shadow ship was one of those moments. I finally decided I had to confront the beasts within, a bit like repairing the CD player. It had to be sooner rather than later.

The constant fear of ships, of storms, of being lost, of faults in the boat and even ghosts walking around in the cockpit, were rearing their ugly heads more and more often. I decided to sit and meditate and clear the mind, focusing only on the sound of my breath going in and out with the rustle of wind on the water and the shaking of the sails. Meditation had worked before when I could block most thoughts and leave the nasties behind, but it couldn't stop them now. I couldn't keep my eyes closed longer than a couple of minutes, as I was riddled with worries and constantly searched for ships all around, with the uncertainties of the voyage and all those what-ifs that were invading my mind.

Somehow, I needed a superior mindset to overcome these lower mind assaults, as the reactionary forces in the old limbic brain were causing me depression and my thoughts were terrorising me, battering away the serenity of the day, making me a victim of myself. I realised I couldn't fight this fear with anger by stomping my feet and shouting angry words to the ocean, I had to be smarter and challenge myself to an arm wrestle over certainty and uncertainty. I had to give in, I had to accept defeat again in order to win.

Suddenly I was back in Malta 12 years ago, in a wrestle with the Mafia about the fate of *Sundancer* where the same uncertainty was familiar, I was out of control of my fate and felt powerless. What to do? I had been lured to Malta to work for a cruise company who wanted to purchase *Sundancer* as a sail trainer between Italy and Malta, due to her history of 6 circumnavigations and racy looks. She fitted their profile.

After getting on their slipway and working to get her ready over 3 months, it became apparent that the deal was going bad. They weren't going to let her off the slipway and I had nearly lost all, including my freedom. I was unable to move forward or back and was at the mercy of someone else. I was a slave again looking down the barrel of defeat. In Malta there is even a local law that says that if you go into dispute with a local, he has precedence and any legal case may not come to court for years so they can wear you down over time. If you leave the island the case is over. I met a Swedish entrepreneur who had lost his miniature submarine worth millions, through identical circumstances to mine, so I realised that I was in deep trouble.

I certainly needed some good luck and wise guidance to get out of that situation intact, hopefully with some cash as well. I spoke to the principal of the company and said I should not have come to Malta and he agreed. There was no traction there. Then I enquired about the cost of getting *Sundancer* off the slip and he said it would cost 100,000 British pounds which was a fortune to me. I countered by saying I'd return to Australia, get my money in order and return to take *Sundancer* away, knowing that I could never raise that amount anyway, but he surprised me by saying "on the condition you must never return to Malta with *Sundancer*" and on inquiring why, he said, "it's on my honour."

Now the angel had arrived, disguised in his worries about the loss of honour and I wasn't leaving without a battle. I was going to be such a thorn in his side and threaten his honour so much that he'd have to come to some arrangement. I put up signs on the side of *Sundancer* about the dishonour of the local cruise company and I contracted a lawyer from the rival soccer club. Ultimately, I was visited by other family members with their own axes to grind and soon enough they paid me some money, just to get rid of me. I had won, I had received enough money to escape and more importantly enough money to buy some land back in Australia to start again, and there I built the castle.

Now here at sea, I have to find another tactic to escape the blues that are overwhelming me, unsettling my equilibrium and making me a prisoner of my mind. I have to admit defeat, not try to hide my worries within, but to let them out and let them run. I dropped all the sails, and drifted, trusting in total surrender in facing my fears that had taken these last 2 weeks to peak. I stuffed the turmoil tightly inside my chest, peeled off my clothes, dived in over the rails and swam away from *Millefleurs*, naked and damn cold, leaving her to take care of herself, however she wanted. I gave up caring what happened. I swam for 5 minutes with a deliberate smile on my face, looking ahead and daring fate to come and take me away, anywhere.

Then I stopped and floated on my back imagining I was in Horta, on the beach somewhere, just enjoying a day at play. The water was cold and swelly and dark below, but I had to challenge all, dare a shark or a storm or my fears to take me away, asking my cosmic being to make sense of that crazy uncertain person inside my skin. I felt like a base jumper free falling and refusing to look for a landing or open my chute, and yet I also knew it was boom or bust.

Not caring about a landing gave me the strength where being out of control became enjoyable, became fun and I laughed loudly at the madness of the human condition, where you can risk all just for some peace of mind. I was finding some weird sanity in just letting go, in not giving a stuff what happened.

I rolled over and became rational again. I looked up and spotted *Millefleurs* 200 metres away happily waiting, floating high, dipping in the swells, calling me back, asking why I would leave her alone, questioning my sanity and offering safety and warmth, love and concern, reminding me we had to do this together or both fail. I floated free and unburdened and after a time I swam back slowly and deliberately put all those fears out of my mind, renewing my faith in my will to survive, finding a strategy that would allow me to spiral out into the cosmos rather than spiral into obscurity and self-doubt.

It is said that when it comes to a life well lived, the critical thing is whether you take things for granted or you take them with gratitude, and I had a lot to be grateful for. I had escaped Malta, I had built my castle, I had two great kids, I had a beautiful boat and life looked just great ahead. As Cicero said, way back in Roman times, "gratitude and thankfulness for all we have is not only the greatest virtue, but the parent for all others." I gratefully crawled up the stern lip, grabbed a hull scraper out of the deck locker, put on some goggles and dived in to share my sense of renewal with *Millefleurs*, by scraping the pesky barnacles off her keel and particularly around the rudder. The cold water had rejuvenated me, bolstered my resolve to go on, shocked me into beating those blues. I'm mindful and awake to the deep blue ocean again. I checked the wear in the rudder bearing, cleaned the propeller blades, I swam to the bow and spotted those two dorados that had been shadowing me for days. (Dorado is another name for mahi-mahi or common dolphinfish).

I cleaned the bow where the goose barnacles sure had grown wild and I promised *Millefleurs* that together we had to take our time across the ocean.

She had to keep watch when I needed more sleep and warn me if ships were coming our way, and she had to get me across the Atlantic. I promised to take her through Panama and on across the Pacific and all the way to Hobart, where she was now registered. We made a silent pact to care for each other, no matter what, and she thanked me for calling her *Millefleurs*, changing the name from *Indulgence* that seemed to be so out of touch with her character. We were a team again. We were back on the road and all my fears were gone, replaced by gratitude that *Millefleurs* had waited for me in the Atlantic, when she could have just buggered off. Gratitude that the cold water had buried my blues and given me a renewed sense of purpose and trust in my progress, feeling whole again.

I climbed back on deck and resolved to not eat such large amounts of food again as that addiction to pleasuring my senses has made me vulnerable to the loss of those conveniences I have left behind. The raw truth of experience cuts deep to the soul when one has to leave those thought demons behind. I realise there is a sea inside me that's also full of turbulence and waves of emotion that reflects off the seas around and that's the important sea.

I warm up under the sun and sit quietly savouring all the things that I have around me to get me across this unsettling divide. I go below and make myself a cup of tea, bringing it to the cockpit where I sing quietly to myself and decide that in my own good time, at my own leisure, I'll hoist a new rig and sail away from this spot, quietly and resolutely, leaving those dark parts of my psyche behind. For good measure I gather some salt from below and ceremonially sprinkle it in the water as a talisman.

In defeat I have won, showing kindness to myself after almost throwing it all away which makes me realise that darkness is only restored when more light comes in. Gently I sail away from the westerly sun heading east at 3.2 knots on a flat sea in a steady breeze that promises to last forever. In sailing, the Tao is not to sail the boat, but to help the boat sail itself, and apart from the helming problem that's all I have to do, day after day.

Give *Millefleurs* the responsibility of sailing herself, to catch the breeze, to ride the swells, to lift to the challenges of the Atlantic, and the renewed me will become her best companion, enjoying all the things she has to teach me about sailing. Surrender to all the sailing wisdom that has been impressed into the design, the building and the details of this Hunter, forgiving her weaknesses that probably reflect my own weaknesses, as we move forward together. As one poster I read on the wall of a friend's yacht said.

"twenty years from now you will be more disappointed by the things you didn't do, than by those you did. So, throw off the bowline, sail away from the safe harbour, catch the wind in your sails, explore, dream, discover and become."

So, I sail on relieved, quietly singing "*Me and Bobby McGee*", being broke and busted in Baton Rouge, waiting for another train!

Chapter 15

Sam Revisits

I sail on until the sun goes down and the stars emerge into a clear night sky ahead. I see Scorpio, the largest constellation, high in the sky overhead. Jupiter seems to be the brightest light to the south west and I know that if the night stays clear then Venus will be big and bright later, rising as the early morning star. The Big Dipper is high overhead and a new moon is beginning to show in the west.

I heave-to on a north-westerly backed tack and go below to indulge myself in a warm cup of Earl Grey tea and some crackers, with peanut butter. I bring them up to the cockpit and sit back relaxed, enjoying my small indulgences, feeling confident and content, looking forward to settling in to living just in the moment again, forgetting totally about how far I have to go. I'm blissed out, slightly drowsy and relaxed even though I do know my progress has been painfully slow. Maybe it'll take me another few weeks to make the halfway mark but that is small change to the bigger picture where I am happily immersed in a privileged position, deeply conscious of the treasures all around. The big "black dog" has gone and I am light hearted again ready to enjoy anything just like the guy who swapped his bed for a trampoline and his wife hit the roof!

I release the backed jib, letting *Millefleurs* slowly swing back to the east and reset the jib as we roll east south east at 3.4 knots in an 8 knot south westerly breeze. We've been out 15 long days and I've almost forgotten when I left. I roll on finding a comfortable position with my foot on the wheel and my back jammed into two cockpit cushions. At 2300 hrs I am engrossed in watching the stars and planning how to collect water off the mainsail when it next rains, as running out of water would be much worse than running out of food.

I am sliding along, phosphorescence streaming slowly out the starboard side with small comets occasionally morphing into big blobs, lighting up in sympathy with other blobs at least 10 metres either side of my wake. There's a lot more going on in the water with these sympathetic responses spreading all around us. I am hugging the moment, squeezing the juice out of "life's oranges" back to my usual positive self and that always provides a generous perspective to one's perceptions. Worry does give small things really big shadows and the cold water has corralled my runaway mind, bringing it back to being my best friend, ready to build any bridge towards inner harmony, ready to reduce the seeming complexity of the previous day to an elegant simplicity, ready to hug the journey and feel bigger for having survived my "desperation swim."

Then, a pleasant surprise – Sam's back and he sits down next to me greeting me in that deep southern voice. "Hi," he burbles, "having a tough time man?" That faint vanilla smell floats across the cockpit and I feel so relieved that I have my mate back to share the troubles of life. I respond with, "You're right about that Sam, got a little down today but it's sure great to see you're back for a visit…best thing that could have happened to me, I sure need some fun company."

He says, "You're getting all those years of negativity out of your psyche, you're cleansing out, and it causes changes to occur that aren't always pleasant. But remember this, nothing valuable is ever achieved wholly from within your comfort zone. There is nothing more self-evident in the universe that gives you pleasure than sharing the best that humanity has to offer, even down to the design of this sail boat."

He continues, "Here's an old saying that you know 'if you always follow the lead dog, the scene never changes!' The followers have always been the same for centuries, blinded by promises that deliver the same pain and angst."

"Do you think we connect by chance or is it because we have shared experiences that allow us to resonate together?" I ask Sam and he adds, "You know man, Joseph Conrad, one of our shared writers of the sea explains our bond somewhat in these words, that do him proud." And he begins to orate in an old sailor's voice that is rough and gravelly as if he were in a movie, mine.

"Between us there was a bond of the sea. Besides holding our hearts together through long periods of separation, it had the effect of making us tolerant of each other's yarns, and even our convictions!"

Sam's presence seems to add a depth of feeling and a pool of warmth that warms my soul. He enlarges this small cockpit, fills up my bowl of friendship and I feel that I have won some dharmic award that I want to hang onto. I want to keep him captive, tie him down, hold him here but this also seems unreasonable. And then I ask "Sam, you'll come again? and he says, "if you call, and we resonate then I'll be here, but only time will tell."

Then he invites me to join him in singing before I head off for a sleep while he keeps watch.

We sing together starting with my favourite, *'Me and Bobby McGee'* and continue with other songs I love like *'Irene Goodnight'* and the *'Wabash cannonball.'*

Music like life highlights its own beautiful soundtrack and it reconnects me back to my country music roots back there in the Tasmanian bush, where living high was imitating your very own artist, flooding your whole being with familiarity and nostalgia and those sweet feelings of love.

Soon I'm wishing Sam well, locking the wheel, dropping the rig and heading off to my bunk.

As I turn in I'm joyously content, pleased to be here in this space, pleased to be empty and light and free from the confines of order and protocol and even logic where all that Sam said would have been dismissed as being nothing more than an illusion. With that I fall asleep, wrapped in the protective arms of the cosmos, knowing someone has my back out here, knowing there is a space for sailors like me who come out here to find what lies deeper within to resolve all those conflicts from one's past.

Chapter 16

Gerhardt, the Survivor

I wake at 0530hrs and go on deck to take a look around. The sky is streaked with a new orange dawn promising a fine sailing day. The air is definitely warmer with a south-west breeze of 8 knots and some spectacular cloud banks to the north-east as the rising sun glints yellow off the higher formations. I decide to hoist the rig and make some breakfast later as I'm really keen to make miles today reflecting my more buoyant mood, helped by Sam's generous visitation. I lubricate the jib track so that it flows more evenly and hoist the working rig with a full main. I hook more southwards into the gentle south-west breeze, hoping to find warmer winds further down south and I sit in the cockpit meditating and mulling over Sam's summary of life. I stare at the sun as it rises and imagine connecting myself to those solar fields. It's marvellous how a new idea gains such traction, almost as if the fun of something novel increases the placebo effect, while the solar gazing gives me new hope for the day with more positive feelings.

As the morning sunrise glints across the horizon a soft breeze gently flows over the water's surface, providing that shattered glass effect, seemingly to reflect from a million mirrors all at once as I imagine myself containing every ripple, reflecting every striation of light as there is only me here, honouring this beautiful day and being aware that the more attention I give it the more it dances for me.

It reminds me of psychologist David Gilbert who challenges us to consider happiness. He asks "who is happier, the man who loses his leg or the man who wins a million dollars?" the answer isn't so obvious as a year later both are just as happy as they were before the event.

I look at the horizon so far away and yet so close and I realise there will always be another horizon framing the ocean, no matter how fast or slow I go. And yet the slower I go the more living I can fit into this gap, into this piece of ocean as the ocean is really like experiencing humanity. The slower I move through humanity the more I can appreciate each drop, each person, each unique individual and the more I can appreciate myself in reflection. This is happiness for sure, but I'd rather have that million dollars than lose my leg!

At 0900 hrs I rig lines to the wheel and go below to make some breakfast. I mix up some rolled oats and dried fruits, some nuts and honey and add some milk powder slowly and deliberately as steering from the galley is the balancing act that requires all my attention. There's no way I could eat below whilst steering and still enjoy the meal. I return to the cockpit, take off my jumper and long pants and sit in the sun on the edge of the cockpit and savour my feast of flavours. I realise that I don't eat for quantity but for the intensity of flavours and out here each piece of dried apricot gets my full attention for a good 30 chews and sometimes even more. I have all the time in the world to eat, relax, and appreciate mulling over a thousand things that take my fancy. In years to come I know that I'll envy this time crossing the Atlantic and realise what an opportunity it is to take stock of life and make new plans for deeper contentment and enjoyment that each new day brings.

I settle into the day and imagine that I'm off to see my old German friend Gerhardt for lunch. When I was building my castle in the 1990s Gerhardt came into my life through the local chess club, and when I trekked out to his place deep in the bushland, way behind my place, I found another castle. He had been there for 40 years, after escaping from Europe for the freedom of the Australian bush. He had raised his daughter alone out there after his wife had died.

He knew every tree and kangaroo and magpie by name – they were his friends. Imagination allows me to visit him out here today as I roll across the ocean for our lunch together, where I'll also use it as an excuse to stop and take some sights, to get a position fix that adds to my chart below.

Gerhardt had the most amazing life one could imagine, full of tragedy and survival and hope that made one feel small in his presence. His castle was a ferro-cement structure like a giant mushroom with windows made of tree bows in-filled with cut glass and a waterfall in the middle of the main room, fed from the cliffs above. He had no electricity, he cooked over an open fire but he had the world at his fingertips. He said he loved to live like a river, captured by its winding banks, going with its flow, continually surprised by the river's reality unfolding as a pure reflection of his own state of being.

He played chess beautifully and also played the classical guitar with feeling and discipline that was astonishing for a man in his late seventies.

Not long after I met Gerhardt, I asked him how he had come to settle in Australia, being so far from his childhood home in Germany. His story was long and amazing, reflecting the paradoxes of life as he was born in the late 1920s and lived through the 1930's depression that had hit Germany particularly hard, whilst they were still paying reparations following World War 1. He said his only solace was found in playing the guitar where he was able to earn a little money to help put food on the family table. Then in 1940 he was conscripted into the army and became an army musician which saved him from the need to fight.

After the war the Russians came and took him and the rest of the German army to the Gulag in Siberia where they were slave labourers for the copper mines. Out of a camp of 5,000 soldiers only 2 survived and it was music again that saved him, as the Russians greatly valued musicians.

From there at the age of 33 he returned to Germany, but his whole family had died in the war, so he left for Ibiza in Spain where he became a leather master, using the techniques he had learned in the prisoner of war camps. He built himself a small business and for the first time in his life had money, freedom, food and good friends.

This was the time of the hippie revolution where they came in their thousands from America and Europe to find sun, sand, sex and lots of drugs to quell their disillusionment with two world wars and the lost patriarchal establishment.

In 1963 Andy, an American came to Gerhardt's stall, admired his leather skills and befriended him, bringing stories of travel around the world and a possible life in America. However, at this time Gerhardt had fallen in love with an Australian girl and she asked him to come to Australia to begin a whole new chapter of his life. He was torn in two directions, America or Australia? Coincidentally the American, after befriending him had asked Gerhardt to make a special leather shoulder bag of a particular design, and Gerhardt had done so over a period of weeks. Then when Andy returned and Gerhardt handed him the leather shoulder bag which he immediately loved, Andy couldn't help but admire how elegant it was and how beautifully the leather was embossed. With great sadness Andy informed Gerhard that he had no money and was very sorry for over reaching his slim budget. He intended to go away, earn some money and then return for the bag, but Gerhardt, knowing what being poor meant, gave him the bag. Andy thanked him profusely, promising to return.

And return he did, 2 weeks later. Andy returned, again without any money, but he gave Gerhardt something far more valuable - the original formula for Hoffman's LSD, which apparently had no side effects, as well as the detailed instructions on how to make it.

At this time LSD was the wonder drug for the hippies, but many were reluctant to take it as many of them were having bad trips and some were even dying due to the impurities in the mixtures. Hoffman's original LSD had none of these negativities and it was known as the elixir of all psychedelics.

Over a period of 6 months Gerhardt sought and found the acids, bases and other ingredients, while searching for the real elixir, "rye grass mould" which was the most difficult to procure until he discovered that the local gypsies had a supply. Next, he went to his chemist friend Alfredo and asked him if he would be prepared to mix it.

He agreed, but said it was risky and he would charge Gerhardt US$100. This was considered to be a fortune then, as Gerhardt was living on US$1 a day, Alfredo agreed to accept payment after Gerhardt had sold some of his LSD. So, they mixed most of the night, and by early morning they were putting the last of the mixture onto blotting paper, 1 cm square, for each drop, ready for the market. "When I tallied it up" Gerhardt said "I had 5,000 tabs and I went to the market hoping to sell each tab for US$1, maybe even 100 tabs in the day so that I could pay Alfredo."

Soon the word was out and by that afternoon Gerhardt had sold the lot. He said with a smile "there were people stoned and naked on the beach, others talking to flowers, others climbing trees and others lying on the roadway oblivious to the crowds around. It got so crazy that the local authorities closed the streets."

It became unofficially known as "the day Ibiza stood still." Gerhardt had turned a simple market scene into both bedlam and a bonanza. That night he said he went back to Alfredo with US$5,000 in a huge bundle and said "Alfredo today is our lucky day, we are rich", Gerhardt happily peeled the bundle in half and gave it to him. Alfredo looked at it for a while, tossed it up and down and then he peeled off US$100 and gave him back the rest.

"I was a rich man," said Gerhardt. "In today's currency it was probably equivalent to US$200,000."

Over the next week he sold all he had, gave away what possessions he didn't need and with his girlfriend flew to Australia where they found these 160 acres of bushland south of Sydney which he bought with some of his money. This was where Gerhardt built his castle. He was "free for the first time in my life, free to make a family, free to grow food and build a house, free to swim in our own river and free to make friends with all the animals."

Gerhards' story continues, "we had a daughter, but my wife sadly contracted breast cancer and she died when our daughter was 2 years old, so I brought her up on my own living the life of a hermit, not sad or blue, but rejoicing in my new-found fortune after 40 years of struggling just to survive.

Now I've been here for 35 years and each day is a full meditation. I have the world in my backyard and memories to last a lifetime. My early struggles have made this simple life a paradise and here I shall happily die" he said with a deep smile.

Once, after playing chess for 3 days straight and smoking a little hooch, I asked Gerhardt, who was an avid student of Gurdjieff, the great 19th century mystic, philosopher and spiritual teacher, what was his lifetime's wisdom?

He told me that first, you need a language to talk to your higher self beyond the influences of all other men. The great liberation for any man is the removal of influences from those outside ourselves and the second is liberation from the fixed beliefs inside ourselves. He considered that the only language able to do this was the cosmic language of numbers, interpreted by yourself, after you understand the rational language of number resonance.

Our greatest mistake in life said Gerhardt, is to seek a guru, a god, a dogma that programs us to follow and not to lead. When asked further about numbers and life's journeys he said "I am a one, a beginner, a starter, energiser and you are a 7, a philosopher, teacher, traveller, seeker" which put our relationship into a perspective that a thousand words couldn't have done.

After learning the Pythagorean language of numerology from Gerhardt I applied it to the many crew members I had travelled with over the years and found it described them very well about 95% of the time. Gerhardt emphasised that there is a deeper wisdom to life if one appreciates one's own search over all others as the real deal, and I believed him. I well remember the day I sold my castle early in 2004. I received a distraught phone call from his daughter saying she had found Gerhardt dead.

He died of a heart attack and not more than 3 days before he had visited me at the castle, where he had brought his favourite chess set and before leaving had given it to me as a present, to remember him after I left the valley. We had had a lot to say to each other in our short friendship, and we had made plans to go to Goa in India, after I sold the castle.

Now as I seek to meet Gerhardt for lunch as an imaginary exercise, I look to the north east and there, not more than 3 miles away is a cloud that is close to the water, being back lit by the bright sun, forming an arch with misty rain that seems to be falling inside the front part of the cloud. It is so unusual that I imagine that it is Gerhardt's doing, he's brought his castle out here somehow and I laugh and cheer and gleefully gybe over and head for it.

Slowly over half an hour I gain on the cloud as it's also moving with our shared wind and the entrance grows huge and higher like the entrance to a cathedral in the sky, reaching well above me. Here is an opportunity to live that "generosity of observation" that Gerhardt and I had often talked about.

If one sees the beauty in a scenario and then offers gratitude for feeling that beauty, one is enhancing one's real appreciation and quality of life. They say life is not measured by the amount of breaths you take but the moments that take your breath away. Each of us create those moments by this simple act in that "generosity of observation." This sight is definitely taking my breath away!!

"So here I come Gerhardt, ready for our lunch appointment" I shout out like a crazed man. The sun glints orange and white around the front of the cloud and rain showers can be seen pouring down in the entrance like waterfalls. I imagine sailing into it, even collecting some sweet rainwater for my barrel. Slowly I gain on the cloud as it hovers above the water, getting to within half a mile, wondering whether I should reef the main in case there could be a waterspout forming.

As I sail closer, I'm imagining Gerhardt watching me, smiling, but the cloud slowly rises and disperses and soon I am left with just a fading image and no rain. Reality turns to illusion. Life is a highway of self-meaning and my imagination was surely running riot. Gently I gybe back southwards onto my old course and decide that my meeting with Gerhardt was somehow cancelled. We missed lunch but he did a magnificent performance on my mind, showing me the beauty of the day in that one beautifully arched cloud.

I sail on until near noon when I heave-to with the jib backed, the mainsail flat pointing north-west, as I lock the helm and go to get the sextant. I'll try to get noon latitude and then longitude by time, so this sight will take all of half an hour, but it'll tell me how much progress has been made over the last two weeks. I put on my only classical guitar CD and imagine Gerhardt playing over lunch, while I make simple chess moves towards getting position lines on my chart.

The positional fix eventually gives me a latitude of 55.12 deg west and 37.18 north, which means I'm about 70 miles south of Horta and 1600 miles to the west. It's a long haul yet, at least 20 days more at this rate so I'd better keep a close eye on my food and water supplies. I make a lunch of crackers and cheese along with a cup of tea and then let the jib fly, haul around to the south east where at least it's warmer, and get on the road again. The wind is about 9 knots from the south west and I could put up a bigger jib, but lassitude has me in its grasp so I'll just jog along, satisfied with the day, waiting for the next interesting intrusion in my life.

Chapter 17

Charlie and Morovo Lagoon

I look up from the cockpit and see a trawler crossing my stern about 3 miles away. He surprises me as I thought I was all alone. I assume he is deep water trawling as his booms are out and he's travelling slowly south. The deep roar of his motor initially alerted me to his presence, reminding me of the beauty of silence that we all appreciate after the loud roar of our society. It reinforces the thought that only by going alone in silence can one truly get into the heart of any wilderness and the ocean is the biggest wilderness that we have. I appreciate the trawler, not by his arrival, but more as he slowly departs, not wishing to contact him or have his noise occupy my space any longer. He's an intruder that I can well do without.

At 1600 hours I heave-to again, lock the helm and take to the bunk wishing to get some sleep before another long night of helming alone. I sleep till 1800 hours and then make a small meal of pasta and chopped salami, onions and mushrooms. It tastes fantastic and I top it off with a cup of tea, realising that I need to make some sort of inventory of the food I have left, as there are still a lot more days to go than I originally thought. It's going to be much closer to 40 days than my original belief that 25 would put us close to Horta.

The sun still has a good two hours in it and the sky is clear with a few cirrus clouds up high, offering more wind later in the week. But now calm conditions prevail and tomorrow offers more of the same. The ocean swell is low, long and steady and we barely roll as I take the steering lines aft and sit on the water container to get a different angle of my situation. I play with new ideas, bouncing them back and forth, even imagining the trawler dropping me off some squid or oceanic prawns, if they exist.

Then I realise that playing with new ideas is like being a child again, playing with a new toy, figuring out how it works and practising each new extension of action it provides. Oh, the fun of an idea, the novelty, the joy.

By playing with new ideas we change, we re-shape reality and we experience things never before considered and we expand our awareness. Things have a life but ideas last forever and are much more powerful. As George Bernard Shaw once said," If you have an apple and I have an apple and we exchange those apples, each of us still has one apple and are no better off. But if each of us has a good idea and we exchange them, we both have two ideas and we are transformed."

I let my mind wander to previous experiences and reflect on my friend Charlie from Morovo Lagoon in the Solomon Islands deep in the south Pacific. The Pacific is so huge and pluralistic and is the most feminine of all the oceans.

Taking adventurers through the Pacific in the 1980s was a delight in itself, as every island reflected its own magic. There's even a saying amongst old sailors "if the world could travel through itself, it'd take a sail boat ride through the south Pacific." I regularly visited Morovo Lagoon when we cruised north of Australia, as there we could experience one of the wonders of the world from our own cockpit.

Morovo Lagoon in the Solomon Islands is a totally enclosed lagoon, with a narrow opening either end and extending for at least 60 miles, full of islands and fascinating tribal groups and is alive with so much sea life.

During World War 11 the Japanese hid their entire naval Pacific fleet there, safe from detection by any other Navy. Here was another universe where Charlie was supremely happy as the village elder on Telina Island, and he didn't want to change a thing, but I understood him from a different level.

It's a little like Sam and me, he's on another dimensional level, not any better or worse, but with a bigger perspective than mine. I saw the limitations in Charlie's life that he wasn't aware of.

I formed a happy, enjoyable relationship with Charlie, a 40-year-old fuzzy headed Melanesian who lived on his traditional island home paradise which had a population of 130 people. His ancestors had lived there for as long as anyone could remember and Charlie was now the island's wise man leading his people forward. He administered traditional medicine, understood the seasons and all the nuances that traditional life brought. He was satisfied and content and I often said to the crew, to impress them of the wonders here "this is where I'll probably end my sailing days living in a hut on the shore. Maybe I'll even come back as a volunteer teacher bringing books, mathematics, science and stories of the outside world hopefully expanding their perspectives on life." But then reality hit me one day as I walked with Charlie around the village asking him about the unnamed beautiful island half a mile from their shore. I was intrigued as to what was over there, as no villagers seemed to venture in that direction with their canoes. "Nothing," he said, "bad spirits live out there, along with swampy ground, coconuts and some big rats." "Any coconut crabs?" I asked, to which he replied that yes there were many.

"Charlie, "I said, "let's go hunting for coconut crabs tonight" and he agreed.

Now, coconut crab hunting is an art form that the Pacific Islanders know well. The secret is to attract them with fresh coconut baits at night, then sneak up on them with a torch, then catch them and bind their claws together with strong fibre before they attack you. If they grab you with their one huge claw they never let go, and if you survive the pain, you have to cut off their claw. Their claws are like the Tasmanian devil's jaw and if you poke them with a medium sized stick they'll snap the stick like a guillotine. After all, they can tear open a coconut with that one claw, so it's mighty powerful.

The best thing about them though is the wonderful taste of their flesh that tastes like a cross between coconut, crab meat and caviar and it is almost addictive. They are by far the greatest and rarest delicacy across the whole Pacific and perhaps even the world and the wise Vanuatuans even have ingrained them on their coins as good luck symbols.

A new adventure was on the go and after dark 5 of us eager novice hunters rowed ashore from *Sundancer* to collect Charlie and some of his clan, and off we went rowing slowly across to the island in the moonlight, ready to meet any nasties on shore. Charlie and his brothers were reluctant to go beyond the beach because of the bad spirits, but we heathens plunged inland, set 10 traps of split coconuts on 3-foot stakes and then settled down with the villagers to wait for a few hours, quietly talking about the paradise that the natives lived in and sharing stories about some of the places we had visited around the lagoon.

We made a cup of strong tea with plenty of sugar accompanied by some biscuits and the local islanders were in heaven. We talked about the fact that coconut crabs are rarely seen in the day as they hide in hollow logs or underground in a solitary existence waiting for the sounds of falling coconuts, and then like big rugby players they bear down upon them, tearing the coconut to pieces and feast upon it. Around their nests are piles of coconut shells and like anything in nature that has a monopoly they also have their rivals, big black rats that race to clean up the shells after them. Like the coconut crab they are black, shiny, sleek and fast. As for the coconuts there are about 10 stages of coconut maturity that the natives understand well.

Their language is rich with nuances about coconuts and if you ask them for one they understand that you want a drinking nut that is young, effervescent and sweet. Each stage of the nut is used for various ailments particularly by pregnant women and for the old men who use very young nuts to restore their vigour.

The meat nuts range from soft jelly to hard coconut which they scrape out and add to hot water to get coconut cream. Without coconuts the natives would surely starve as the coconut tree provides food, fibre, building material and medicine, and we in the west are finally catching onto the benefits of coconuts as a refined food source. If the coconut is left for a while it eventually fills up with foam like fairy floss, and that is also a delicacy. It then sprouts a new plant that is also enjoyed for its green shoots.

Soon we were off inland, hunting with our torches, sharing bravado and the excitement of the elusive hunt until we arrived back at the beach with 5 jet black shiny coconut crabs of various sizes. Their claws were soon immobilised with coconut strands and they were gingerly put in the bottom of the dinghy so that we could happily row back to the village, keeping our bare feet well away from their savage claws.

On shore I told Charlie to take 3 crabs and we'd take 2 but he declined them all, saying they no longer ate coconut crabs, even though they did enjoy catching them. I was surprised, presuming that Charlie was reluctant to take the crabs because we had caught them.

That night the whole crew had a feast of coconut crabs on a bed of rice with mayonnaise and fresh garlic and they loved the experience, thanking Charlie in absentia for being so generous by raising a glass or two of Bundaberg rum. The next day we baked bread and the 3 loaves that I took ashore to Charlie were a hit with the kids and adults alike, even though they made their own bread irregularly, baking it in the stone ovens which they had built.

I offered to buy some chickens from Charlie but he said the village didn't keep any which was surprising, and then I asked about any pigs they may want to sell and he said they had no pigs either.

I then remarked to Charlie that I was surprised that they didn't eat coconut crabs, chickens or pigs which had been their staple food for generations, and he said "we only eat special meat now, with rice and coconut."

On enquiring about this special meat, I began to realise that the Seventh Day Adventist Church members had arrived as missionaries and subsequently had taken over the island, convincing everyone to join their church. Now they are locked into not eating creatures that crawled, ate offal or picked through the rubbish. Nut meat had become their staple food, and the islanders had to make artefacts and carvings to sell so that they could buy this 'meat'. Simplicity and self-sufficiency had gone walkabout as they were now on the religious treadmill.

Their lives had changed dramatically on the "new ideas" scale of others which is so common in indigenous cultures. They had traded their self-sufficiency beliefs for a new idea that was putting them into a lifetime of debt.

The next day I was walking with Charlie through the village and I asked him what they needed most on the island and he said "a school." I pointed to the only building on the island that was substantial, painted white with gardens around it and asked him why not this beautiful building. He was shocked and said "oh no, that is the church and it's only for God."

I asked him how often it was used and he said Saturdays and Wednesday nights and the rest of the time it was closed. I suggested that maybe it could be used throughout the week as a school, but I was definitely stretching his limits. Charlie was a good man trying to do his best but his inability to think outside the square was limiting the progress of the whole village.

The church was also providing education for the children at a cost of US$130 per term and if the natives didn't pay, their kids were excluded.

It was the only source of education in Morovo Lagoon and no doubt the Seventh Day Adventists were also doing their best to create new Church communities, but their "superior beliefs" were causing much pain and anguish amongst the natives.

We sailed away wiser men for trying to understand how cultures are often overrun by other cultures, using religion as a self-righteous sword to fracture old established traditions creating new and better patterns of living. New ideas keep humans from suffering entropy but new ideas also bring pressures to bear that can cause a great deal of harm. It's the balance that is important, the use of empathy and understanding and the virtues of humanity that should form the guidelines for releasing radically new cultural ideas.

Around 2030 hrs the sun begins to sink in the west and I realise that soon we'll have the longest day of the year and the more daylight hours there are, the less chance I have of being run down by a ship. I get motivated and just on dark I drop the working jib and hoist the blue no. 2 jib which is bigger and better suited to these light airs. I probably should have done this 2 days ago, which makes me realise how flexible time has become out here. A day has little meaning and I always tell folks that a day at sea is 30 hours long, a week is 10 days and anything longer is too far away. The oceanic mind is more jelly-like, more flexible and more in tune with the rhythms of the ocean.

My speed through the water picks up from 3 knots to almost 4 as I increase the rig. The stars begin to emerge and I'm in for a beautiful night sail with a steady south west breeze of 8 knots, a slight swell and some bright moonlight. This is the first quarter of the new moon so for the next 2 weeks I'm going to have gorgeous moonlight nights where the skies are clear with lighter breezes emerging from more settled weather. I can't imagine having a better scenario for cruising across the Atlantic.

I sail on heading south east towards a clear horizon lit by a bright moon where the light ripples across the ocean and bounces around our wake creating magic.

This is my novel and I am in it. Some research indicates that novels are almost always about people who fit in, who follow society's rules, who have lives similar to us so that we can relate and vicariously share their experiences. This novel is also about us, you and me, sharing experiences. This is not a short story because they are all about people who don't fit in, who meet trauma and accidents and illness, facing the intense pressure of malevolence and loneliness. Short stories are generally about our shadow side, our faults and admissions and teach us about what not to do and that was probably why that "Aussie guy" swam past the other night. That was a short story written by a disturbed mind, mine, as I quietly hallucinated through tiredness.

I look at the moon, now my only mandala in the sky and imagine it's connecting me to the moon's etheric field, downloading its feminine energies after the all-day sun's masculine, doing its balancing act that nature always provides. It is said that the moon is the lost lover the romantic turns to and that's the amazing thing about our mind creating scenarios that enhance our well-being and giving reasons for me to keep going, whilst drifting on a wing and a prayer. The placebo effect for example where the power of a drug you believe will do you good, is 56% dependent on your belief and not just the chemistry of the drug.

Mental toughness is also something that has intrigued me a lot, raising many questions about those I have met, whether they are mentally tough or just crazy, leading to whether I am also tough or just crazy also.

Was Gerhardt mentally tough living alone out there in the bush or had he painted himself into a corner, escaping the dreadful experiences of his youth?

What about Tony, another friend of mine in Tasmania, who had retreated from his business, creating a bunker mentality where he believed the world was on the edge of a nuclear holocaust and he needed to dig a big hole in his hillside, line it with cement walls and fill it with food. Was he mentally tough or just paranoid? He very definitely was persistent.

What about those Jehovah Witnesses who stand on street corners trying to convince people to change their ways? I couldn't do that even if they paid me a fortune. Are they persistent, deluded or delusional? I know a past friend who joined the Jehovah Witnesses and then gave away all his possessions because they said that on Friday 27th May 1987 the world was ending and he wouldn't need anything. On checking I found that the group had done the same thing 5 times over the previous 30 years, but on telling him that he said I wasn't his friend anymore.

My other friend John, the base jumper, who had joined the 500 club, was he mentally tough? I thought so and wanted to exhibit the split-second decision making he so often had to face.

And then me, hiding below in a storm, too buggered to stay up and endure the cold and the wet. Was I a confirmed wimp? And then I realised mental toughness has to be a combination of tenacity but not stupidity, making mistakes and then trying again, being able to focus on details when you're dead tired, to trust in your own instincts and feelings and doing things you don't want to do to keep things going, like leading when no one else wants to follow.

Mental toughness does not remove pain and unhappiness, dilemma or the pain of choice, but it does put the individual in charge of his own life where real life and experiences become your one and only religion, not the dogmas of others.

Faith in yourself creates mental toughness and self-reliance and in experiments on mental toughness it has been found, oddly enough, that high spirituality and strong connections to others, plus strong self-belief lead to higher mental health, while high religiosity, rituals and dogma and strong beliefs in others, lead to a decrease in mental health.

At 2300 hours I decide to take a break as the moon has gone down and the night is getting colder. My mental toughness cannot compete with the cold or the need for sleep. I heave-to with the helm locked as an 8-knot southwester blows gently through the rigging and go below to put on warmer clothes and make some tea and grab a snack. It's much warmer below and I decide to put on a Willie Nelson CD and enjoy my first cup of tea for a number of hours accompanied by crackers with cheese and peanut butter. The cheese is the yellow plastic stuff, so common in the USA, but it still satisfies my taste buds and warms my heart. I wish I had some much-loved Aussie Vegemite to increase the flavours.

I take my cuppa back to the cockpit, settling in for a long night, releasing the backed jib and head east again at 3.5 knots, gently cruising through the long hours of the night enjoying the gentleness of this big wide ocean.

I look at the stars and focus on Canis Major or what is commonly called the Big Dog and in particular Sirius that is its choice navigable star, being the brightest star in the sky. I politely call it the dog's behind. It always twinkles, changing from red to green, to white and purple in a constant kaleidoscope of colours. Anything brighter than Sirius is a planet and in the south east tonight that's Jupiter in Scorpio. The night sky is my only contact with the vast cosmos out here while the day is all about the sun and the solar system and yet we are connected to both.

I like to see the merit in those who say that Sirius is where humanity came from before settling on earth and I give it more generosity of observation than any of the other stars, feeling that direct connection to it may be just me giving it more meaning.

It's aspirational for sure but it is an expansion of self, allowing me to transcend both the experiences of the ocean and the realisation that I am caught in this cosmic alchemy, while also wishing to connect to my own infinity. And the bliss, the contentment comes strongly when I am quiet and still, contented and calm, throwing my dreams into the cosmos like a kite, never sure what will return. I realise I have been out 18 days and nights and yet it feels like I've been sailing forever. My whole life seems to have focused into this small trajectory of my journey and yet it's a space pregnant with all sorts of possibilities.

There is a real discipline to this journey that I've not experienced to the same degree in any of my past ocean miles. Before, there were others to share the journey and the privations, to share stories and hopes and here there is just me. It's like a profound but rich emptiness and is the same emptiness that others talk about meeting on their journey to themselves.

I sail on until I can stay awake no longer. It's close to 4 in the morning and nothing has changed. The stars are bright, the sea and wind are the same, the coming day offers the same as yesterday and I heave-to, lock the helm and go below to sleep and dream, leaving the hatch open, the breeze blowing in. I wrap myself in my sleeping bag and drift off.

When I awake full of beans and enthusiasm, the new day is filtering through the hatch. The moon is sinking, the sea is flat and from horizon to horizon there's nothing but this vast Atlantic ocean and my little *Millefleurs*.

I make some breakfast with rolled oats, nuts and dried fruits and sit in the cockpit with a cuppa admiring the day.

There will be many more horizons today on towards the east and hopefully more birds, some flying fish and maybe a whale or two. This is my 19th day and I'll celebrate when I get to the halfway point sometime in the next week, unless I'm becalmed for a few more days.

Then there's a sudden unexpected clap of thunder and I notice that a dark cloud is rapidly making its way towards us, low to the sea and I can see rain ruffling the sea's surface in its shadow. It's disturbing the quiet ocean like a naughty child and then there's an applause of thunder (many claps) and that dark cloud is approaching fast with sparkles glittering rainbows out of the base. Maybe it'll miss us, but my hope is it'll bring some rain for me to capture in the mainsail catcher. Between helming I rig the catcher, put a bucket under the spout and grab the shampoo from the cockpit locker. As the cloud moves in with it's quiet rumbles I take off my clothes and fish up a bucket of warm sea water then lather up as I steer with one foot. Then the cloud is over us moving faster than the breeze, but showing no malice now, not even wind gusts on the sea's face. It begins to rain and I lather up again keeping my eye on the catcher and rushing to collect fresh water from bucket to container as I keep the boat tracking joyfully east while having a beautiful, languid bath.

The rain is very cold, much colder than the ocean, but a whole lot sweeter as it drips off my hair down my face and into my opened mouth. I drink it in like the best spring water. I catch one bucket and then two and then the show is over. It lasted all of 10 minutes as the cloud rumbles off to the north-east almost under its own steam, grumbling quietly as it goes. There are now 10 litres of fresh water in the buckets which can last me as fresh drinking water for 10 days. I'm proud of myself for spotting the cloud before it hit us and happy to challenge its threatening behaviour, just like I've gone a round with the local bully.

I look to the north and see the lights of a ship heading west. They are low down on the horizon indicating that he is over on the other side of the horizon while his front stack is lower to the west. Occasionally I catch a glimpse of his port steaming light. I imagine there are 25 or more crew aboard, they have finished their dinner and are getting ready for a night watch. Some are complaining about a 4-hour watch and some are 'netting' to their families and others are having a quiet drink in the mess. Boy would I like to swap a few hours with them and enjoy all their luxuries for those hours! They're probably an Asian crew because they are cheaper to employ and non-unionised. The ship is probably registered in Panama or some other port of convenience. And then I imagine the collective stories of all those crew with their extended families and realise that that passing ship is literally carrying hopes, ambitions and struggles of a significant portion of humanity.

The sheer mystery of it all always intrigues me and aren't we all interested in spy novels, detective stories or adventure yarns where the main character is out there somewhere, searching for something beyond his grasp, just as we all do, contributing to this amazing panorama of life. And isn't there always something inside ourselves that we reach for, that leads us on, that makes the load bearable, the day brighter and the living easier?

We sail through the day and into another dark night with a late moon and the smell of another intrigue and mystery comes slipping over the rails like a ghost and slides into my nights abode as my mind wanders off to St Helena.

One of the most unusual mysteries I came upon whilst travelling was in

1991 when I visited St Helena Island in the south Atlantic ocean, when *Sundancer* was heading north to England after leaving Cape Town, South Africa. St Helena is quite small and has been a part of the British Empire for centuries with 2,000 people living there, with an amazing ratio of 7 females to every male. The males go off to work in other countries and don't return, which is a shame as the women are quite beautiful, being a mixture of many races. The only connection to the island with the outside world for them was a ship from Cape Town that brought in all the supplies, and an unreliable, perpetually poor radio telephone link.

There was no airport or easy connection to the rest of the world and they seemed to like it like that.

They are at 15 degrees south of the equator which means it's a balmy warm tropical climate and the people are very friendly and all speak "old English" with an easy twang. We anchored off Jamestown which is to the south, and organised a tour of the island in an open topped 1930's vehicle that could carry all 12 of us crew members. We saw the Governor's house which was palatial, and Henry the 200-year-old tortoise who probably had had enough of visitors, as he slowly and deliberately headed for cover when he saw us.

But the real highlight of the tour was seeing the residence of the French military leader Napoleon Bonaparte who lived there on the island after being exiled there in 1815 after the Napoleonic wars. He lived there with his maidens until 1821 when he died of bowel cancer and was buried in the valley below. He was obviously a small guy as his bed was only 5 feet long. I spoke to the caretaker of Napoleon's cottage and asked where Napoleon was buried. He told me that Napoleon had wanted to be buried in a nearby valley, called the Valley of the Tomb, where he often took afternoon strolls with his maidens. I asked him what happened when the French came to take Napoleon's body back to be buried in France and he said "we gave them another body - Napoleon's body is still here resting in the valley, according to his last wish." He even offered to take us there, but unfortunately, we were out of time.

This, he said, was the secret of St Helena. I'd love the French to do a DNA test to see if Napoleon is really in St Helena or France. I was high on the fumes of intrigue and I giggled to myself wondering what the French would do if Napoleon's body was really still in St Helena and if they'd ever allow the truth to emerge.

Mystery is part of our DNA as we love mystery, intrigue and double dealings as much as we love wine or sport - that's probably why the Mafia do so well!

At 2200 hours the wind backs to the north west over a period of half an hour as I gybe away to port tack and it begins to increase, quickly. I race forward in the dark and drop the big jib and get back to the helm to keep trucking on the main. The wind increases to 20 knots and the sky begins to cloud over from the north-west so I consider dropping the mainsail as well. The old saying is if you have to debate whether to put a reef in it's already too late and I am at that stage. I hold the main and tighten the preventer and hope for the best even though I am now on port gybe, heading east south east at 5.5 knots. Fortunately, I have my wet weather gear in the cockpit beside me and am able to kit up while still on the run and settle into the cockpit seat ready to make lots of miles while also hoping the wind doesn't increase in strength.

Then a huge rain squall comes beating down on my back as I try to huddle in a small ball behind the helm sailing on compass alone, unsure whether I'm enjoying this or whether I'm just a pawn in the game of fate.

The inertia of discomfort takes over as I huddle in my cold gear, water dripping down my face and running up my right sleeve. I sure wish I was sitting in that truck with Bobby McGee singing all those songs whilst just keeping warm and dry. Belief is the best placebo and so I play a mind game with myself trying to turn this cold Atlantic weather change into a friend.

At this latitude I guess I'm squeezed between the Atlantic highs south of me and the Atlantic lows to the north and if I work further south I'll get out of this squally weather. I deliberately angle a little further south, heading for the tropics and that feels even better as I feel that I'm back in control.

I look around searching the horizon for ships' lights knowing full well that my present visible range is probably only a nautical mile. My life is regularly in the hands of fate and yet I'm reluctant to admit it. It's that control issue again, I want freedom but I want to be in control, only allowing ships that I can see to come into my circle.

The wind again begins to gust higher and we surge away under the main and soon I realise I have to do something about this mainsail otherwise there could be a wild broach, or a crazy gybe particularly as I get tired, with possible damage to the rig. I have to get the mainsail off and soon. I round up to the breeze heading north and let my speed fall to a couple of knots with the main flapping wildly as the wind seems to howl louder and more brutally. I race up to the mast with spray flying all around, wrestling the main down to the boom and lashing it tightly. It takes much longer than I expected and by the time I get back to the cockpit I'm completely buggered, having used up all my reserves of energy. I'm shivering from the exertion and the release of all that adrenalin. This blow has come quickly and hopefully it'll go soon as the wind gusts to 35 knots and we lie beam-on drifting south east at a knot, riding easily like an albatross between feeds.

Tired but secure, I'm ready for this blow to pass through. The night is definitely dark, cold, misty and scary and I don't have a lot of bravado up here in the cockpit, I'm feeling like I'm parked in a ship's freeway praying for more dharma. I know that if I took the average person comfortably sitting in their lounge chair drinking coffee and watching TV and beamed them out here for 20 minutes, they'd all say they have just been to hell.

There's only one worse place than this and that would be on a battlefield with shells exploding and people dying around you. That would be really bad karma.

Then the lightning begins up to the north-west and rolls our way with huge bangs of thunder and brilliant flashes against an absolutely jet-black sky.

This is not just claps of thunder or applauses but staccato thunder that is irregular and concerning. A huge black cloud rolls over us and the lightning becomes wilder and more erratic, striking the water around us. I'm really scared now. I look at the masthead and see that the masthead light is on, but I haven't used it for days. Then I'm reminded of St Elmo's fire where the static charge in the air causes the highest point on the boat to discharge.

I have to sort this out before we are also struck and I dive below and grab the battery charging cables that I stowed on board from the van, and I crawl forward along the deck and attach them to the rigging and tie them to the rail and let the ends drag in the water. If we're struck at least the rigging won't be fried and the cables will let the charge flow into the ocean. I'm not sure if this is the way to treat the problem but I feel better for at least having tried while the lightning and thunder crashes malevolently all around us.

The mast continues to glow and the sea gets rougher as we wallow like a dead whale hiding from all the panic. Waves crash into the side and spray is everywhere and my quiet party has been interrupted by a gang of crazies. The air is heavy with peril and if this is an omen then I hope it's quick as things can't get too much worse, or so it seems. Then the ominous black cloud moves off taking the lightning with it leaving disturbed water and gusty winds behind. It's heading south east and boy am I happy that it's got heaps of fresh horizons that don't include us in its tantrum trail. I leave the charging cables attached to the rigging for later retrieval, even though between the wind gusts I can hear them rattling on the hull.

I'm over these power bursts of nature as I've used up a week's worth of adrenalin in 10 minutes. My whole body is shaking and my ears are still ringing from the crash of thunder. The waves are still steep and irregular and I have only one choice and that means I have to sit this out, keeping watch, staying alert till dawn and then raising the storm jib to get me on my way.

I don't have the energy now to drag myself up to the foredeck, hoist the storm jib and get rolling. We may be lying ahull after escaping another dangerous moment but the good feelings of pure relief say this is a beautiful moment in life that I'll remember for years to come, balancing on that knife edge of possibility, looking out over the valley of waves below, embroiled in the turmoils of nature. I'm riding down waves on this big surfboard, smiling with adventure and distance made.

In the paintings of old sailing ships they are invariably shown standing tall, fully rigged, barrelling down wild seas with dark ominous clouds above as the threat of an approaching storm bears down on them. They seem to be at war with the ocean as well. If you'd never been to sea then your expectation would be of a wild dangerous place and yet the war scenario and the wild sea are also reflections of us. The sea that the artist produces, full of action and bravery is just a reflection of the images that his culture fed him about the ocean. Very few of the paintings show a fully rigged ship sailing happily across a flat sea with the sun shining brightly and the crew having fun, and yet that's what happens 95% of the time. Perhaps the new era of cruise ships full of happy travellers in trade wind seas, that is now capturing the traveller's market, will change our collective image of the sea's face as friendly and benign rather than dodgy and savage.

In the tropics there are few storms out of season and you can sail for 3-4 months in the trade winds without a blow, but in the Southern Ocean below 40 degrees south, a storm comes through about every 4 days. If it comes through at 20-30 knots it'll last for a whole day. If it comes through at 30-40 knots it'll last for half a day and if it comes through at 60 knots it'll last about 6 hours, as fronts are usually only 300 miles deep.

A hurricane like Barry though that engulfed me at the beginning is very different as it is heat driven rather than being a cold front, and it always moves towards the west which is contrary to other weather systems, until it finally comes over land and loses its heat vortex. If it continues over warm water it increases its speed from category 1 to category 5 when winds can get up to 200 miles per hour and that's why hurricanes are the most powerful wind systems on earth. The good news is that even a fierce blow in the Southern Ocean is mild compared to a hurricane in tropical waters and fortunately they are fairly rare. Oceaning is not an exercise in weathering storms, it's really an exercise in participating in the power of nature at its best with an ocean disturbance just bringing another form of beauty. I often play a game with each blow when I'm feeling mischievous because if you go half speed at anything you do, you create twice the enjoyment. So, I deliberately play this mind game with myself saying "I'll be disappointed when this blow is over because the seas will go down and the ocean will lose its majestic power and I'll eventually have to start catching wind again, rather than spilling it, and that will be hard work."

So, that's what I have to do now…or at least when morning comes, when I'll have to gather my energies for another long day in the ocean's office.

Atlantic Ocean – Early Days

Solomons, Chesapeake, Maryland, USA

Panama - 2008

Cold and alone in the Atlantic

Millefleurs, Graciosa, Canary Island, 2007

Millefleurs, Atlantic Ocean

The Author

Arrival into the Azores

Lisbon, Portugal

Journey's End – Burnie, Tasmania, Christmas 2008

Chapter 18

Tired and worn

It's 3 in the morning and the wind has settled down to about 25 knots and I'm slowly drifting away to the east, lying ahull and being pushed along like a lost log. I'm tired but feel the need to not push my luck. I stay on watch longer, huddled down in my wet weather gear, taking short naps and then looking around. Standing up to look around is too painful, so I discard that idea, balancing comfort with my safety and immersing myself in this challenge of spotting ships and staying dry. I just pop my head out for short observations and shrink back into my sailing hood. I have to immerse myself in this movie that I've started, as it's right here and now, and the present moment is where I am confined. If I try to escape from this moment then it says I must be unhappy with this portion of my life and then the game's over. I need to practise acceptance and just enjoy the moment, even though the water has run up my arm and then slowly crept down my back and it feels very cold, sticky and uncomfortable.

I feel penetrated by malevolence. Besides, my butt is sore and I am left alone thinking about wearing down the dawn and eventually putting up some rig to get out of this place.

The sky is beginning to lighten to the east and I've come through the night again unscathed and my surfboard rolls on to the east. The waves didn't get big, they were sizeable as they rolled through while they smiled and waved as they carried me to Horta. I thank the ocean for its endeavours, almost like an appeasement to its immense power, particularly for those wild lightning displays.

In the Southern Ocean the waves are usually bigger but rarely dangerous. A big southern wave is most often regular and long, and as it lifts you to the crest it is like driving through hilly country.

You look down into the valleys and marvel at how deep it is down there and then you're soon down there looking up while also being sheltered from the 60 knot south wind blasts. But a rogue wave is vastly different as it can come at any time with a sharp crest on the top, like another wave within a wave. It springs up at random moments and showers you with spray as it malevolently separates from the main wave like a passing terrorist, crashing into the boat's hull like a runaway mortar shell, exploding randomly in cold heavy spray that soaks all. One of my crew members from the 1994 around the world said the waves at Cape Horn were small compared to the biggest wave in the world that he had ridden in Western Australia.

Terry was a hang glider pilot in the late 1980's and had taken his glider to Burketown on Australia's Gulf of Carpentaria to ride this huge wave that comes through yearly but only when the monsoon seasons are changing. This air wave is a spectacular meteorological event that occurs just after dawn within a 2 month window around September when the conditions are just right. There are few people who have the fortitude to ride this spectacular "morning glory" as it can be up to 3,000 feet high and hundreds of miles long and sometimes a mile deep. It's like a giant rolling pin as it emerges from the ocean and sweeps inland travelling from west to east at up to 30 knots.

Terry said he camped on the coast and waited for 2 weeks before the word went up that "morning glory" was on its way. He, along with many others, launched his motorised glider and was up at 2,000 feet before it swept in like a huge white rolling surf break. He said he rode it for well over 2 hours, flying like an eagle on the top edge of the wave, staying high so he wouldn't be sucked under, dipping his wings into the cloud, tacking up and down the front and finally dropping out the back exhilarated and totally exhausted.

He landed in the desert to radio in his GPS position so that the ground crew could locate him.

He had ridden the wave for 50 miles and said it was the most amazing god-like adventure of his life, melding the beauty and power of nature into a raw flowing stream of pure energy. Later, Terry climbed Mt Everest and then most of the 50 14,000ft plus peaks of Colorado with some being free climbed, without any ropes. He was a real adventurer.

That's what I really loved about collecting a bunch of adventurers and rolling out into another ocean expedition - it was a privilege to travel with the cream of humanity. I had the added fun of being their leader, taking them to unique, beautiful and wild parts in nature that only a big sailboat allows you to explore. It was surely a blessed life that I still savour every day.

We roll into day 20 and I finally decide that I must sleep even though the dawn arrival has given me new energies. I'm a morning person and function best when the sun comes up while night owls tend to sleep in the morning. Research has shown that night owls are more driven, smarter and get more booty while morning people are happier. I've always found morning people easier to live with, probably because they belong to my tribe, but now with the sun heavily blanketed by thick cloud and the sky a steely dull grey, I'm going to sleep for an hour and get sailing before the wind dies right off, which looks to be the case as it is now down to 12 knots.

I leave the deck, locking the helm and considering what rig will be needed when I emerge later, acknowledging that it's going to be a real sailor's lottery. It's 0800 hrs when I emerge and the breeze is down to 10 knots from the west. I make some breakfast and a big cup of tea and sit in the cockpit drawing energy from the ocean and debating what the day will bring. Logic says that blow is over and a high will settle in more from the south, bringing settled weather and light winds, so I decide on the big main and the no. 2 jib.

I always make my bunk early as it's the most sacred thing on the boat beyond the wheel, but I have certainly neglected the galley as its been little used lately. In fact, I've hardly cooked in days but now in this lull, I put on a pot of rice with one third sea water, let it heat up to the boil and then let it sit where it'll cook in its own heat and be ready for later meals.

There's little chance of any navigation today and I decide that this is really going to be a "no day" where we may achieve a few miles after that short blow, while better things are coming with warmer air and steady south westerly breezes. I'd love to take some time to read and edit the diary that I've been keeping. I brought along 6 books with great promises for consumption, believing I'd be able to sit by the self steerer, expanding my knowledge with some fun esoteric and psychology texts about high achiever's experiments. Plus I've brought a soft-covered sailing book about adventuring around the Bering Strait which sits just below the Arctic Circle, separating Russia and the United States. But none of my books have been opened yet as I just don't have the time even though it seems that I should have so much free time.

Even making time for washing up is a bit of a drag and then I realise I haven't put out the Jesus rope for a couple of days as it's been coiled on the aft deck and it shakes me a bit as lassitude seems to be overcoming my simple safety rules.

The Jesus rope was a very useful item on *Sundancer* as it became part of our daily adventure routine. There, when one climbed out of the bunk in the morning and went on deck, the first action was to leap over the side, swim sideways to the Jesus rope, glide arm over arm up the knots and climb back on deck to lather up with cheap frothy detergent and leap over again, rinse off and climb back on board cleansed, challenged and ready for the day.

The only time we didn't go out on the Jesus rope was when we were going faster than five knots or the water was too cold. The joie de vivre and the energy it added to the day challenged crews to stretch their limits. It was a new form of ocean surfing where you climbed on your board, paddled out and caught the proverbial ocean swell before breakfast. The challenge of not missing the rope was crowned by the relief of grabbing onto one of the knots as *Sundancer* surged away like a frisky pony.

Fortunately, we only had one person swept off that Jesus rope and it was Dan, a tall Texan, crossing the Pacific with us in 1992. He foolishly went out on the rope when the boat was doing 7 knots. We were 10 days out of Panama and north of the Galapagos Islands, almost halfway to the Marquesas with the fresh trade winds driving us down a choppy, sloppy sea. Dan was no slouch - he was a fit ex US serviceman who had joined us to experience more adventures in life. In Honduras he had led our boat crew in a successful basketball challenge against the locals and in Colon, Panama, he stared down a knife-wielding crook who tried to steal our gear. In the Las Perlas Islands outside Panama, he rescued Mick the Englishman, who tried to swim to shore and nearly drowned. Dan was our big fella and I found his one weakness only a few days before he was washed off the Jesus rope.

One morning on dawn watch he and I wickedly conspired to catch and eat the booby bird that had taken over the bow of the boat, diving on flying fish as they scattered before our bow wave and then repeatedly pooping all over the deck. We had let the ferocious hunter take over his bow position on the pulpit as it gave us lots of entertainment, but the resulting mess it was making was getting out of hand and eating him seemed appropriate, particularly as we'd never heard of anyone putting one in the pot before as they are just too difficult to catch.

Its final act of ungratefulness came when it sat in the rigging overnight and caused a huge white mess down our brown sails. We scooted him off with dire warnings and the evil eye as his novelty had finally turned into a damn nuisance. Dan was keen to eat him as well because when the sun peaked over the horizon and Mr Booby took up his position on the bow we could clearly see the awful mess he had made - his goose was literally cooked, he had betrayed our trust.

Dan and I discussed for over an hour how we were going to catch him and more importantly, how we were going to cook him. We decided slow cooking in a curry with lots of coconut would do the sucker the honours of "real chef cuisine" served with turmeric rice and evening rum sundowners in the cockpit. It was going to be a Galapagos ceremony we'd never forget as we charged across the Pacific. Dan was going to be the first to have his bowl filled and regardless of the taste was going to loudly proclaim "booby bird, the best chicken I've ever eaten" in his big, loud Texan accent.

So, the scene for more adventure was set. Dan was going to position himself midships and I was going to creep forward and shoot Mr Booby between the eyes with the air-rifle that we kept onboard to scare birds off the rigging. Andreas from Austria who had just emerged for the morning watch was keen to be in on the fun, so he took over the helm and the movie of the day began to roll. As soon as I shot the bird Dan would dive overboard, grab him by his dangerous beak, drift aft, claim the Jesus rope and we'd grab the bird from him. As we were sliding along at only 3 knots there was no danger of losing either. If the bird fell on deck Dan and I would leap upon him and pin his dangerously hooked beak with a lump of cloth that Dan had ready in his hand. We were primed. It's a story you plan to share when you're old as you tell your grandkids that booby bird is the finest cuisine you've ever tasted and you have the whole wild story to tell them why.

I crept forward behind the life-raft, around the sail bags and past the first mast, then the second mast and then the third. Finally, Mr Booby turned around to see what was happening, fixing his big blue eyes upon me at a range of 20 feet, and then 15 feet on the crawl, as he fluffed up his feathers to say 'this is my area'. He'd never been hunted before, he was the ocean master and I was the alien. I could feel Andy and Dan's eyes upon me, willing me to hit Mr Booby right between the eyes, knocking him out before the real drama began.

I took careful aim and bang! He unfortunately fell over the side with a loud squawk and my job was done, it was up to Dan now. "Grab him Dan!" I excitedly sang out, "grab the cheeky bastard" but I could see Dan was hesitating as Mr Booby drifted past him, flapping wildly away in the water. "Grab him you god damn Yankee bastard" echoed Andy, but Dan continued to hesitate and then sang out "he's too dangerous" and the moment was gone - our big game hunter had dropped the ball and booby curry was off the menu.

Fifty yards astern Mr Booby recovered his senses and flapped wildly away and Andy philosophised on his long-lost chance to eat a booby. Dan sat quietly nursing his ego and I put away the gun and hoped we'd catch a dorado for the day as I streamed out the fishing lure instead.

Whether that was the catalyst for Dan to go out on the Jesus rope 2 days later at 7 knots to restore his reputation, and then be washed off as a wave caught him a full body blow, snatching him away, I'm not sure. The first I knew about it as I was sleeping below was the man overboard alarm, wailing through the boat and everyone rushing on deck to take up positions around our MOB (man overboard) drill pattern that we practised weekly.

When I hit the deck, Mark had released both the orange life-rings but the Dan-buoy with its tall flag was jammed and caught up in the stern holder.

Mark took over as spotter and we saw Dan frantically waving as we prepared to organise ourselves and get back to him. But as we began to tack with full rig in a 12 knot trade wind breeze we found the number one headsail jammed on the windward tack.

The lazy sheet had been deliberately cleated by Chris who found it interfered with his sunbaking. He had been warned about the problems it could create, but he was one of those guys who always knew better. We failed to complete the tack with a backed headsail and fell back onto the old course gaining more distance away from Dan.

The sail had to be completely dropped, as the pressure on the sheet was beyond anyone getting it off the cleat, and in that focused drama we were drifting away quickly. In the fracas Mark unfortunately lost sight of Dan in the swells so we sailed back to windward trying to regain our lost ground over the next 10 minutes but there was no sight of Dan. We tacked back, going onto a tight close reach to get back to where we believed he had come off the Jesus rope, but after another 10 minutes of sailing there was still no sight of Dan.

The sun was glinting off the water, the white caps were everywhere and we'd lost Dan. Sadness and despair were creeping in for a good man down. We continued to cover more ground where we believed he could be and time stood still. It had been 25 minutes since we'd lost him, so we dropped all sail and prepared to motor upwind to somehow find him, not knowing where the hell he was. Andy climbed the mast as I prepared to get the motor started and all was quiet on deck as we digested the drama that was now unfolding.

Then the angel appeared with Andy shouting that he could hear him," he's up there!" he pointed from the spreaders and we could faintly see Dan waving the life-ring above his head amongst all the whitecaps, shouting for his life.

We hoisted our rig again and ploughed to windward with two spotters and Andy up the mast, till we tacked above Dan, letting the sails fly and then drifted down on to him finally dragging him up the leeward side in the flat water.

Thankfully we'd finally won the battle with the sea that almost took him away. On board Dan was very quiet, he never went out on the Jesus rope again and we all thanked our lucky stars that we hadn't lost someone on passage.

Years later Andy came to visit me in Australia and as we sat digesting that voyage over a beer he said "you know we shouldn't have bothered rescuing Dan." I was shocked at his casual words and asked the mild-mannered Andy why? and he quietly replied, "because Dan died of an overdose in Amsterdam."

As I head for the Azores with the Jesus rope trailing astern I raise my cup of tea to Dan and Andy and remember the good times we shared and the way chance runs one's life. I then remember the old Hasidic saying "man is afraid of the things that cannot harm him (boobies) and craves the things that cannot help him (drugs)!"

Dan was a tough guy with his own demons and he obviously came on the Pacific crossing to face some of those. He was likeable, keen to try new things and one day somewhere, sometime we'll sit and talk of his journey across the Pacific and his brush with an earlier death at sea, and maybe he should have taken that choice, rather than dying alone in Amsterdam. I'm not sure if he was chasing a dream or running away from a nightmare but I'm damn sure the next time we meet I'll ask him!.

In all those 11 years of doing share expense cruising at $15 per day most crew were fantastic and fitted into our lifestyle of 3 months and 5,000 ocean miles. I well remember all the characters I met on that "long, wet and wild road between countries".

The odd few like Chris were "know-alls" and headstrong, believing the only advice was their advice and were a constant danger to themselves and to the rest of us. On *Sundancer* we dived, we explored but most of all we long haul ocean sailed, with the boat doing 33 expeditions and 3 times around the world, both east about and west about, with us enjoying a rollicking, wild, outrageous lifestyle that you only read about in books. So the Jesus rope is there to remind me that safety can't be ignored particularly after some of the blows we've been in and being too casual on this journey could cause me a lot of concern.

The other problem is that I have to take the Jesus rope out of the water when I stop to sleep as it could wrap around the rudder and cause serious issues. At 0830 hrs I prepare the number 2 jib and hoist it on a backed jib sheet. It seems pleased to be chosen and shakes its happy shoulders.

I hoist the full main trusting that the wind won't increase beyond 15 knots and then settle at the helm bringing *Millefleurs* around till she is going south east at 4 knots and all seems well with the world. Then I put out my trusty Jesus rope as I pass some more interesting flotsam. One bigger piece is a plank of wood about 2 metres long, floating gaily with few barnacles covering it, indicating that it was probably tossed from a recent passing ship. Give it another few weeks and it'll be the centre of a whole new school of sea life and one day if the Teredo worms don't eat it, it'll wash up on some distant shore with many intrinsic memories.

A while ago it was a tree, and now it has taken a journey out here on pure luck, where chance will determine its whole history. It's on its own adventure and we're passing mates for as long as it takes to drift away astern.

I sail till noon, the sky clears slowly and the sun comes out in short bursts lighting up the ocean and turning grey into majestic blues. I debate whether to take a sight but postpone it till tomorrow.

I know I must be getting near the halfway mark, but I'd rather find I'd crossed it and was on the downhill run than still climbing up the west face. It's peculiar how we define up and down as the concept runs deeply through our thinking. In the southern hemisphere up is always north and down is south while those guys in the Chesapeake that I shared time with were fond of saying up was towards Washington while going down to Annapolis, which was also north. Sailing across a featureless ocean means that the compass becomes very important and headings are constantly parts of one's conversation, it gives us something common to hang onto.

At 1530 hrs I stop for a short sleep, lying hove-to with the mainsail up and vanged out and the jib dropped loosely on the deck ready for a quick hoist. At 1630 hrs I'm up and off again with an eagerness that surprises me. I didn't even make a cuppa or a cracker as that someone inside me just wants to get on the road again.

Perhaps we have passed that magical halfway mark and *Millefleurs* realises we are off downhill as we skip along through the slight swell with a balmy sunlit sea sparkling away under a soft breeze and a few white caps, heading 120 degrees. This ocean is a live painting that I am crossing, with its deep blue coat and it has me in its arms finally, like a loving mother. I feel safe and at home, alive and joyful and I hold that feeling tight without any thoughts that could snatch it away. I purposefully focus my attention on the tip of my nose and allow the changing flow of breath to reduce my insatiable desire to think and small talk to myself. As the distance between the land and *Millefleurs* has slowly increased, I'm finding less need for thinking, while the talking out loud has certainly increased. I find myself talking out loud about the weather, the rig, passing flotsam and conversations with people who are not here.

This then brings to mind another one of Leo's favourite t-shirts that said, "Of course, I talk to myself, as sometimes I need expert advice!"

Chapter 19

Flying fish and dolphins

For the first time this trip I sail through a patch of flying fish and they take off to the south rising up into the breeze, gliding along its shoulder and splashing back into the ocean 200 metres or more away. I must be getting into tropical waters for them to appear, as the warmer waters are full of rising krill that feed those flying fish. Flying fish are the favourite food of dorados and I imagine the two dorados underneath the boat passing messages to each other about these prospective meals.

Often the dorados surf on the bow wave and then rush out when flying fish are disturbed, chasing them as they glide away and pouncing on them as they hit the water. I imagine having a boat to hide under, like this one, disguising their approach, gives them an added advantage in their hunt, but I don't see any of this happening today, indicating possibly that my dorados are probably novices in that game. Flying fish are easy to catch in the tropics. They are usually found on deck in the early morning after crashing into the rig in flight during the night and they lie quietly in the scuppers waiting to be collected, often along with lots of small squid.

I usually place both into the pan together. The squid take a minute to cook and are then devoured with lots of black pepper and lemon juice, while the flying fish are always cooked till crispy, particularly their wings, and then crunched up between the teeth as they are full of tiny bones. They are a delicious treat particularly when food supplies are low. The Pacific Islanders love flying fish and they go out into the lagoons at night with a lantern on their boats and a net set up high. They then rush around disturbing the flying fish and when they fly they head for the nearest light, are caught in the net and then fall into the boat. Some flying fish can grow to 10 inches long and they live in huge schools plying the tropical waters in search of tiny krill.

The frigate birds often fly above a passing boat also waiting for flying fish to be disturbed, and then they dive on them in full flight creating a wonderful spectator sport, with most sailors betting on the fish. I expect I'll see more flying fish as we get further south and east. The wind is definitely heading more to the south, south west and I angle to the east almost directly to Horta and realise that the wind gods are certainly on my side today. The day has evolved into a beauty with wind in the right direction, the sun full-on and I'm directly on course to my destination without any expectations.

Now, imagine if I had to get to Horta quickly to meet someone off a flight. That would be hell, as every wind change would be measured as good or bad, every day would seem to drag, and eventually there would be the anger of disappointment through sheer frustration with the weather. Getting ahead of ourselves is the big mental disease of my age. There was a saying my Grandma used to use often that I well remember but usually forget, "the hurrier you go, the behinder you get."

Going sailing with expectations is always painful because there are so many things outside of one's control. Life just happens while you are making plans and plans not met bring frustration, pain and eventually ulcers. If I had too rigid a timetable for this voyage it would be seen as a total failure and I'd be one annoyed and cranky sailor. Just imagine if I was racing across the Atlantic - I'd be tearing my hair out by now.

The reason I guess those old explorers were able to go on very long expeditions, over many years, and make huge discoveries, was down to a very simple mindset. They travelled largely beyond time, often without clocks and calendars knowing that the pace of change at home was so slow that when they returned nothing would be any different. What a luxury they had, time was not their keeper as it is today.

Today time is even the hunter and father time slays those who lag. But there is also a wisdom that says when we die there will be many things we haven't completed no matter how fast we go and equally there will be many things done that we couldn't have contemplated. Before the mechanical tick tock of life, the changing of seasons and the rhythms of nature determined when you hunted and when you rested. Now we deal with time as a powerful mental dimension that goes into all our plans, into most legal contracts and is used constantly to co-ordinate when we eat, sleep and work. Out here on the ocean I've had to forget father time, as he interferes with my well-being and if I let the mind influence my happiness I'm in a vicious circle.

Time definitely needs to be understood as it is a critical dimension in our consciousness growth and we need to be in charge of that dimension and own it, rather than becoming its slave. Research is now showing that when we rush for appointments or worry over wasted time we are straining our heart and measurably shortening our lives, while bringing sadness to our whole being. We use time well to overwhelm uncertainty feelings and reduce the unexpected to tangible measurement. With time under our control we feel that in the modern world we are finally in charge of our lives, and yet reality, which is the only truth serum, ambushes us all the time. That's till we realise that contentment and happiness are enhanced only when we go with the flow and avoid mental time. If we go half speed we realise we create twice the enjoyment, and there is even a mindful meditation that practises going slow. This voyage is reminding me painfully that if I rush forward under the tyranny of the helm, I invariably kick my toes. If I mindfully move forward letting the boat do its own thing and go with the flow, then the end result is the same and my toes are much happier.

I'm still off course but not overwhelmed. I'm able to change sails methodically and carefully and my plans are simpler. I know that when I get to Horta and finally tie up, I'll realise that there will be another wisdom confirmed, go with the flow, don't paddle against it.

In Sedona, Arizona I saw two cowboy truisms written on a wall about going with the flow. The first one said "never straddle a unicorn" and the second said "never squat on your spurs" and my helming problems seems to cover both.

I sail into the late evening, remembering that this is one of the longest days of the year and after sitting on the stern steering with the lines attached to a rod that I have rigged as a secondary helm on the stern, I change the lines to the galley and go below to make a drink and a snack. I put some of the rice I cooked yesterday into a bowl, add soy sauce, some sesame seeds and a few pieces of salami and return to the cockpit with water and a fine meal that will sustain me into the night ahead. After the meal I still feel hungry and I go below again with the steering lines in my hand to settle that hunger demon. I decide to splurge and make a warm milo drink with some honey and cinnamon. The milk is powdered and I get the lumps out by adding a little warm water, stirring it carefully around the cup and then adding the milk and honey before the hot water. I take it back to the cockpit and settle in for the long night haul as the sun sinks slowly behind me.

The sweetness seems to satisfy my need for affection that comes with loneliness and it is like a homesickness that I'm sure will diminish the further I get into this voyage. When Mary, my first wife, expressed milk for Cameron before she went to ballet, I'd warm it and taste it first before giving it to him and I was really surprised by how sweet human breast milk is.

We humans are obviously attuned to sweet things from birth and when sugar was first brought to Europe in the 16th century, it was literally worth its weight in gold. The demand for sugar was equivalent to the present demand for cocaine and the results were about the same. The demands for sugar from the West Indies caused a growing revolution in agriculture requiring slaves for labour.

The subsequent "black birding" practices, with the huge rise in European sailing ships going to African ports, luring negroes on board with all sorts of offers and sailing away, loaded with captives, created dreadful ramifications for later racial inequality and poverty. The racial dogma that swept Europe was that negroes were thick skinned, bone headed, only good for work and breeding and easily fed on a salvation mentality that continues even today, creating some of the greatest inequalities within humanity.

The cocaine trade causes a similar demand for sweetness in people's lives, helping them transcend the grinding numbness of day to day living, often providing immediate gratification but causing slavery, poverty, fracturing of families, crime and violence and the increased rise of the police state. Like all wars the war on drugs has been lost and our western prisons are 90% full of foot soldiers from the drugs trade, while the real slave masters buy themselves out of prison, and like those sufferings from the sugar trade, the echoes will go on for decades.

Sugar overuse has created obesity and huge health problems that threaten to overwhelm any decent health system, just as the drug trade threatens to swamp any justice system. Perhaps we could see sweetness and drugs as our conscious foray into preference and choice that sometimes threaten us all. To grow ourselves through free will and choice we have to realise that all strong preferences are double edged swords. What makes one person strong poisons another and the stronger your preferences, the stronger your antipathies.

When my preference for foods with spices and flavour becomes addictive my acceptance of natural foods becomes worse. Equally my preference for quietness and solitude on land is challenged by my annoyance of irregular beats, strobing lights, loud Harleys, barking dogs and head banging music. My preferences have also created my own hell and that's the deep lessons of choice.

At 2100 hours I heave-to and sleep for an hour, then I hoist the wind chimes that I bought in a lovely Goodwill store near the Solomons, and they tinkle away quietly as we sail on as the last of the light begins to fail. The night is soft and gentle and we roll along without time or concern, enjoying another beautiful night sky with some classical music playing softly below and the chimes above. I've almost given up looking for ships as we've had the whole ocean to ourselves for days, so around midnight I heave-to without the masthead light on and collapse into my bunk with absolutely no thoughts of any passing ships.

I'm becoming more secure in my invisibility, in my dream-like state of sailing for as long as I can, for as far as I can and then sleeping briefly followed by some more sailing. I can't honestly remember when I wasn't sailing and I can't remember what I ate yesterday. My memory has gone to sleep probably from sleep deprivation and yet my body pushes on like a robot looking for a phantom harbour somewhere out in front of me. I sleep for an hour which seems to be standard practice now, get up, make a cup of tea and start to roll again. I sail on till the dawn emerges from the east and the ocean changes from its darkened somnolence and lights up with streaks of scattered sunlight and streaky white caps, as my slow weaving wake stretches out behind.

I stand with my back to the helm and steer backwards trying to keep the wake straight, but it still wanders back and forwards with its own tenuous trail telling me that I'm only a small part of this process. The Jesus rope snakes out behind while the buoy at the end bobs up and down with a life of its own, almost in unison with the trill of the wind chimes. I sit in the cockpit practising steering, not thinking, just being in the moment and drawing in the sun as if it's my life blood. There's no place other than here and that satisfies my insatiable mind. There are no signs or goal posts, no passing people or vehicles, no vegetation or landscapes and I can't imagine a more anonymous place to be.

No critics, no interpreters, no advertisers, just us and a little music. One's life journey should be a statement of whom you are rather than about getting richer or smarter or better. What a place to retreat from the world for a brief time and just enjoy being me. It's a place you couldn't plan, buy or change. It's all mine and anything that stops me enjoying it has to come from me. I'm finally 100% responsible for the whole scene, the whole voyage and the whole day and I like it like that. I sail on through the morning on the same 12 knot south westerly breeze heading eastwards with the sun rising in the sky and the day slowly shaping into a gentle stroll down a soft laneway.

I rig some lines to the helm and go down to the galley to fossick for some food and a hot drink. Today it's strong Chinese tea and some crackers with peanut butter and that'll satisfy me till much later in the morning. I have no priority list today, nothing to fix, no lines to repair, just miles to make and that sounds like a recipe for a sailor's joy. I want to challenge the modern sailor's belief that you should never waste a good breeze, you should go as fast as you can with the biggest rig and you should continually adjust one's sails to get the best out of the boat. Forget that, I'm not a racer I'm an explorer, I'm out here to enjoy the whole drama of the day, not just the sailing menu.

The sun is wonderful and I stand naked drinking in the warmth of the day feeling like Hercules as he stood at the gates of the Hellespont, daring the world to come and join him. I take time over my tea, I roll parts of the cracker around my taste buds, I imagine peanut butter as the elixir of life and peanuts as the greatest gift to mankind. I once saw a sign on a t-shirt that said "peanut butter makes you horny!" and I asked the owner was it true and his girlfriend just raised her eyebrows!

Americans even claim that George Washington Carver, an American scientist, invented peanut butter but its history apparently goes all the way back to the Incas and the Aztecs.

Carver did extend the uses of peanuts into shaving creams, shampoo, antiseptic soap and lamp oil so it's obvious that peanuts have saved the planet from itself and hopefully some town in the south of the USA will put up a statue to the humble peanut.

I heard that Carver even made substitute coffee from peanuts but the most remarkable thing about Mr Carver was that he refused to patent any of his inventions, saying that everyone should have access to them. The best thing about peanut butter for me is that it doesn't need refrigeration or any form of preservative and it tastes heavenly and whether it makes me horny or not, I'll just raise the other eyebrow!

I sail on quietly until noon and heave-to with the helm locked and go to collect the sextant and notebook. I take a sight and the time, mark it on the notebook graph and then wait for a few minutes till it increases and mark it again on my rough bell curve till it peaks and begins to fall. Then I wait patiently till it falls back to the first reading I took, and I take the time again, averaging out the rise and fall to get my maximum reading over the time taken. This reading with corrections for the centre of the sun and biases in the sextant finally gives me a relatively correct noon latitude and longitude by time. It says I'm 36 deg 18 mins north latitude and 51 deg 36 west longitude and after plotting my noon position on the chart I stand and silently celebrate.

It's amazing how some simple mathematics and a few measurements can change your whole day like the tug of fate that reassures you things will get better. I am a few miles past the halfway mark. I'm on the downhill run now and I get a bowl of cereal and some nuts and honey, make myself a cup of Earl Grey tea and sit on the stern in the sunshine watching the Jesus rope snake out the back with its marker buoy going nowhere. I celebrate with a huge smile. It's 21 long days of being on the roll. Another 5 days will be full moon and hopefully the weather will be quiet and steady and there will be more warm water, more flying fish and birds.

I feel pure relief that the first half of this struggle is over with the best hopefully yet to come. I mull over whether I should take a swim just for the hell of it and finally decide to get back to sailing and leave the swim for even warmer water days, as we get further into summer.

I put away my navigation gear, mark a big day 21 on the chart, boil the kettle and, with a big smile, make up a half bucket of hot water. I wash my hair and my beard with shampoo that smells heavenly and I collect a pair of scissors and hack away at both the long hair and knotty beard. Then I apply some razors to my face and eventually get myself looking "society ready" again as I scoop up the loose hair and toss it overboard. My towel needs a wash so I get more fresh water and rinse it out and hang it on the rail and imagine myself arriving at Horta and heading for the closest laundry spot with a big bag of smelly clothes. One of the worst aspects of sailing is that salt water clothes never dry completely and after a while you just get used to being slightly damp and slightly smelly.

I can't think back beyond leaving Norfolk, Virginia. It's so far away that it hardly seems real, while today is so big and bold and bright with promises hard to imagine. Life is so good, so fantastic, so amazing that if you had told me 10 years ago that I'd be here in the Atlantic, alone, 21 days across the ocean, I'd tell you, you were dreaming. But it's all real, I've served my apprenticeship with this new boat and this new ocean and I feel like I belong at last. I'm no longer an intruder into this ocean, this space, this spot. I own it as much as it owns me and we share things together that are unique to both of us. We have surely grown together.

I look to the sky and see a billow of clouds to the northeast and remind myself that some call a bunch of clouds a soufflé, probably from the French. I muse on those weird words we use for bunches of things like a laughter of monkeys or an embarrassment of pandas or an alley of clowns and I wonder why we call a collection of sailors 'maties'.

It's probably why in Australia, where we were settled by sailors, we use the word 'mate' so often.

I clear the cockpit, wash out any loose hair and get prepared to sail on eastwards. I go below and put on a Kris Kristofferson CD and let *"Me and Bobby McGee"* sound out across the deck as I hoist the full main and the working jib and settle down to broad reaching eastwards for some more serious sailing. The breeze is still about 12 knots and we are making 4.5 knots on a flat sea. Tonight, to honour the soon full moon, I shall dress for the occasion with the purpose of increasing my generosity of feeling when the full moon blooms. I want to sail under the glow of the full moon with music playing and the wind chimes ringing, imagining I'm somewhere in paradise, dressed to the nines, wearing the big cowboy hat that Mike gave me to shelter me from the sun. I haven't worn it yet - in fact I'd forgotten it. It's the bit of heaven that I want to grasp to reward me for coming this far and finding how beautiful it all is without mind noises and routines.

I'm still holding all those promises to make this voyage special in my life, honouring Mike and Leo and Gerhardt for helping me to grow my dreams and particularly Leo who gave me that big tub of peanut butter that he had especially bought for his rats.

More flying fish take off, disturbed by my passing and I begin to count them and make guesses where they will land. The ones that interest me are the double flyers as they seem to have something extra that needs rewarding and I send them a "hooray" when they perform. They're the flying fish that take off and fly with the rest but as they hit the water they refuse to disappear, taking another flight seemingly propelled by vigorous tail waggles that gives them lots more airborne time. Some do a third flight, but all flights get shorter as they eventually succumb to gravity.

I wonder if flying fish were the first birds as their fossils have been found in many parts of the world, even as far inland as China.

Unlike birds they don't flap their wings, they just glide through the air propelling themselves by a splendid tail wobble. Apparently there are about 60 varieties of flying fish around the world.

They all look the same to me and they all seem magical out here as they're joyfully taking their flights of fantasy, much like whales breeching. Just then a pod of whales appears alongside, starboard ho, 200 metres off, and I welcome them with loud whoops and lots of hand signals. They play around with each other spouting as the smell of "fish breath" blows my way more as a welcome, and I enjoy their fishiness, their closeness, their immensity as they travel lazily along matching my 4 knots. There are two big whales, two smaller ones and a tiny one that seems to be riding high occasionally, probably being lifted by the other whales. Maybe it's their form of piggy backing that I've never seen before, but it makes sense to help out the young as they migrate those huge distances.

At 1800 hours I heave-to for a sleep under the same steady breeze and a flat sea with the few white caps around. I sleep longer than usual and emerge ready to make a meal, do a few odd jobs below and get ready for another long night under a bright moon. Then I notice that the mainsail has been chafing around the lower batten pocket whilst hove-to, and the batten is half out of its pocket. I drop the rig knowing I'm in for a few hours of getting the sail off onto the deck and bringing up the sewing machine to reseam the batten pocket and all the bits and bobs that that entails.

This reminds me of the wisdom of the powerboat broker back in Annapolis who said, "motor all the way, it's a lot easier!"

It's another reminder that I am fairly self-sufficient in making and repairing sails, setting up rigging, doing mechanical repairs and keeping all the parts of a sailboat meshing happily.

The only thing I find difficult is electronic repairs. Ordinary electrical circuits are easy, even enjoyable as you can get into the mind of the people who first laid them down, but those electronic guys, they're another breed. They run on intuition much more than logic, they have a feel for interfaced equipment that I just don't understand and they speak another language.

By dark I have the mainsail repairs done and dusted, and I put away all the gear methodically and carefully, almost as I'm in a trance, going deliberately slow which is not my nature, going to the rhythm of the ocean as it all comes together, without any haste, and we are soon ready for another long sail. I put on my warm gear for the night, make myself a cup of tea and some more peanut butter crackers and hoist the jib this time before the mainsail, letting it languish on a loose sheet while I hoist the main. The repairs were a little more extensive than just one batten pocket, as I had to re-sew a few more seams that were chafing on the leech. The full main goes up and I head back to the helm and steer off to the east while I arrange the preventer and sheet the jib in halfway.

The breeze is slightly softer at 10 knots this time, and we're making about 3.5 knots into a soft horizon with the moon high in the sky, shining down across the water like a huge solar searchlight. I settle in the cockpit with my wet weather coat hooded up to keep my neck warm and a cushion jammed in the starboard corner for my worn butt. I feel tonight is going to be fun. I'm so pleased that my sights have put me across the halfway mark and into the final leg of this long road to self-discovery. I wonder if I'd feel any different if I still had a few more days to go to mark that halfway point and I seem to feel it wouldn't. Time and distance have lost their impetus, lost their yoke and I'm enjoying being free of their reins.

In this expansive space, freedom rides the big white stallion and I've almost lost concerns with the weather, with ships, even with the rig as I drift along slowly to nowhere and everywhere. Nirvana, that I've pursued for years within adventuring and oceaning, is nowhere else but right here and that's difficult to hold, when I remember all the conveniences of shore life with phones and food and entertainment. There's a Zen-like quality to "deep life", to being out in the universe somewhere all alone and I'm lifted up, immensely present and wildly alive and it's hard to imagine that one could eventually find contentment out here on the edges of beyond. Perhaps it's true that the health of our mind comes from its ability to extract nourishment from the environment.

The reality that my expectations are now for a 40 day arrival in Horta, after initially predicting about 25 days, has changed the whole equation for this crossing. This boat is not fast, and the helming requires constant attention, but the motion is gentle and her pace sedentary, reminding me of an older style, well-dressed lady from the 1950s. But we're in this together, fate has handed me Mr Hunter's 1984 design baby and I'm the test pilot taking her for her long ocean run. I'm pleased I didn't read any ocean reviews on her performance as I'm sure I'd be disappointed, so I feel that my own review of her capabilities is positive and nothing is perfect in life. All things, including boats are compromises. It reminds me of the old saying," only the guy who isn't rowing has the time to rock the boat" and I've been rowing here for quite a while.

We sail deep into the night and I don't see any ships or planes. I seem to have left all those distractions behind and am out here all alone, but I know when I see the next ship I'm bound to feel vulnerable again and start sleeping with my masthead light on.

One ship shall break the ice and then I'll feel there are many coming my way. Funnily enough I've deliberately been avoiding looking around the horizon for ships, just in case my reverie is broken and another sombre reality comes knocking for recognition, changing my whole environment.

The moon is so bright, the seas so soft and the chimes play beautiful melodies that are totally irregular, yet enjoyable. Each wave passing through sounds out its own unique tune and now I listen to the passing waves rather than feel them. Old ships had bells but I've found a new use for Chinese wind chimes and I have no doubt that they also took them on their long sea voyages. I look at the clock below in the moonlight and see we are a little past 2300 hours and then, once again out of the blue, Sam sits down beside me with that lovely vanilla smell and a whole new chapter of life begins.

I say "Sam where have you been, it feels like weeks since you were last here?"

He replies "I've been out there keeping the world sane."

"How the hell do you keep the world sane?" I say and he slowly answers "as the consciousness sink of humanity, those of us beyond physicality are acting positively like the keel on a boat, keeping the proverbial Noah's ark afloat."

"You mean after dying you still feel a responsibility to humanity?" I ask, and Sam says, "all of us are part of humanity and we 'over souls' outnumber those in physical bodies at this present moment by factors beyond ten, so we have a huge influence on the consciousness of the human spirit."

I say," Sam, does that mean we are just expressions of each other meeting at the crossroads of a shared reality?" and Sam says, "we are expressions of each other, otherwise we could not recognise each other as we look within our own realities."

And then, just as quickly as he arrived he's gone and I am left wondering whether I'm losing my grip on reality.

Sam's visitation has left me energised and slightly cosmic as I hold all the journeys of the night into something more real than a dream.

I imagine I'm in some strange space like a Japanese tea ceremony where the Zen of sailing alone, the wind, the water and the heavens are synchronising into some mystical ceremony that is allowing me access to other parts of my mind. I feel perfectly lucid and sensible and yet I also feel empowered with having peeped through the walls of illusion and have been assured there's only myself in charge.

I feel like the Australian Aborigine following his song lines through the desert connecting to his ancestors who slowly open the door to the never-never. That never-never was the cathedral of my mind connecting to the infinity of the universe and the lost Shangri-La of humanity and the bright sunny day before me.

It'll take time to put it all into perspective and rather than burying it under the carpet, there's time to enhance my long deep belief that every experience is there for some damn good reason.

Chapter 20

Message in a bottle

I put away my notes and cup and let the jib fly and we track back on course, heading south east to a 9 knot south west breeze. The day promises lots of miles with a few more whitecaps and hopefully some flying fish and maybe dolphins. I sail along till near noon and heave-to again to go below to collect an empty vinegar bottle with a plastic cap that I have been saving. I write a note, make a drink and log myself on the chart with the extra miles I have made since the last sight. In the bottle I tightly fold an A4 piece of paper with my name and address in Tasmania, my position and the message:

> single handed sailor crossing the Atlantic 26th June 2007 in Hunter 34.
>
> 23 days into the trip heading for Horta, Azores.
>
> sailing free, sailing on. contact me when you find this message with the position where you found it and your details.... small reward offered.
>
> keatingontheroad@hotmail.com

I roll the paper into a cylinder, covering it in green plastic, tape it tight and slowly insert it into the bottle and then silicone the lid on. I didn't realise the effort required to put a message into a bottle and then aim to preserve it for years, as it floats across the ocean. I ponder on the number of bottles out here on the ocean just waiting for people to find them.

I decide to have a bath on the aft deck and boil up a kettle of salt water, while also cooking up some rice with a couple of eggs in their shells and some dried Chinese sausages along with a tin of peas with a hole punched in the top. I then set it on the spare metho burner where it'll take a good 25 minutes to cook.

I enjoy the efficiency of Chinese cooking where everything is cooked in one pot which is a food simplicity and a wisdom that other cuisines don't have. I take the hot kettle of water up to add to a half bucket of cold sea water, shampoo my body and hair and rinse off with the rest of the warm water. I dry off in the sun and lunch is ready, so I sit in the cockpit eating and enjoying feeling fresh, fed and content with my independence and freedom.

I'm having more troubles with the damn CD player again as it often fades out in volume and becomes impossible to hear, so I dismantle the speaker and try to find any problem with the wiring. It seems ok, so I reconnect and play another CD but it also begins the fading trick, so I search the wires to the speaker and find some green verdigris about a third of the way along the wire and realise it's been damaged somehow. Salt water is getting into the core again. I cut the wire, remove the damaged piece and reconnect, and it plays without fade. I guess the damaged wire has changing resistance and all I need to do now is to keep a watch on the join. I start the player on medium/loud and go upstairs to let the jib fly and track back to the south east with many more miles to go.

I'm enjoying taking the choice to stop when I feel like it and not feel guilty anymore. Music plays below with Willie Nelson crooning away and the breeze blowing softly through my streaming hair as we rollick along at 4 knots, heading into the afternoon and hopefully another bright night.

I remind myself that what emerges from Sam's visit is an understanding that as I sharpen my perceptions to all that is around me the greater my enjoyment becomes. Once again it reflects the power invested in the generosity of being where every bit of appreciation one can apply to the taste of food, or the beauty of music, or the sense of joie de vivre for a beautiful day, returns fourfold. As soon as I invest in my appreciation then I enhance my wellbeing.

It seems far too simple that a life rich in awareness is also rich in meaning. Out here that is gold, as once again I can take charge of all my feelings, all my thoughts and remove the things beyond my control, like scary ships or sharp weather changes or broken rigging. By actively reducing the negatives and enhancing the positives it puts me back in charge of my journey and turns this simple voyage into a very valuable exercise. I am learning more about myself and I guess that's what I came out here to learn, the real survival mentality for living well.

The day closes in and I welcome the soothing night train as it rolls along its rails, swish, thump, swish, plop, uphill and down another valley, swaying lightly in the breeze. The night is cold and soon I'll lose count of the hours till midnight, with a short sleep and then another long session till dawn. Nights are for nostalgia and those long forgotten memories and I muse on the Hindu saying that illuminates those old hazy memories "it's difficult to hold in your hand the bird that has flown," while tomorrow is another day of promise and joy and bounce and hopefully more wind, as this night train merges into my boat again.

The sun seemingly draws me on as it rises and pushes me away as it sinks, and I smile at the simplicity of it all while the struggle going east has been turned into a real gift. The Azores are just over my perceptual horizon as Sam showed me, the moon is very bright while only another 2 nights will bring a full moon, and I'm reminded that this June month has 2 full moons, which is quite rare. The last full moon was at the beginning of the hurricane blow which was unusual for sailing, because full moons usually offer settled weather, and this next one hopefully will bring a bright clear sparkling night, a gentle breeze to blow us east and no nasty swells, where I'll be able to steer comfortably all night while enjoying the whole performance. My restless mind wonders when Sam will return because he is certainly entertaining, and I wonder if I'll ever get an answer to my message in the bottle. I have a thousand other questions that linger at the back of my mind, queuing for recognition.

The CD is playing below and the haunting sounds of civilization float up the stairs, drifting into the sails, rolling out across the Atlantic towards the horizon. I'm in heaven, even though there's an ache in my butt from sitting here as still as a mouse but unwilling to break the spell all around. I suddenly see white lights coming from behind and then I see the green starboard lights of a freighter as he overtakes me, moving well off down my port side, charging eastwards. I sail dark knowing he is unaware of me and is probably going to Europe or the Azores. In either case it means I am probably south of both shipping lanes now, which explains why I have seen few ships in the last week and that gives me a mental boost.

My desire is to keep heading south east before making that last-minute surge northwards onto the latitude of Horta. It means I can at least sleep well, knowing only the occasional maverick fishing vessel may be on my track, while the vast majority are well over my horizon. At 2300hrs I stop, drop the headsail, back the main and lock the helm. We sit still on course fore-reaching slowly as I go below with the intention of sleeping soundly, till only my body clock wakes me. When I awake two hours later, I go on deck, take a leisurely look around, have a pee over the side, make a cup of tea, pull out a muesli bar and sit quietly going over my notes on Sam's visit. It's quite remarkable how well I remember Sam's visit, the sojourns we took and the words that resonate with me. It's like a 3D movie that I aim to capture in as much detail as possible, particularly his words about cosmology and experiences, reality and humanity and then reduce it all down to an understanding that enhances this voyage.

I realise that some of Sam's words could not have come from within me. There are concepts and thoughts there that are puzzling to me and many I've never heard before. The witness in me wants to bury Sam while the magician in me wants to polish his lantern. Rather than split the images I've turned the critic and the cynic off and have gone with the feelings of wonder and awe and the mysterious.

The interesting question is whether I'm able to tell others about Sam's visit when this is all over, with a straight face, or have them question whether I'm losing the plot. Only time will tell.

At 0100 hrs I hoist the jib, release the helm and get back to sailing again. The breeze has eased to 8 knots and we roll along under a bright moon and clear sky at 3.5 knots, heading south east into warmer waters and fewer ships. I've not seen an aircraft for days so I must be well below their Atlantic route from New York to London, and as I head north I'm sure I'll catch up to plenty of ships and aircraft again.

As dawn approaches after another 20 miles at the helm I'm ready for some breakfast, but first I need to re-rig some steering lines and sit in the stern enjoying the magic of a new day, focusing on the sun rising ahead, enjoying the gentle pull of the sails and feeling the sweetness of life in all my sense.

I'm gradually replacing the need for honey or sugar or my favourite raspberry jam. I am practising just being content without the need to fill myself up on food or thoughts about Horta, or even practise meditation as I feel complete in what I have. I try to read the wisdom of the old sailors giving clouds special meanings, along with the low swell and the sun glinting off the higher clouds in bright orange. The old sailor's adage 'red sky at night is a sailor's delight, red sky in the morning is a sailor's warning" is interesting, but I'm not sure as a novice how close red is to orange in the scheme of things. I try the solar gazing for another few minutes and I take the lines below and put a Willie Nelson CD on. I then heat up the kettle to the sounds of *"Georgia on my mind"*, sit in the cockpit holding the helm and listen to *"Someone watching over me"* and one of my favourites *"Blue eyes crying in the rain."*

Dolphins appear, come rushing up to us, swimming alongside, dancing and choofing as *"Faraway places"* wraps itself around the rigging and suddenly we're all sailing along together with my crowd of admirers all dancing to a newer rhythm.

They cavort and glide, listening to another repeat of Willie and finally as Willie hits *"Help me make it through the night"* which brings tears to my eyes, they slide away as one, heading south east leaving little specks of foam for me to follow. I'm getting emotional again as feelings heavily outweigh my thoughts now. I'm learning big time to not chase happiness, but to embrace joy, the joy of the dolphins, the joy of Willie, the joy of just being. Willie resonates with me out here in a voice not unlike Sam's, and I wonder how much of Willie is in Sam. Willie's words have a cathartic effect on my psyche and I realise that solo singers with guitars and beautiful songs all affect me in the same way.

They're part of my ideal, showing how I'd like to develop in the future and where I've been in the past. They're like déjà vu in that you recognise the personal impact in some way, but as soon as you interrogate the memory it fades away and leaves you floundering in its wake, knowing something resonated to you, but it didn't leave any residue.

Another pod of dolphins suddenly swings alongside and life is again getting crowded. I rush below, put on Bob Dylan, turn up the volume and scoot back to the helm to see the dolphins' reactions. I feel like a lion tamer dishing out treats to see if I get any response, giving me added status in this no man's land. Bob begins loudly *"Knocking on heaven's door"* and I'm sure there's a newer dolphin reaction as they come back from the bow and frolic alongside, where I can enjoy them more. Then Bob gets *"Blowing in the wind"* and they like that too, with one dolphin getting very close to the hull and lying there listening as if in a trance.

Maybe I'm attaching human behaviour to them because I need the company, but when *"Hard rain gonna fall"* hits the sea waves my tranced dolphin suddenly shoots out 50 metres and goes gliding off, on up to the bow. Maybe he couldn't take it anymore as the music was too loud or else he's become bored.

All of Bob's songs seem to apply to the ocean. I suspect he's a closet sailor and I enjoy being the choirmaster as I perform for the concert of dolphins, rolling along, rocking away, tapping my feet, flowing sad to the lyrics…this is living…this is the generosity of being, of appreciating all the joys that civilisation brings me out here. Particularly those amazing advances we have experienced in music in the last 30 years as we've moved from records to tapes to CDs. What's next I muse and it's hard to see where the creative technology will lead, but you can be sure someone in the future will be out here sailing and playing music to the dolphins in a very different way.

The dolphins leave and head south while an occasional bird wheels around in the distance, hunting the ocean for food as the day flows into noon with the breeze holding steady at 8 knots while the rig draws us to the south east on solar energy alone. There's next to no swell fortunately, otherwise the wind would get regularly knocked out of the sails and they'd slat and bang in protest, causing angst all around my deck. We hardly heel at all and I'm quite in awe of the designer of this Hunter as the designer has done well in producing an easily driven hull without a lot of weather helm, that's also very responsive to the helm. The swept back spreaders are novel as they simplify the rigging, reducing the need for an aft lower stay, allowing the mainsail to swing further out for those runs downwind. The stern lip not only encourages access from the stern but also extends the waterline length, smoothing the wake and reducing drag.

Yacht design reflects history and fashion like any other designs and yachts are now getting fatter and lighter and sit on the water rather than in it. They're built on the newer duck design rather than the traditional fish shape and I'm confident that the new move into catamarans will change the history of yachting forever. When Captain Cook sailed into Hawaii in the 1770's in his slow old square-rigged ship "Endeavour", it displayed the peak expression of European sturdy boat designers.

But amazingly he found the islanders were skimming across the waters in proas at 20 knots, with up to 100 oarsmen and families, often travelling very long distances between islands. Their designs sat on the water rather than in it and this whole new technology stunned the European's traditional mindset. Finally, after 300 years our yacht racing designs are catching up, with the America's Cup catamarans now skimming across the water rather than sailing in it. Even the military are now using skimming craft rather than displacement designs. The only drama with a catamaran as an ocean crosser though is the jerkiness of motion, particularly when going to windward. A mono hull wallows up wind gently, while a cat belts up into the waves accelerating and decelerating, pounding and crashing along going much faster, but shaking the daylights out of the crew. It's the newer drama of speed over comfort.

I'm pleased that I chose a mono for this trip particularly when it became super rough. I expand the comparison and wonder what amazing new designs for living will emerge when humanity meets some cosmic tribe in the future and swaps various technologies for crossing oceans. The fusion of new designs and the discarding of old beliefs will create a revolution in both humanity and the aliens that will resonate in each other for hundreds of years. Firstly, though we will have to drop our fear of invasion, our fear of the stranger and be prepared to welcome change on a grand scale. Perhaps the dolphin who was mesmerised this morning to the beat of Bob Dylan was on the same path, discovering a whole new world about us.

Noon comes and goes to its own rhythm and we creep slowly towards another horizon with the music still playing and the surface of the ocean twinkling lazily under a hot sun. I'm mindful and awake to the ocean and I'm present to the beauty of the ocean bouncing all around, carolling to the gentle breeze, rolling with the swells, fluttering in the bright sunlight. It's almost tropical but the wind is still light and I'm forced to head more to the south and further away from Horta to keep us rolling gently along.

There is only one cloud in the sky dead to windward and as it comes over it drops a fine rain shower for 10 minutes that hardly wets the deck but is a welcome relief under this hot sun. The rain is so soft and gentle that I refuse to try catching some as the cloud drifts off alone to the north east, like a travelling salesman selling expensive and rare presents. I wish I had studied clouds somewhere in my journeys, developing a language that explained them to me, rather than just high or low, dark or light in much the same way that I'd studied the psychology of peoples.

In my travels I've found that past cloud artists like John Constable from England even had a cloud exhibition in 1822, reflecting the interest of the public in clouds and wind, particularly when sailing ships were at their peak. The sky is definitely the source of light in nature and the clouds do provide an ambience to all things.

Trent Dalton, an Australian writer, once said "Nobody ever whispered a trivial word to the sky. The sky gets all the big important words from us. Help me. Thank you. Why me? I love you. So, sky talk is serious business, beautiful business…there's more than clouds or sky up there. Our pasts are up there, our successes, our failures, our futures."

Clouds are a backdrop to life and there are even cloud whisperers, like tea lovers, who speak in whispers and tell you your fortune by trying to read the messages overhead.

There are cloud physicians who take particular interest in cloud formation, growth and precipitation in the atmosphere and there are even cloud seeders who head out regularly to impregnate sexy clouds so that they can create more juicy rain for the farmers. And I've even met cloud romantics who lie on their backs in grassy fields, delicately chewing dandelions and muttering soft words to their lovers, as they get naked and mate to the rhythm of a passing stratocumulus, or at least I think I did! Now that was a wild thought!

In London where I lived in Surrey Quays on *Sundancer* in 1994, I endured the sad drawn out cloud banks that regularly covered the city for days on end, bringing introspection and often mental myopic shrinkage within their tiny world, covered in greyness and sad old trees.

In Australia the sky is big and the clouds are high, while out on the ocean there is a dimension that is in between. There are lots more clouds over the ocean than the land and I'm sure our nature focused ancestors imagined that they probably saw their wind gods in the sky riding fairy wagons as they trotted by, tossing blessings from their saddles!. Now big business is awakening to cloud potential as computing moves into new arenas like big data and artificial intelligence and a new cloud language is forming that will transcend the old one, taking the language we know from cloud Utopia, and morphing it into technology that seems both familiar and revolutionary.

I particularly love the native American's story about cloud and coyote expressing the characters they see in both. Cloud and coyote ran a race according to their legends. Cloud bet on a storm and coyote on good weather. They started off in the south and for a while coyote was in the lead. Then cloud made fruits of all kinds and coyote stopped to eat, cloud skipped by and won. According to the Indian lore this is why we have more storms in spring.

The Shawnee Indians on the other hand have as their matriarchal figure "cloud women," and young maidens pray to the clouds for the delivery of a young buck who may come in the form of a cloud and wrap around them like a tepee, no doubt with plenty of fire in his hearth.

As a sailor I should be more aware of clouds and the messages they send, but today there are few messages, no young bucks in the sky and no menace from "storm cloud". Perhaps the next time I have a few clouds ringing me I should set up a conversation with the clouds like; "Mr Cumulus I see your cirrus strips are a little ragged today but hopefully by this evening you'll be able to reach for the stratus violin and play me a light rain melody!"

I guess this whimsical scenario shows my need for conversations as random thoughts run wildly through my head, forming, mingling and dancing like storms in my own cloud mind and maybe this lack of cloud cover is having some influence on me here just hanging out below!

At 1400hrs the breeze begins to increase to 10 knots and we surge up to 4.5 knots again, heading more eastwards as I increase the pressure on the preventer and flatten in the jib. We broad reach along on starboard dig with the wake becoming more serious and the course more wandering, as I settle in for another long challenging haul if the wind increases. I decide to hang out the wind chimes again when I get the helm steadied down, and I stand beside the helm wedging my knees into the wheel and reaching into the deck box to retrieve them. Rather than hanging them from the stern arch with the need to steer by lines as I do it, I helm with my foot as I reach up and hang the chimes from the dodger. It's a little close and also a little louder, but I intend to enjoy the music as I surge away swapping it for the CD greats.

The more natural tinkles of the chimes give me a completely different perspective to the afternoon as gradually I realise the volume of the chimes becomes related to the strength of the wind. I've now got a virtuous music circle going that I'm enjoying immensely.

We sail on into the evening as the sun sinks in the west and another school of dolphins comes by, parking themselves up on the bow.

We seem to be going their way as they came from astern and it looked like they were going to go right by, till one lead dolphin came racing back to say hello and then the others, who were well out in front, swung back also.

I can't go up and say hello, but I do rush down and put on some loud Inca music as I've done before, to entice them to stay longer.

They oblige by leaping around the bow, coming by the stern and parking alongside in the moonlight, rolling and twisting, snorting and tail wagging and, as I tap on the side of the hull they all gather alongside for a conference that increases my taps, starting with one tap and then working up to 9 and going back to the beginning. Perhaps it's the first maths lesson they've ever had as they hang around for longer, obviously interested in this Hunter dolphin, cruising east with Inca music and Asian wind chimes and someone tapping out number sequences. Maybe I've made their day, just as they've made mine.

The wind increases slowly to 12 knots and we surge along nearing 5 knots at times, which excites the dolphins as we begin throwing spray wildly out to the sides, glittering in the moonlight with bright stars standing out in the sky big, bold and bright, turning the cosmos into a near Da Vinci scene.

There is a deep magic to be found sailing at night with my appreciative dolphin audience, my music, a solid breeze and a bright sky so close that I feel that I can touch it. This is a perfect example of the sublime practise of appreciation that turns this whole experience into transformational living. I cannot imagine a more complete scenario to fill my heart with an appreciation of pure living, making the soul sing for the joy of being human.

We sail on for hours and the dolphins eventually depart and I happily let them go wishing them sweet journeys and wild freedoms, hoping they will send others to say hello, somewhere down the track. At 2300hrs I decide I do need to sleep. this is my crucial time. If I can sail past it then I can go on for hours, but tonight I decide I'll take a break and rest up for a few hours. What's more, the strengthening wind has taken a lot out of me and I can't heave-to in this breeze, I'll have to drop the whole rig otherwise serious chafe will cause me trouble.

I drop the main and tie it loosely to the boom and belay the halyard. I drop the jib and do the same and *Millefleurs* becomes a tepee again in the ocean, as I drift dark to the north-east at a knot. I go below, leaving most of my gear on and fall asleep almost immediately. I awake at 0300 hrs and am surprised at how long I have slept. I go up on deck and check for ships, but there's just a clear horizon with the wind now at 10 knots and a low swell from the south.

I boil the kettle, make some muesli for an early breakfast and putting on a beanie, head for the cockpit. The stars are bright along with the moon and Orion stands out with his big star sword ready to attack Taurus the bull and if that seems futile, then he's ready to head over to see the 7 little sisters in the Pleiades. I sit silently taking in the vast cosmic scene realising how small earth is in comparison and wondering how humans could have made the earth the centre of the universe when we're really not very important.

I go forward and hoist the mainsail with a small reef in it and then the number 3 jib that is lying ready on the deck and we're off again to the east, rolling along at 4 knots with a bright wake out the stern and the familiar rhythmic lurches as we crest each wave. I'm ready to sail through till well after dawn following that huge 4 hour sleep without dreams that I've just had. I'm ready to close the gap to the Azores, ready to face the beauty of a whole new day. There's a full moon tomorrow and we're now 25 days out and 3 days past the halfway mark. This is getting better.

Today I'm going to take a sight at noon and have a swim in the ocean as each bucket full of sea water seems warmer than the last. We're getting well south into warmer waters now, below the easterly shipping lane and I'm curious how many miles north I need to go to get to Horta. It's a nice dilemma as I intend to stay down here for as long as possible.

If I miss Horta then there are other islands in the Azores chain where I can clear in. Dawn comes with another gorgeous day in the semi-tropics and I meditate through the dawn hours and into a whole new day with few clouds, a 9 knot south westerly breeze and bright sunlight. There are few birds around which surprises me, but there's a lot of flotsam that I've given up chasing.

The game is too big and after eye-balling hundreds of possible treasures that turn out to be measly fishing floats, or plastic bottles or pieces of wood, I realise I'm not likely to find a full bottle of whisky or a barrel of rum or even a watermelon or coconut to sample. I sail till 1100 hrs and then I drop the rig and drift, ready to take a swim before the sight near noon. I walk the deck, take off my t-shirt and shorts and leap in to clear my head and frolic in the joys of this vast ocean. I float free on my back looking at the rigging and then see the side of the boat with dirty marks all the way along the hull indicating that I've somehow sailed through the oil slick of an oil tanker emptying his tanks at sea. I also realise I'd never be able to climb up the sides of *Millefleurs* if I fell in, they're just too high, so the lip is definitely a lifesaving measure. I roll over and dive under the hull coming up the other side of the boat seeing the same dirty oil slick on this side as well. The oil tanker bastard has no idea that washing his tanks out at sea causes so much damage to fish, shorelines and beautifully painted boats like mine.

It takes a long time for humans to consider the damage they do to the earth while they are unconsciously sleepwalking through life. I climb up the stern and shampoo my hair and body and leap in again with the water a lot warmer than before or else I've just adjusted to it.

I rub my hair vigorously and duck dive wildly like a seabird washing itself, coming up for air when I feel exhausted. I feel replenished and free and I swim around *Millefleurs* again at a fast clip, to get my heart rate up. The old tired me, the sleepy sea dog finally comes alive, ready to find his position in the Atlantic and then celebrate with a fine cooked lunch and maybe even a coffee that I've not indulged in for weeks.

I climb up the stern after inspecting the Jesus rope connections and all seems well. I feel like I've swum 1,000 miles to get here and I sit in the sun focusing on my breathing, absorbing the fun of a whole new day and realising that the secret to all of life is not where you're headed but where you are. I've let go of the couch and the TV, the safe job and the superannuation, the castle lifestyle and most everything else, and I've ridden my horse out here so I can just roll in the sand, light a campfire and live free. Buddha in the wind-chimes tinkles his agreement and the passing swell quietly goes on its way to a meeting somewhere unknown, north of me.

I go below to collect the sextant and notepad and prepare to take a sight to get my noon latitude and my longitude by time. I take the first sight at 1145 hrs and begin taking more sights every few minutes, rocking the sun to get the horizon at the bottom of the curve and increasing the shades to counteract the sun's brightness. By 1230 hrs I've finished and I sit to calculate my position with the aid of the nautical almanac. This is fun, it's the best bit of magic I know that the old sailing captains passed down to us, and is an art form that is slowly being lost, replaced by the surety of the GPS.

I calculate our position as 35 deg 20 min north and 41 deg 12 min west. That puts us at 750 miles out of Horta which means we are about 10 days out with this increased breeze, and well south by about 190 miles. That's just fantastic and indicates that we are in some sort of east sweeping current down this far south and I'm happy to take every mile I can get.

I go below and put away my sextant and tables and log our position on the chart in a joyous mood. I put on the kettle and cook up some rice and add a tin of mushrooms and a tin of fish and let them slowly simmer away. I try my first weak coffee while poring over the chart. The coffee is certainly delightful with some added sugar, but I feel it giving me a high after all these days of gentler food and I don't even finish drinking it, tossing out the remainder.

I take a drink of water to balance the effect, promising myself not to hit the familiar coffee trail when I get into Horta. I smell rice cooking and soon I'm into rice, fish and mushrooms with hoisin sauce and I'm in food heaven. The tastes are superb and all I need is a bottle of red wine, a delicate Greek pastry and I'd be King of the world.

At 1400hrs I decide to add to my pleasure by getting ready to go sailing for the whole day, as if it is the first time in days. It's all heady stuff, but I deliberately focus on each step by drawing it out into a meditation on life. I clear the decks, wipe down the cockpit, reorganise the cushions and go below to wash the dishes, pack away all the cooking gear, make up my bunk, fluff the pillows, put on a mixed CD and potter around to the wonderful 7 minutes song of *Hallelujah* by Jeff Buckley. His song captures the magic of making life into an art form. I make a cup of tea with the leftover hot water and get back into the cockpit for another sailing session. I intend to stay well south of Horta till I'm about 3-4 days out, and then angle north east.

That decision seems to be rewarded with the arrival of a white-tailed boson bird, who flutters around *Millefleurs* looking for a place to land, but I project my authority by telling him in colourful language to find somewhere else to roost. The bosun birds are tropical and I'm sure they're related to the big white Australian cockatoo as they flutter around in the same manner. Both appear to be poor flyers with jerky wing actions, but both cover vast distances, exploring the environment for food, content in themselves, often being alone for long periods of time.

I begin hoisting the mainsail, shaking out the old reefing lines, checking the battens and slides for wear, applying medium halyard tension to give the main some belly for lighter airs, while also easing the foot tension by winding back the outhaul. The mainsail has lots of life in it yet and will get me well beyond the Pacific crossing and well into cruising those familiar Australian coastal waters.

I untie the jib, attach the halyard and hoist it by hand, topping it up with the winch for the last few feet. It flaps free in the breeze and the loose sheet gives me a playful slap on the thigh, letting me know we need to reach off, beam to the breeze to build momentum and as speed builds we begin to broad reach to the east. The breeze is somewhere around 10 knots from the usual south westerly quarter and we roll along at 4.5 knots, sailing along in a light swell with the boson bird out to the north-east keeping us as his marker, as he hunts the surface for food. He occasionally dives down into the water and then flutters up again. He keeps me entertained as he swings around us in huge circles and unlike other predatory birds he doesn't hunt in our wake looking for food that we might bring to the surface.

Some flying fish take off to the north-east quite near to where he is flying but he doesn't seem interested either, which means he doesn't hunt for them. He's an intriguing seabird. In the south Pacific his close cousin is called the red-tailed boson bird. In the old sailing ship days the boson bird was a talisman for good weather and steady winds and killing one to get his gorgeous plumage was considered a very bad omen.

There's a real magic in this sailing, in efficiently harnessing that invisible wind, capturing the free energy by squeezing it into pockets in the sails and exchanging the sun's energy to drive the boat.

It's green energy at its best and, unlike the old square sails, the newer Bermudan triangular sails capture the most wind when they push upwind, allowing modern yachts to sail in all latitudes, rather than the old downwind sailing ship. Nowadays the spinnaker is the old square sail for driving downwind and unfortunately, I don't have one, so I can't run square off the breeze.

One of the improvements in sailing though has been the replacement of hemp and flax fibre with dacron that makes the sails so much lighter and stronger while also vulnerable to sunlight. If left out in the sun for a year the modern dacron sail would perish so the sign of a good sailor is he always covers his sails well when passaging is done.

Hemp fibre has been the staple in many countries for centuries but now it has a bad name as the modern hemp contains lots of THC that gets the hippies rocking. Henry Ford even tried to build car bodies out of hemp fibre in the 1920s. But in 1934 hemp was banned in the USA when Dupont Chemicals muscled in on the fibre market and backed cotton, because it needed more chemicals to be grown, being subject to many more predators as compared to the old hemp plant that could be grown almost anywhere. Dupont saw an opportunity to supply chemicals to the farmers and lobbied hemp out of the market and it's been that way ever since.

The only exception was during the World War 11 years when hemp was allowed to be grown again for the fibre needed for military clothing, and then it was again banned in the USA when the war was over.

I'm "job jar free" today and there's no alarmist in my mind telling me to sail more efficiently, tack to the north or head straight for Horta. I'm living by my own timetable, sailing when I like, and diving and swimming as I please. They say there is only one path in life, yours, but modern tick tock living often makes it difficult to celebrate that path when you are working 9-5 with 3 children and a mortgage along with birthday parties and shopping.

Here there are no timetables, no deadlines and the concept of forever is a little closer when modern life and limited language have put it out at the ends of the universe. I like Woody Allen's description of time, "Forever is a very long time, particularly the bit at the end!" and I smile at the way words, when put together in unique patterns, bring out the wisdoms of it all.

I tell myself a joke out loud, pretending that I don't know the punchline and laugh long and hard at it, as I focus on helming to the east. I try a longer joke that I remembered from years ago and laugh out loud again letting go of any inner tensions and bringing a big smile to my day, trying to avoid the drama of helming.

Humour fascinates me, along with all the subsequent laughter, as they're both connected to our smiling behaviours. It is said that a well-developed sense of humour is the pole that holds the balance to your steps, as you walk the tight rope of life. I like that image, especially out here, putting up with what most people would call bullshit. I do know though that the best crews I've had were those who had a great sense of humour, and when one long haul sails the discomforts can be awful, while a good sense of humour is certainly needed to provide a welcome relief from it all.

You need to humour yourself particularly when you're doing night watch and a flying fish slams into you or when you're up changing sails in your driest gear and a wave completely drenches you. I also know from experience that the ability to take a joke, not make one, is the real proof that you have a sense of humour and mine's been challenged many times. But as long as I can vent with lots of screams and other dreadfuls, I'm soon back to normal.

In Australia we tend to exaggerate or satirise in our humour and the best humourists are those who can make fun of themselves, rather than others. Squeezing out those weird idiosyncrasies we all have and exposing them to wild ridicule amuses us immensely. It is said that terrorists have no sense of humour and I truly believe that. If you could only laugh at the stupidity of blowing yourself up you'd try something else. They're really picking up red hot stones to throw at someone they dislike, and the real humour in that stupidity is it's burning their own fingers to the bone in the process.

That reminds me of the Irish joke which is all about making fun of yourself as the Irish are prone to do.

Mary says to her husband Paddy, "if you were stranded on a desert island who would you most like to be with you?" "My uncle Mick," replies Paddy. "What's so special about him?" asks Mary. "He's got a boat," says Paddy.

Someone once told me that imagination was given to man to compensate him for what he is not, and humour to console him for what he is. So I like Paddy's humour as it is something we can understand and take on board. I'm sure there are many jokes floating around the world, told at the expense of the relevant 'national jester' in their own particular culture.

The breeze has been slowly coming around to the south and now I can reach along under sail, which is the fastest point of sailing with this wind square on the beam. I'm gaining on the Azores and still keeping warm as I roll along at 5 knots with a slow rising swell from the south. I think this is just an afternoon deviation as the wind often follows the sun and by nightfall it'll probably be back in the usual south west corner.

There's colour out here that is engaging, the many sky-blue shades that paint the fresco between the sky and the sea and the white pastels are reflected in the foam of our wake. There's deep soul art as each wave trundles through, leaving memories of itself behind in sparkles and splashes that stay only for a moment, like one's life in the seconds of the universe. I feel like a wallflower waiting for someone to ask for a dance around the deck. And there is meaning in all this motion and change and hustle.

There's something beautiful here that one holds fleetingly and would like to capture just for a few moments for savouring, but it's gone, replaced by a thousand other movements that go on endlessly, a thousand photographs away.

I decide to cook while on the roll and set up lines to the galley where I prepare some tinned chicken pieces rolled in egg and oatmeal and fried in the pan. The exercise is a bit of a brain teaser as I have to watch the telltales without a compass below, while I prepare the food and then cook it over hot oil while still keeping us on track. I feel suitably rewarded with a whole bowl of goodies and I head back to the cockpit, sit beside the helm steering with my foot, and slowly devour the lot. Oh, the beauty of taste with all its subtleties as an amazing variation on all those colours around the horizon and I practise mixing and matching both, trying to taste those blue hues and sunlit sparkles and the creamy foams.

Oh, the beauty of being an artist appreciating all around without changing a bit, drinking it in like fine wine, sharing and enlarging what nature has to offer.

I helm along on instinct alone, my own without thought, just tracking on the feel of it all, keeping us dancing and the boat shuffling and rolling along without any effort, as if one were born to do this one's whole life. I breathe in as the boat rises and breathe out when it falls as the ocean breathes me. There's feeling here, deep feelings that don't have to be understood, just shared.

A good helmsman looks at the compass occasionally while most of the time he steers from fixed points on the horizon or the feel of the rig or the angle of the tell-tales. The position of the boat comes naturally so that even when you are below you can feel how well you're sailing.

On *Sundancer* we even issued certificates to those helmsmen who were afforded the honour of helming while the rest of us ate our meals in peace, with the very best helmsmen being able to helm and eat at the same time.

A natural helmsman was afforded the honoured certificate when he/she could steer a reasonable course with eyes shut for 10 minutes and not get more than 10 degrees off course. Trips with good helmsmen at the wheel were privileges in motion, as it turned wild rides into gentle exercises, mellowing the motion of the wind and waves into a symphony of progress. A very good helmsman is even better downwind, where small changes in course double the effect of the breeze, so we doubled their rum rations to keep them on the helm on rough and wild nights, as that was when they really counted.

I'm sailing along at 5 knots eating my morsels of delight and smiling for the fun of it all. I realise I'm involved in sailing for pleasure, committed to getting to Horta and the subtle balance between commitment and involvement is like the one between ham and eggs. There the chicken is involved but the poor old pig is committed, and that makes all the difference. Here I'm definitely the crazy pig and I'm committed!

The sun begins to sink slowly in the west and the sky begins to colour up with "marmalade butter light" drenching the last few light "cotton wool" clouds with oranges and yellows and golden hues, providing an element of beauty that is surreal. These are moments of secular beauty where the sky is a pastel painter's paradise and as the night takes over the moon begins to rise ahead of us.

It's big, full and bright as tonight is a huge full moon, meaning we've been out 26 days and it's all come to this. A beautiful night where I can sail all night and appreciate having all the vision possible.

I race below and put some classical music on repeat cycle and push the volume way up, racing back to the helm as we've started to round up to being close hauled. It takes some effort to get back to a reach where the sails are settled and the boat feels happy again.

It's such a beautiful night with a steady breeze and a flat sea compelling me to spend more time trying to make *Millefleurs* self-steer. I've tried various techniques before but this time I'm going to use 2 shock cords attached to the top of the wheel and onto cleats either side of the cockpit and then alter the pressure on each so I can get some kickback. That will help self-correct the changing rudder pressures. I've thought about doing this for days and if it works it'll be a real bonus. I set up the cords and begin adjusting the side pressure to duplicate the corrections my hands are making. It works occasionally and sometimes it holds course for up to 20 seconds, but then we go off course and generally round up to the breeze.

I adjust the sails as we reach along easing the mainsail to reduce the weather helm tendency and tightening the jib, and that makes it a little better. Sometimes we sail for 30 seconds without adjusting the helm. What a bonus and I begin to live in a few 30 second bursts, enjoying just being able to relax my vigilance for that brief time, even lying back occasionally and staring at the moon without a care in the world. It's like being released from prison and standing outside the gates, free from all worries and cares or getting a letter from the medical board proclaiming that you're now free from cancer.

This is magic that can't be duplicated, a bonus that only comes after banging your head against that proverbial wall for days and then, thankfully, the wall disappears.

But *Millefleurs* is still inherently unstable and I realise that after 2 hours of adjusting the shock cords and altering the rig balance, it's the best I'm going to get out of her. The whole exercise is repeating what's happened before, causing me further frustration when I cannot improve the situation. The hull shape is the real problem as her wide beam alters the waterline so quickly, even when she heels just a tiny bit, causing her to gather weather helm and round up. I'm sure that would occur even if I took the mainsail off completely, as I've let the main all the way out till it's feathered with the subsequent loss of speed, but the weather helm always kicks in when a swell goes through.

It's disappointing because tonight I was half hoping for a solution to my helming woes as I'm really a slave to this cockpit. My original plan on leaving Norfolk, Virginia, was to spend days lying back in the cockpit with Henry steering and reading the great books I have brought for the voyage. Up to this point I haven't read a line, being continually attentive to the helm, and after 26 days it's getting bloody tiresome, while my hopes for a better helming future have been slammed into the dust bin again. The only gain has been the way I have decorated the helm with lashings all around with the many fancy knots that I've learnt from years of sailing. It's a work of art and instead of reading I spend hours altering, improving and finally producing a knot that I'm sure Picasso himself could hang in the Greenwich Sailing Museum. It proves the point that it's an ill wind that blows no good.

How wonderful, some visitors to improve my mood. A small school of dolphins turn up and begins surging around hopefully, listening to the music as I whistle and bang away on the hull, turning the steering into my own art form, mixed with corrections between taps on the hull and stamps of my feet.

I wind up some Hawaiian hulas to the sounds of Beethoven. They seem to enjoy my first performing private concert as they huddle close alongside the cockpit, with me waving the winch handle like a conductor's baton and tapping my feet wildly in the bright moonlight. They hang around giving me encouragement and when they finally depart, having listened to the same CD and the same conductor's peculiar actions too many times, I feel a little sad and relieved all at the same time. It's been a good work-out and I feel quite hot under my heavy wet weather gear while relieved to have given my very best in the face of all adversity.

They say nothing has meaning except that which you give it and now I have a special performance to give to any passing dolphin, a bit like spreading bread for the seagulls, whereby I maybe can value add to both our passing journeys, with each of us richer for the experience.

Once again, it's that generosity of living where the more value I place on my performance the happier I am. No wonder they say the wise man can walk through a battlefield, amongst all the chaos and destruction and smile all the way at the folly of the crazies.

The wind chimes replace my loud underground music and I sit back in the cockpit imagining what supper I'd like to make for the full moon midnight feast. Everything centres around helming along at 5 knots because tonight I intend to make at least another 50 miles towards Horta, while the intensity of balancing both cooking and helming will enhance the final result.

I imagine one of those trans-Atlantic planes dropping me a simple hamburger with fries in a bag, and me sitting back glorying in the wonders of life. But if I can do it all myself then even better, as I plan the special feast. Wouldn't it be great if a ready-made sandwich could just turn up out of the blue occasionally, just for my simple pleasure? And then I remember one of Leo's stories where the ham sandwich walks into a bar and orders a beer and the barman says, "sorry, we don't serve food here!!"

I pull down my beanie over my ears as it is rather cold and then tighten the wet weather hood around my neck and decide whatever I make has to be hot, sweet and delicious, and every bit as good as any ham sandwich. I balance helming and getting myself a tin of baked beans that I warm in some hot salty water and then mix some spices and some rolled oats and get back into the cockpit with my goodies along with the customary cuppa. I'm going to spend a good hour eating it, no matter the taste, with me turning this plain galley food into a gastronomic delight. Then I notice ship lights ahead and I quickly calculate he's going to pass down my starboard side if I alter course more to the north-east. As I change course I pick up the second steaming light and soon I see his green starboard light as he chugs to the west, and soon with our combined speeds he's past me with a string of lights down his side making him a possible cruise ship, heading for the USA and well off the shipping lanes.

They're the dangerous ones. I imagine he has come out of Gibraltar and is heading for New York. I raise my plate to him and quietly remind him that there is no one on board who is enjoying his passing more than me, as

I mix and match my simple midnight feast. His stern lights soon come into view and I smell motor fumes as he slowly disappears over the horizon, leaving me to my solitude as the only owner of the moon in this quadrant of the ocean. What a privileged life with automation taking over the life of a ship and guiding them from one port to another. Soon there will be unmanned ships, called robo-ships, with just a few engineers on board to attend to mechanical problems, hauling across the oceans with no lookouts. They're the ones I really would worry about.

It's 0230hrs and I notice the log says I've sailed 57 miles since midday and by the end of tonight I'll make another 18 miles which must be some kind of record as I've only averaged about 65 miles per day since setting out.

Life is never quiet on a sailing boat as there's a cacophony of sounds beating their own time and rhythm. There's the thump and bump of a passing wave, the rattle of the wind in the rigging, the creak of the gimballed stove as it adjusts to its levelling position continually, the clack of the boom in the goose neck and the tap of the block on the traveller. There's also the dull thump of the sheet block on the deck as it regularly relaxes under the changing strains of the sheet, easing out its tension like a chained guard dog.

In the cabin there's the tick of the clock, the ever-present tinkle of my wind chimes and other sounds that I can identify if I focus on them. As I relax and cease identifying the usual sounds they come to me unfiltered and I hear the whispers and sighs and groans of a boat that is alive with its own mysterious story, telling me all sorts of things if I only listen quietly, a bit like life itself.

My thoughts take wings again as I imagine the older couple who owned this boat before me, taking it out on Chesapeake Bay, talking quietly in the background, coming down into the galley to make a cuppa, admiring their beautiful sailing machine, anchoring around the bay and enjoying themselves. I feel their energies around the boat and their spirits as I sit here absorbing the ambience of it all. Their resonances are definitely left behind and I imagine Mike still here playing chess and Glenn talking sailing and Leo laughing and joking and I realise the memories we all carry are there for mining for our whole life. How we are in the small moments of our life is how we are in all aspects of our life, and these small moments in the cockpit with the moon beaming brightly down must be just as valuable as any moments I've ever known.

Chapter 21

US Navy

I stop musing and concentrate on the moment to moment flow of things around me. The restlessness of my mind has been the greatest discovery of this voyage and I find I can now helm away without thinking anymore, keeping my focus on breathing slowly and enjoying just living in the moment for no other reason than feeling expansion.

I drift over to the Grand Canyon in the USA for no apparent reason and walk with my memories from years ago. In 1995 when crossing the states from Boston to Los Angeles in an old Chevy station wagon, I promised myself that I'd head down that steep trail into the canyon and then out to the Colorado river, which took much longer than I thought. Then that hard grind back up to the rim in the heat of a hot August day, climbing the steep trail out long after dark, into the cold night air of the canyon rim, eventually collapsing into the back of my station wagon and falling asleep, utterly exhausted, but powerfully rewarded.

Down there on the canyon floor at midday I met a fellow traveller, Dave from Washington state, who asked me why I was down there with just shorts and soft shoes and I told him that was all I had to wear, "it's my sailing gear!" and he lectured me, saying sternly, "you need to come down here with the right gear man!"

Feeling a little apologetic I told him it was probably because I was born at a very early age and the trauma of that meant that I couldn't speak until I was 18 months old, plus being so poor when I was young meant I couldn't even afford to pay attention, and that's why I had come so poorly prepared!!.

That went straight over his head and he apologised for blasting me, asking me where I was from with my rather strange accent.

"Tasmania." I replied. He said "you mean that little island south of Australia where they have those crazy bears?" I was surprised that he had a good handle on the geography of the world, particularly places so far away so I rewarded him by saying "few Americans know where Tasmania is and lots ask can we even speak English" and I always say "we speak a little English, but our strange accent comes from paying $5 a month for accent lessons before the ages of 12 and then we pay $10 a month for more intensive accent lessons, up till the age of 18, when we finally get a certificate for speaking the way we do. If we don't get the certificate for our accent then we can't vote, and we would all sound like your southern rednecks!"

He was suitably impressed but my humorous, novel explanation also slid over his head, and he asked me what was the best thing about Tasmania and I confidently said "it's the honeymoon capital of the world," he countered that by saying loudly "no way man, that's Hawaii" and I laid an ace on the table with "no man, it's Tasmania" and he said "why?" and I replied with a perfectly straight face, "it's the only pubic shaped island in the world." He told me I was surely furked!

Then he asked me if there was anything else special about Tasmania and I told him it was the first place in the world to get telephones and they'd even named a town after it. He incredulously asked what the name of the town was and I said with a wry smile, "Ringarooma" and he said "I'll check that out."

He asked me to visit him in Washington state which I did, and we laughed a lot about our earlier encounter.

Dave finally came out to Australia in 1997 when I was building the castle and he began practising the special Aussie accent that I taught him, so that he could go home and make out he was also an Aussie, able to speak deep down his throat and also talk about that pubic shaped island in the sun. Ah, the fun of strangers meeting and sharing their stories.

Mark Twain once said, "all stories are true, except some are made up!" I can definitely vouch for that.

I helm along while laughing about my chance meeting with Dave, mentally drifting around the world, acting as a tranquil observer to all my "memory capital", remembering the wisdom of the Hindu philosophy that says, "in all things tranquillity is the greatest emotion, because it lies beneath all the others" and tonight, beneath the magnificence of all that is around me lies solitude, harmony and tranquillity that make me a very rich sailor indeed. The tranquillity amongst all these sounds and movement comes from my being here experiencing it all. I am the bringer of a whole new energy to this boat and together we roll down each horizon. Hopefully when *Millefleurs* is gone from my life, somewhere in the future, the new owner will take her out on the ocean under another full moon and commune with her as well, sharing the memories and ambience of what she has done.

I re-attach the shock cords and attempt to get *Millefleurs* to sail herself again, but she resists, promising only to hold course for 10 seconds at a time, before she becomes unstable. In that 10 seconds I dash below and put on my Willie Nelson CD and rush back to the helm with Willie following me up the ladder singing about lost love and the dreams of tomorrow.

He is a real character for me, singing from experiences, gathering the images of the saint and the sinner with the sadness and the suffering we all experience and then transforming them into songs that we can relate to. I well remember going to Willie's statue in Austin, Texas and standing there admiring the way an artist had sculptured him as the "wild noble savage", but then I imagined that it would be even better if Willie's statue had a dollar chute where, after dropping in your money, he poured forth a song to amuse us all.

I'm sure that in our technological 3D future all statues, noble figures and icons cast in splendid materials will come to life, giving out renditions of their famous speeches, singing their songs, offering advice for the future in an interactive process that connects us to their spirit.

I think that might be my next business idea after I get off the ocean, as my imagination drifts wildly around my universe, writing short stories for my own entertainment.

A falling star streaks across the sky from the north, leaving a fiery trail that seems to both fall and rise from the ocean dead ahead. I am so shocked I begin imagining it possibly could have been a flare from a yacht that I thought I may have seen in reverse. Maybe it was a flare that was coming down. I run downstairs and turn on the VHF radio and race back up to stand on the side deck peering intently ahead and listening for any emergency call or for any more signs. After a while I decide it must have come from the sky and not from the ocean.

Sometimes one must test the truth when it could literally mean life and death for some poor soul, possibly drifting out here in a life-raft, hoping for a boat to come by. I finally dismiss the drifting sailor idea and decide the truth can only be one's decision, after weighing all options. Guilt only comes when you cease trusting yourself. I now know I'm not sailing past a distressed sailor and that flare was definitely a falling star.

In previous journeys whilst sailing at night I've often seen fabulous falling stars lighting up the sky overhead, as they're hard to miss when you have this huge dark panorama, clear as a crystal, not being obscured by any lights when a long slow flash of light suddenly appears. It's one of the reasons I like to sail dark, as the glow of the masthead light tends to become annoying, obscuring one's night vision and bringing the city to the ocean, modernity to tradition, changing one's appreciation of being minimalistic and living closer to nature.

Furthermore, in trusting myself, I've claimed those falling stars as messengers from the heavens directly for me, just like the Aborigines claim message sticks from their ancestors. I decided a long time ago that falling stars were my message sticks as they've often highlighted synchronistic events, indicating dangers ahead or directions to go, or where an island finally lies, and with experience I've begun to trust them as my own personal oracles. This falling star is possibly telling me that I'm on course for Horta and all is well in my universe. I sink back in the cockpit and enjoy the flirtatious 12 knot breeze filling up my solar gas tank through a full working rig, driving us steadily on.

Finally, after a long night the ocean dawn creeps through the portholes in slices of bright yellow and burnt orange that add sparkle to this new day and as the sun rises ahead I am gently reminded of the only truth I know in sailing, "Sailing is long, long periods of boredom, interspersed with intense periods of activity, rather like a marriage!" while ocean sailing for me was a way of life and a source of perpetual uncertainty. Eventually I found that it was really a search for beauty in the natural world. A sailing vessel is alive in a way that no motor vessel can ever be because it begins to reflect things about nature and the ocean you've probably never considered.

It's the necessity for self-discovery that always leads us on to expand our repertoire and out on the ocean one finds that soft feminine spirit bound into the vessel (all ship's names are feminine), with that harder male spirit living on the land and the differences between both that a sailing vessel bridges, offers multitudes of perspective. As I've mastered the negativity of my own thoughts over the years I've been able to re-experience the beauty of each ocean day with a generosity of being that turns every glorious expanse of sunset, all the magic in a wild stormy day, all the fun of uncertainty rolling it's dice, as the experience of being a true noble adventurer into the purest form of living I've known.

Now that's real living. and I've been forced to comprehend that the now moment on the ocean is not a razors edge between the past and the future that we often fill up with concentrated bursts of energy, but an endless plane stretching from horizon to horizon, sandwiched between a faded past and a distant future.

All the positive sailors I have known have one great thing in common, they are always hugging the now moment that stretches right throughout the day, generally with a smile and a good sense of humour.

With the sun well above the yardarm I drop the rig, lock the helm, take a look around the horizon and go below to fall straight into my bunk and take that glorious deep dive into sleep that only comes when you're dead tired and also completely happy with your lot.

I wake at 0920 hrs and lay there enjoying the soft roll of being becalmed on a warm day on a flat sea. Curiosity finally overtakes me and I get up and stand in the stairwell looking out across the ocean to a clear horizon with a few puffy clouds, a deep blue sea with razor bright sunlight shining off my bare skin. It's going to be another quiet day in the lee of that full moon, and I wonder what the day will bring along for us to ponder upon.

The wind is down to about 8 knots from the south-west and I remark to myself it's an awesome experience to be out here alone searching within my own infinity to live this dream I am in, as if it's never been done before. I make a cup of tea and am reminded of the Chinese wisdom that says, "you drink water to slake your thirst, you drink wine to gentle your melancholy and you drink tea to raise your spirits." I toast the Chinese wisdom and go and sit quietly on the stern, practising my own form of raising my spirits that magically turns this ordinary day into something remarkable.

I look up to the north west with a huge smile and remember one of the secrets to life is whether we take our pleasures for granted or we take them with gratitude, because as I stand here focusing on the horizon I see coming towards us is a long line of white half broken water almost to the horizon, like a dangerous coral reef along the shores of an uncharted atoll. Along this line are at least 20 frigate birds wheeling and diving in organised frenzy and I realise it's not a squall line that I first thought was on the march, but rather a school of fish, maybe tuna heading south, covering a huge arc in their millions as they migrate to newer food supplies. The splashing continues heading our way and slowly behind the tuna schools emerge lines of dolphins leaping and gambolling and chasing the tuna, with the birds picking up the leftovers from amongst some giant feeding frenzy. The tuna school seems much smaller than the dolphin mob as they cross my path, with the frenzied tuna being driven ahead of a long line of dolphins.

It's not so much the tuna that are remarkable, but the size of the dolphin migration as they extend all along the west to the northern sector of the ocean. There must be hundreds of thousands of dolphins heralding some mass movement as they plunge south for the summer warmth, away from the cold but rich hunting grounds of the north, for that joyous tropical south where they rear their young. They're all travelling at about 5 knots in one big carnivalia and as they pass a few take up brief stations alongside, milling frantically around *Millefleurs*, but moving on quickly.

I watch for at least 30 minutes in awe as more and more pass through and apart from the novelty of it all, I take it as a personal sign of endearing good luck for the day. I idle around the deck with my cup of tea in hand looking, lingering and enjoying this whole new day, finally deciding to make a breakfast of rolled oats and dried apricots with honey and powered milk and get on the roll, later maybe putting out a fishing line to catch a lazy tuna.

I make my breakfast slowly with another cup of tea and relax on the stern, sitting on the water containers immersed in this gentle roll of *Millefleurs* as she floats like a duck, becalmed in her own giant swimming pool. She rolls steadily to each passing swell, while the black tell-tales flap gently in the 8 knot breeze that is impatiently waiting for us to hoist our rig, and get on the way.

I take my time with breakfast, sliding slowly into the magnificence of the new day, deciding that today is the day I'll change all my clothes for a new stash which are wrapped in heavy black plastic that I've patiently secreted in my well stowed travel bag.

I put away all the gear and emerge in a dry pair of old jeans, a bright red t-shirt, a navy-blue jumper and a pair of old leather deck shoes I'd been using back in the Solomons. I love to feel their genuine familiarity, they seem to have gone mouldy around the tops, but with some fresh air and sunshine they'll soon be ready to walk me around the Horta waterfront, proudly displaying the knowing that they've come a long way to get there.

I feel like a new person in these familiar travelling clothes that have all come from second-hand suppliers, with that used feel no "up-market store" can provide. I patiently hoist a working rig of full mainsail and no.3 jib and release the steering brake and we're soon moving off, flapping our sails like an albatross beginning to run across the water with fully outstretched wings, gaining forward momentum, ready to burst into a whole new day.

We're heading east again at 3.5 knots which puts us south of Horta and I consider the fishing line that I've set up on the stern with the heavy line and long shock absorber ready for release. After due consideration regarding the drama involved, the poor old dorado or tuna along with the excess of fish that I'll have without refrigeration, I put the line away and wisely decide to eat all the food I have first, before going down that killing trail. I don't want to waste resources or sacrifice some gorgeous piece of nature for my small appetite.

I'm not really a lover of fishing, even though trout fishing as a child in the Roger River valley in Tasmania, was a big part of my youth, and a focal point for my youthful freedom and valley adventures. In fact, I dislike those big game fishermen who spend huge amounts of their resources to power across the ocean, spewing forth foam and diesel fumes, hunting for deep sea fish with the agenda of catching 15 different species of fish before you can eat at the "special fisherman's trophy table". I call them fish torturers as they don't hunt to eat, but to torture fish by bringing them up to their boat, robbing them of any energy they have stored up, pulling them aboard to weigh them, taking a picture and then letting them go sometimes with a kiss, so buggered that they usually die. There's no purity of action in that, no equality of struggle, it's might versus right, it's David verses Goliath in reverse and if they're really big into it they have the poor bloody fish mounted on their hunting wall, so that they can gloat to their mates about how many thousands of gallons of diesel it took to capture that one sailfish.

So it's no fishing for me today, I'd rather go hungry till I'm right out of food before I'll risk the suffering of my ocean mates to satisfy my poor organisational skills for not bringing enough food.

I well remember being in Sydney in 1987, ready to leave the wharf at Birkenhead Point for a long haul to the Pacific Islands, when an old "worn out" grey headed guy came padding slowly along the wharf in his old deck shoes, and stood there admiring *Sundancer*, obviously casting his discerning eyes over our rig, our deck gear and other points of interest. Finally, he decided to make himself known to me by saying "you fish much?" and I said "yes we do, but only on passage" and he said "what sort of fish?" and I replied "mainly dorado or tuna" and he nodded his head knowingly.

Realising he was leading up to something important I cast my curious line into his mouth by asking "what's your favourite fish?" and he said" Murray cod!" and I said "I've never caught one, what makes them so good?" and he said surprisingly, adding to my very limited fish knowledge with the true words of experience, "best fish in the world. You can cook them so many different ways - bake them, smoke them, chowder them, even dry them and they're always delicious."

"Now" I say, so I can add to your own knowledge as the reader of this saga, expressing my deep interest into his Murray cod experience, "what's the biggest one you've caught?" which is the most expansive way to get any fisherman to roll his biggest and the best movie into the wider world out here, which includes our world right here this morning.

He replies, "can't tell you, I never weighed him!" and me being intrigued said, "there's a good story in that, come on up here and I'll make a cup of tea and you will no doubt educate me on the huge Murray cod story, that's probably only been whispered over a cold beer in the back bars of some Australian Murray river hotel."

On deck came Jack the Murray cod hunter, all 5 feet 6 ins of him. As he sat down on a cockpit cushion he rolled a drum smoke while I made the cuppa with three spoons of sugar for him, some milk and sweet biscuits as requested, and then we sat down to talk. Every fisherman always begins his story with "it's a long story" and I always say "tell me more as I'm actually writing a book on fish stories and I bet your story could make a whole chapter."

They love that introduction, as they often fluff their feathers like a well satisfied seagull after a feed of stale chips and then Jack, suitably lubricated and inspired begins, and I quote him word for word with his croaky old voice, as his story now plays out like a well-oiled panorama in my mind's eye.

"I'm 71 now, but two years ago I was down the Murray river on Sunday morning with me dog Bruiser, sitting in my outdoor Coles canvas chair, listening to Macca over Australia on the radio. I was fishing with chicken guts, on a 200 pound line that you only use for Murray cod, wrapped around a hand reel as rods are useless down there with all the over-hanging branches, when I hooked the big one."

He now takes a noisy sip of tea and sucks on his rolly for emphasis and then the words, all without a break, begin to flow again. "I know he's a big one as he draws away from me without any tugging, just a long straight draw that goes on till I feed him more line and then more line and then I realise he's too strong for me to hold back. Then he begins to head up river with me and Bruiser following, with me trying to hold him back as he's well hooked by now, but he's got me going at a good walking pace and I'm jumping over logs on the bank and squeezing through bushes while keeping the line free from being fouled. Well, you're not going to believe this but he drags me up the river for a good mile, with me huffing and puffing and Bruiser barking like mad, and the other fishermen looking at us as if we're mad and just when I'm nearly buggered he turns and heads down river, going twice as fast with the current, and now I'm really battling, my dog is going butcher's hooks and I'm determined to try to slow him down without a lot of success. I'm not sure now who is really hooked, me or the cod as he drags me bodily through the sandy patches and over branches testing my resolve to the limit!"

Jack's getting very excited as he relives his adventure.

"So," he says, "I aim for one last big effort before I'm done and he's going to take all my line. I dash ahead a bit and with the dying energy of my fading youth, wrap the line around a tree and stand firm. Now I know I'm winning as he battles with the tree, jerking it back and forth but after half an hour he eventually gives up and I drag him ashore, head first up onto the sand.'

Then Jack takes a break from his story and has another long sip of tea and another longer slow drag on his drum rolly. He's got me hooked as well, as I say "wow, that's amazing!"

Jack says, "I'm not done yet, there's more to this story, even though he's the biggest Murray cod I've ever seen, as I crouch there in awe, thinking what do I do now?" (feel free to go and make a cup of coffee now as this story may get bigger if you wait longer!)

"So,' he continues, "I get down on my hands and knees and feeling sorry for him, I decide to get the hook out of his mouth to let him go, as you can't kill something like this, a fish that's older probably than me, a fish that has spawned thousands of others, a fish from history." So, he says, "I get my Joseph Rogers pocket knife out of my jacket that my grandfather had given me, and, reaching down his throat I try to find the hook, but I drop my knife and being sentimental I decide I'm not going to lose the damn knife. So I get inside his mouth on my hands and knees, and start looking for it. Now while I'm doing that with my head down his throat, a guy rides up from inside his belly on a horse and says, "what the hell are you doing up here?" and I say" looking for my pocket knife and what the hell are you doing down there" and he says, "I've been here for a week looking for a mob of lost sheep!"

I smile and encourage him with a long loud clap and Jack says, taking his last sip of cold tea, "to cut a long story short, I didn't weigh him, I couldn't, but I did take a photo of him and the photo weighed 14 pounds!"

That fisherman's yarn has given me more fun than the cup of tea and time spent with Jack, possibly the greatest fisherman I've ever met, who's also immortalised in my extensive memory capital of big fishing stories and is also now part of yours.

I sail on at 3 knots knowing that if I angle further to the south-east I'll be able to get more speed, but it'll take me further away from Horta. I'm really well south now, so I trundle on keeping the main from banging by tightening the preventer and letting the jib out further. I probably should pole out the jib, but that's just too difficult without some self-steering and I've even given up on the use of the shock cords as they hinder more than help, causing me to become a little frustrated that this is the first yacht I've owned that won't self-steer at all.

My mind is rather drifting like the proverbial country radio station as I go deeper into the things I have discovered about this boat and I really don't need my mind trying to develop more strategies for self-steering. I just want to be left alone like the fisherman on the banks of life, letting the current take me along, tasting the sweetness of life, immersed in this journey, even though I'm a reluctant hostage to the helm. There has to be something worthwhile in all this as Oscar Wilde said a long time ago," experience is something you can't get for nothing." I feel like I'm also a puzzle in minimalism or a personal marker for emptiness, being immersed in this vast space all around me like humanity in the cosmos.

Humanity is a giant puzzling mystery in the universe until we eventually find some other and maybe we are the scouts out here hunting for solid ground, so we can establish our own position in the whole scheme of things.

Perhaps the vastness of our inner space reflects the enormity of that universe out there and definitely being beyond the reach of others and alone with just myself, my mind seems to magnify that knowing. I wonder in a thousand years' time how much of our inquiring minds will have grown to close the circle between humanity and this vast amazing cosmos we occupy?

And just to get back to reality one of the frigate birds has grown tired of his chase with the dolphins, and has joined me, circling overhead watching to see if there is any food around this slowly moving piece of flotsam. He circles and wheels and soars like an eagle, never once moving his wings, it's like he has his own hang glider built into those angular struts. The old sailors called them the "devil birds" because of the split in their tail and their ferocious fighting ability particularly when other birds tried to steal their catch. I just admire his ability though to fly free out here, a long way from land, sometimes flying for weeks on end and yet strangely he can never land on the water.

His Achilles heel is the lack of oil in his feathers. If he gets them wet he can't take off and he drowns. His dry feathers certainly help him to soar but not float on water so the frigate must be the most unlikely ocean survivor of all birds, sleeping on the wing all night long, gliding across the featureless ocean alone for weeks, watching for fish schooling and following them for days, waiting for their leftovers after a feeding frenzy. I feel some connection to this bird, we're both in the same boat. I can't survive out here without my pieces of equipment and he can't without his dry feathers, and yet we both do quite well taking our special advantages for granted.

A line of clouds is building ahead of us looking a lot like the beginnings of a huge bushfire at sea. I can see the smoke and even some lightning flashes at times, just as if land was close over the horizon. The thunder rumbles ominously, cracking open the sky and threatening to strike all around. It's no threat to my sailing, unless it moves back against the wind. Very slowly other huge thunderheads form ahead, well beyond us in their pinks and creams and glossy whites as if they are rehearsing for a local cricket match.

Slowly I begin to gain on the formations growing taller in front of me, with the very top peaks of the clouds doing a Michelangelo, with just me as the sole appreciator of their fine flowing style.

A whole range of bullet clouds are also forming on top of these skyscrapers and I hear louder rumbles as the storm's base orchestra gets underway. If this is nature's art show then I'm trying to make sense of the surreal, because in this storm there is enough energy to compare to a nuclear explosion say our scientists, and yet all over the world 10,000 other storms are happening continuously. I slip below before the helm knows I'm gone and load John Williamson's CD onto the player. I'd almost forgotten that I'd brought it all the way from Australia. His music adds to the storm effect with *"True Blue"*, and *"The Boomerang Café"*, and for long moments there I'm back home with familiar music and then when *"Waltzing Matilda"* comes booming up the stairwell, I'm even a little teary with nostalgia, feeling like I'm back in the country fire brigade steaming towards another bush fire disturbance.

It's amazing how familiar music creates such longing in one's soul, as I imagine I can smell the smoke. Soon I feel I'm back with Sam on the stage as I loudly sing *"It's raining on the rock"* to our own surreal audience, remembering how big the country is back in Australia and how similar the people are to Americans, in so many ways. Australia and America are the two big immigrant and experimental countries of the world, creating a promised fusion culture that will last for centuries. England used America as a convict destination up until 1780 when the colonists revolted. Then the convicts were sent to Australia, beginning in 1788. So, the British Empire birthed two brothers, Australia and America, while sending their "problem children" overseas and introducing the rule of law and our maverick can-do natures, that have thrust us into the newer promised lands. America has much more religion than the predominantly secular Australia and both grew enormously after the gold rushes of the 19th century that drew record fortune-seeking immigrants from around the world.

America grew from their gold rush fever of 1845 to 1850 and their gunfighting era came at the same time, while Australia grew their gold rush from 1850 to 1855. The very same people, seeking their fortune in those hard times, came from China and from many European countries to far flung spots around the world, opening up these lands, doubling both populations, making each country a reflection of the other in their lawless ways and the rejection of any authority. The biggest difference though was America was the land of milk and honey while Australia was much drier and barren, except for its narrow fertile strips around the coastline. The Australian population never soared like America's.

When I'm in America I'm home, sharing the same language, ideals, foods and ambitions and some of the same humour as Australia. We're brothers, with America being built on the importance of the family and Australia on the importance of the individual.

In America there is a pilgrimage to the car, to the family and to conveniences arising from their amazing bounty, while in Australia the pilgrimage is to the beach, barbecues, the bush and the maverick, reflecting our poorer and more solitary struggle.

Noon has well and truly come and gone, as we sail contentedly into the afternoon, making slow progress towards the thunderstorm that is dissipating ahead. I'm immersed within turquoise blue skies right from my fingertips to the far horizon. I'm a tiny bubble within a bottle, a murmur within a crowd and the bigger the canvas gets the more my fertile artist plays upon it. The great meeting of the clouds in the sky is over and they are dispersing to their chosen corners, having run out of heat and thunder and lightning and what was once a circus is now a just a small sideshow.

I'm still impressed that nature put on a performance for me today and unlike the clock ticking in the empty room I was there to enjoy it all, along with Mr Williamson and his outback CD.

I make a cup of tea between helm visitations and we sail into the evening with the breeze building to 12 knots as we head east at 5 knots with the bigger rig powering us along almost as if it's also in a hurry to get to port.

Sailing is definitely the slowest way to get across the ocean as you move only at walking pace, but if speed is not the main issue then the sojourn is the real story for going, where sailing answers more than one realises at the time. Sailing as a way of life was all the rage in the 1970s and in the sailing town of Hobart, Tasmania where I built my first yacht in 1972, there were 30 other budding adventurers also building theirs. We were a band of brothers, helping each other, sharing our secrets and techniques, creating a whole new fashion in travel, promising to meet at famous ports around the world, creating a future lifestyle others would envy.

Some critics were saying the ocean would soon be full of yachties moving from continent to continent in mass exodus, causing mass disaffection amongst all the stay-at-home public servants. We were supposedly the next promised revolution after the hippies, building our dreams and sailing away to love, adventure and freedom. I rode that wave into the 1980s and I eventually continued making a business of taking adventurers to the islands and around the world, but the movement died in the 1990s and it eventually has morphed into cruise ships for this next generation. With the rise in the green movement of this century and the great impetus for wind and solar power, one would have expected the yachting ideal would be re-invigorated, as sailing free is right up their alley, but I believe that this newer generation is wedded to the security of the forest and the silver of the mountains, rather than the uncertainty of any ocean.

Now yachting as a lifestyle is almost over as marinas are filled up with expensive boats full of electronic toys, taking the ideas from us older vagabonds and value adding for their gain.

The mega rich have super yachts with well-trained crews and they fly rather than sail to their new destinations amongst the beautiful islands of the world. While the old fashioned "bum boat" cruising world is over, with newer expensive marinas eliminating most free anchorages and demanding expensive insurance policies before you enter and solid rigging that can be no older than 7 years. Even countries mandate that you can't leave port without a life-raft, a satellite rescue beacon and a boat full of safety gear. Now it's security and safety and rules for an ocean that could be dangerous and they even promise to pick you up if the going gets too rough.

Looking back on those 30-odd builders in Hobart, I wonder where they went. I was one of the few who kept the dream alive, sailing around the world, becoming an international citizen, belonging to no one, nowhere and everywhere, while experiencing true freedom just like that frigate bird.

Oh, to dream the dreams of the many and to keep that dream alive, fills me with the knowing that even though it kept me poor, I am richer in spirit for the going.

I sail into the evening with the almost full moon rising, without any navigation lights, and just the glow of the compass to keep me on track. I feel strong and alert and re-energised enough to sail through another whole night even though I haven't slept for ages. The sun brings the day, and the moon the night, and I really enjoy quietly sailing along at night with a bright moon, feeling that special energy and renewal that keeps one's dreams aglow. The rapture I get from the moon is similar to the performance of that thunderstorm running through my body, keeping me on edge, encouraging me to bridge the difference between the physical and the mental, in lucid feelings, that I've never experienced before. Rapture is surely an amazing feeling that only comes a few times in our lives.

It's felt after your first child is born, or when you've bought your first house, or when you've left the runway for the first time, or when you're finally escaping the clutches of some dictatorial regime like the Mafia of Malta.

But rapture brought me to my knees in laughter once in South Africa when I saw a huge Zulu with a colourful mohawk and an equally impressive ratty t-shirt full of holes that some yachtie had probably given him. It read; "rapture is what you get when you lift something too heavy!" Rapture though does seem to do something special for our brains that combines feelings and thought into a newer medium, where the brain literally lights up in full-on trance.

Neurologists are now studying it intensely, particularly by testing Buddhist monks and Celestine nuns who seem to be able to go into the rapturous state almost at will, obviously after training their brains for years. In that state they feel perfectly happy for long periods of time in silence, creating their own virtuous circuit of feelings, feeding back into their neuronal circuitry creating harmony and love while connecting them to some bigger feel good "inner space".

I sit here quietly without any worries or concerns, smiling happily at the moon, watching the few stars that are bright enough to show their lights and enjoying the rhythm of *Millefleurs* in this steady home bound breeze. We rollick along at 5 knots making amazing progress as we gallop to the east and I can't waste any of this amazing run of good luck, with warm seas and bright nights lighting up the bigger movie all around. I've not had any problems in the last week as I pour my positivity into *Millefleurs*, practising some of those wonderful moments I trust, where I'm into my own euphoric state of being beyond any negativities or concerns about getting this boat home. I'm practising being in harmony with the whole experience around me as the hours roll by and another dawn comes and I realise I've been out for 27 days.

It's the 1st of July and my food stocks are getting low, the eggs are gone, along with the potatoes and most tinned meats, while Leo's peanut butter stash is staring at me with glazed eyes like his big black rats, each time I open the lid. I still have some rice and flour and some crackers and small treats that I've held back from my stomach for this long, while my supply of Earl Grey tea is almost at an end and there's some coffee that'll send me hyper and a few tins of fruit. There's maybe 10 days to go.

I'll be thin when I get in and maybe I will consider being a forced

Breatharian if all goes pear shaped. If things get too desperate I'll have to open the life raft and get out the emergency rations, but I'm a long way from that scenario yet. Then dawn comes and I decide I must have a sleep and make some breakfast later, giving me more of a chance to face the music and check my dwindling supplies. I drop the rig, take a look around the empty horizon and happily dive into my bunk leaving the world and *Millefleurs* to take care of themselves.

I emerge at 0630hrs and take a look around the horizon while the breeze still runs at 12 knots from the south west, kicking up a few white caps with a bright warm sun overhead. The colour of the ocean is a soft turquoise echoing the shades of blue desert wildflowers - it's an impressionists' painting early in the morning, marinated in gentle oil colour hues. I lounge in the stairwell enjoying the new day, not planning anything as I can flow into this day like a novice on holiday.

I put on Kris Kristofferson on soft volume and let the music waft all over me, bringing my long 90 day road sojourn from Boston to New Orleans in 1995 in my Chevy station wagon-back back to my memory, with *"Me and Bobby McGee"* raging in the background.

And then I recall that fabulous long ride from New Orleans up to Baton Rouge where I was hunting for a place to park and sleeping soundly in some anonymous street late at night, when a huge dog leapt at me through the open window, almost biting my arm.

That then reminded me of the massive guard dogs in South Africa that kept the lid on most mischief. I guess the dog was keeping me honest as well and I left his street alone to sleep elsewhere.

I go hunting in the galley lockers and find some steel cut oats I've stored away, along with some dried blueberries and even one UHT juice that has fallen down into the bilge. Oh, what treasure a little food is, and I make up a bowl of cereal with some added coconut and two almonds as I sit in the cockpit, drifting gently along sharing my bounty with the universe. I imagine I'm at a special whole food's restaurant describing to the masses the magnificence of my morning's feast.

The dolphins and the frigate bird are long gone, but I wish they were here to share my good fortune, so we could raise our glasses together and toast our good health. I'm obviously euphoric after finding that food stash and it'll certainly bring me lots of good cheer. They say to those who can dream, no place is too far away, and at this moment I feel like the world is my oyster, I've been in this same "free wind" for 3 whole days and it's beautiful. It's like groundhog day and tonight the moon will still be big and bright and hopefully we'll sail right through those long late-night hours, possibly gaining another 70 miles.

Now duty calls. I put away my gear and get ready to hoist a rig and get on the road again after a leisurely start to this day. And just like groundhog day the rig is the same, the hoisting procedure identical and my well-practised routine runs much like clockwork. Soon we're off to the east rolling along at 5 knots cutting a turbulent wake across a mirrored sea, leaving traces of where we've been in white patches for hundreds of yards behind.

I spot a ship to starboard and slightly over the horizon coming my way. Then it becomes 2 ships and then 5 and the crowd builds as they come over the horizon and I see that it's the US Navy steaming west, probably heading directly for Norfolk, Virginia, back from a deployment in the middle east.

I run downstairs, turn on the radio and tune to channel 16 and get back up to the helm before we go off course. It'd be a bit embarrassing to do a crash gybe under the watchful eyes of the navy, as they are obviously watching me by now, wondering where I'm going. Then I hear vessel 91 calling vessel 94 telling them the captain is coming over for breakfast, and soon I see a helicopter manoeuvring around between the fleet, probably picking up the captain and practising helicopter transfer.

I attach the steering shock cords and run down to the radio and call 91 saying, "warship 91, Australian yacht *Millefleurs* 28 days out of Norfolk Virginia, do you copy?" and I run back upstairs to the helm and listen excitedly for a sailor-to-sailor response, but there is none. I know they're listening with their sophisticated radio gear and they're probably tuning their radio to my signal, practising "target range isolation". I run down again and say "warship 91 this is Australian yacht *Millefleurs* out of Norfolk, Virginia. I'm 5 miles off your starboard bow and I'm really low on food, any chance of dropping me off a few eggs or potatoes or a loaf of bread?"

No reply, the bastards are starting to annoy me now with no respect for a sailor in possible distress and no reply, meaning they are definitely ignoring me.

I hit the radio again with, "warship 91…my position. Look fellas I fought with you guys in Vietnam like a lot of Australians, and I sure could do with a little food to get me to the Azores. I surely need a bit of payback now!"

I patiently wait but there's no reply and as I correct my steering and long for recognition I'm suddenly mad, I'm pissed with these American Navy bastards and I consider calling mayday, which means they're obligated by international rules to come to my aid. But then I imagine them saying lack of food is no excuse for a mayday and maybe they'll cause me lots more trouble, even taking me off my boat and sinking it for target practise.

I go back upstairs and watch them steaming past beam to beam, range 3 miles, I can even see people on deck. There are a thousand eyes on me now and they're laughing and joking about this crazy Aussie heading east while they're about 5 days from home. There are 7 ships in the flotilla and there's not an ounce of goodwill coming my way. The miserable dirty rotten bastards!! Bugger them, I'm mad now and I need to give them a serve, so I hit the radio with, "US Navy, US Navy ,US Navy. I know you guys are listening and I could call a mayday on you but I won't, but you guys could show a little kindness to a fellow sailor, a little kindness to an Australian whose really low on food and still has a few weeks to go to get to the Azores. You guys could use me as an exercise and drop me a little food, maybe some bread or a cake, maybe some onions and I'll even trade you my Aussie flag. How about that?. But I know you guys have no bloody heart and when you get home I hope your mother runs out from underneath the house and bites you. Now fuck off!"

I close down the radio, go back to the helm and vent my spleen on them as they rapidly steam away, with me refusing to look their way or hold any hope of some change of heart. Sometimes the world is more beautiful when you have it at your back.

I'm really pleased now that I didn't go to Vietnam or fight any war for the bastards, they weren't worth it.

At noon I drop the rig and take sights and am able to plot myself on the chart. I am 35 deg 58 north and 35 deg 10 west, putting me still well south of Horta with only 380 miles to go. It seems so close with just another week of sailing at this rate and I won't need those bloody potatoes anyway!

The behaviour of the US fleet reflects their training, which removes them from the normal every day responses one would expect from the average guy. I'm sure some of the radio operators would have liked to chat and say hello but protocol ruled it out. I do wonder if someone on that fleet would like to tell me why they didn't respond to my calls. My email is at the back of the book. It did reflect the sentiment I once read from the sarcasm society; "National Sarcasm Society, like we need your support!"

Chapter 22

Diving on the hull

At 1430 hrs the wind begins to drop to 5 knots and then suddenly increases up to 8 or 9 knots and down again. This goes on and on and I've only been sailing for an hour into this afternoon. There's no doubt my run of beautiful breezes is coming to an end, as the sails begin to slat and bang, and our speed drops down to 1.5 knots where steering becomes even harder, almost frustratingly difficult as I have to use more and more rudder to get some response and yet more rudder takes away some of our momentum.

This is a little like watching grass grow, things have slowed down, the world is going less than half pace and I begin to watch for those hazy patches of wind on the water where I can possibly get a lift. I soon realise the futility of it all, remembering the saying "a watched pot never boils" and "a dying wind never picks up!" I reluctantly drop the rig and stand watching the other wind direction to the south west and I can see it's run out as well. Its pockets are empty and I'm becalmed, for how long, is the $64 question and I hope my savage tirade at the USA fleet hasn't brought me bad luck.

While the doldrums are here I decide to get my snorkelling gear and attack the fleet of goose barnacles that are slowing us down a lot. They're all along the water line, opening and closing their furry mouths as we roll in and out of the water, waving at me, declaring they have staked a claim to *Millefleurs* that will only be broken when I attack them with a scraper. I'd like to fire up the dive compressor and make the job much easier, but I'm reluctant to get out the dive hose, hook up the compressor, set the limits to air pressure and slip into the water with the hose tied around my waist. The job would be much easier with air, but today I'd rather dive free, putting on just my fins, mask and snorkel and diving in over the stern.

I'm leaving the Jesus rope out just in case a squall comes through and maybe drives *Millefleurs* out of my grasp, causing me to frantically use up another of my 9 lives as I'd be playing catch up. It's amazing how such a simple negative thought expands into a possible reality, causing me to hesitate about diving in, even searching the horizon for possible squalls and ships, and even big white sharks scarily begin to swim through my mind. If I don't bite the bullet soon, other reasons for leaving the barnacles alone will enter my worried head.

Lassitude has a habit of growing quickly and it's so true that if you want something done don't ask someone who has lots of free time on their hands, choose a busy person and he'll fit it in, while the other guy will be still thinking about it. I well remember in the Solomon Islands I once traded a new fishing net with an islander, Mali, who took a fancy to it, telling me how many fish he'd be able to catch and how he'd be able to feed his family and train his sons to make a business out of repairing and selling nets. The net needed floats and leads so I gave him all he needed with the instructions on how to do it and I rowed it over to his beach hut and strung it out between two stakes on extra lines. I spent a couple of hours showing him how to start putting on the floats and weights and then a squall came through so I hurriedly left for a better anchorage on the next island.

The following year coincidently I was back at the same village with a different crew and I went ashore all excited to see how the net was progressing, taking some of the crew to show them how simple technology could change a native's whole life. I found Mali sitting under a tree resting from the sun and we all sat down to share some moments with him, asking about his family and his children and life is general. We took a walk back to his beach hut and behind the hut I spotted the net with the sinkers and floats tossed beside it, nothing had been done since I left. I didn't ask, but Mali had obviously been too busy to finish the task.

I climb into the ocean over the stern and the water is pleasantly warm. I look at *Millefleurs* happily floating in this huge lagoon, realising the amount of work I have to do. Her bottom is really, really dirty. I slip deeper into the water and swim up to the bow looking back at *Millefleurs* floating along like a big balloon. There are barnacles all over the hull, particularly along the water line and around the whole rudder and on to the back of the keel. The prime places of turbulence seems to breed barnacles and it tells me again that there is no anti-foul that'll stop growth in the tropical ocean as a slime forms over it all, and the barnacles grow wildly on slime. I gradually relax in the water and forget about checking to see if a breeze is making up or the sharks are circling. I imagine creating my own little aquarium with streams of sunlight striking deeply into the ocean while life goes on all around me.

I begin to scrape off the barnacles and the two dorados that seem to have been with me forever come over from their hiding place and follow the barnacles as they drift downwards. I can see far below into the depths of the ocean, it's like looking into space that never ends and I feel like I'm floating in an amazing back lit pond. Some tiny fish, no bigger than my finger appear from nowhere, and begin feasting on the free-floating barnacles and pretty soon I have a whole party going on around me. I feel like I'm King Neptune waving my trusty scraper fork, keeping all life around me happy and involved and it spurs me on to get the whole job done. The water is quite warm, probably about 22 deg centigrade, the small fish are getting bolder, sometimes dashing in to get a free-floating barnacle piece a few feet from my arm, and the dorados hardly seem concerned at all with them. They've taken up a new position at the bow, keeping a sharp look out.

I clean the rudder and the propeller which has hundreds of barnacles over the three bladed bronze surfaces, probably because it's free of any antifoul, and also along the complete propeller shaft to the stuffing box.

I clean the keel and along the waterline and around the stern where it's more like a small vegetable garden. I work away for an hour and then I notice a school of barracouta coming up from the bow direction, and a small shiver of recognition runs through my body as I've been close to them before. They look menacing, continually opening and closing their mouths as if they're ready to charge and do a piranha dance on my bones. But these barras don't seem to have the same mouth action that I've seen before, they're not threatening me at all and then I suddenly realise they're flying fish in a school of 6, checking out the scene. Their wings are folded and their eyes are huge and I see the power in their tail as they glide past, quite fast and yet seem to be hardly moving.

The two hidden dorados from the bow streak through the water after them and they all disappear in the blink of an eye. It's all happening in my own aquarium.

An occasional jellyfish drifts around and I'm sure if I hung here all day and had miniature vision I'd find the ocean full of life. The full of life bit reminds me that there are sea lice in the water and I'm getting some bites under my arms and around my crotch so I'd better get out of here soon. In the southern ocean sea lice are so bad you always have to wear a wet suit to dive, or even surf, and if you net a fish and leave it there for longer than an hour, it'll just be bones, stripped bare of flesh. They're like a swarm of mosquitoes and when you get out of the water you'll find them in your hair, your ears and every exposed spot possible, as these tiny critters clean the ocean bare of dead bodies.

Fortunately, there are only a few here and I decide to finish off my cleaning hobby by diving deeper below *Millefleurs* and looking upwards admiring the beauty of the hull shape and her clean lines. Beauty is in the eye of the beholder and in this isolated place there is no greater beauty than this fine sailboat with a barnacle free bottom.

It's wonderful to know the urban myths about Hunter yachts being poor ocean vessels has been shattered as most common myths are almost always negative. It's like someone has some paranoid gossip to tell you that begins like this, "I've got a secret to tell you....and you wouldn't believe this, but Hunter boats are just blobs!" I hold my breath and dive for another 30 seconds looking at the huge expanse below and my tiny boat above that is home. We're an oasis in this huge desert, a safe haven, a platform, an observation outpost, a sanctuary, a cruise ship reduced to a dot in the water and the barnacles find it the same. Holding my breath makes me realise I am floating here without any worries as I feel intuition take over and I feel that deeper connection to the ocean as part of my whole evolution.

I feel at home and content and connected with the strong feelings drawing this tiny part of the ocean into being a part of me. Down here everything is surreal, beautiful and languid and no thoughts come to interrupt the hum of the ocean or the splash of a swell on the hull. I hear the distant tap of the rig as *Millefleurs* rolls gently, I hear the sound of my heart beating loudly in my ear, the sound of bubbles being released and the movement of my teeth on the snorkel. I'm in another world where the familiar creates its own orchestra in unfamiliar tones, but the best thing is that those pesky thoughts about sharks and squalls and barracoutas have entirely left, leaving me free to just be here, hanging in the water wishing for bigger gills to continue my watery experience.

There's a different dimension all around me that I don't have the language to explain in words. The depth of water that goes on till I can't see any end lets me feel like I'm floating in a balloon, listening to the universe, suspended by my breath in some primordial state of being that feels secure and natural and is all nature at its best. I feel I belong here.

I'd like to bring adventurers out here and suspend them in a glass pod deep in the water for days on end, and let them feel their deep spiritual connections to mother ocean and their own watery nature, letting them explore their connections to the earth that the natives feel, where the earth is really mother and the sun is the father, driving all of life. It's a language I've never learnt, a feeling language that only meditation tries to tap into, a language beyond logic and rationality where living in the moment and being very aware of the wonders we create around us in our very own garden of Eden, makes ordinary living just pure joy.

Language nuances like the "joys of life" that are so important in any new situation was brought home to me in South Africa in 1991 when I was on the slipway in Durban. There I met an admirer of *Sundancer* who had vaguely heard of her exploits and had come down to share his curiosity with me.

At that time I needed lots of strong steel poles to make a frame around the boat to keep out the weather and he said we could probably get those poles at a nearby junk yard for a few rand and I was excited. I showed instant interest and suggested in typical Aussie behaviour," lets head down there and see what they have" or in American slang, "lets hustle" but he said "we'll make a plan." I was a little taken aback as any of my plans suggested many steps carefully organised, like a ladder of sequences, that we needed to do before we could go, and what's more I assumed that he just wasn't keen to head on down to the junk yard. Maybe he only wanted to go tomorrow or next week. But when he suggested we hurry up and head off I realised the plan idea was just another way of saying "let's go, do it."

English is definitely a hybrid language, full of nuances borrowed from many other languages, probably because England was invaded so often by the French, the Germans, the Spanish, the Vikings and others back through the centuries.

The French have a beautiful language but it has taken on fewer words from other languages which tends to act as a form of snobbery.

I met an American lady sailor in Panama, travelling with her French husband and children, but confined to some degree by her husband's unwillingness to mix with us non-French. She told the story that when she went to live in France she had the greatest difficulty as a mono-lingual speaker, trying her best to communicate with the French in proper French, always begging their forgiveness and making apologies for her ignorance. She said she loved all the things about France, but in her husband's hometown she felt isolated and inferior. She said "I struggled desperately for a full 10 years to fit in and understand the nuances of the French language, until by accident I discovered that almost all those French girlfriends I had desperately befriended, all spoke excellent English, but they would never reach across that divide to help me out." That alone says a lot about French arrogance and their isolation in the world.

In anchorages around the world there are often many French sailors as they love their cruising and are good at it, but they tend to anchor away from the common international mob, forming their own small cliques. English is also generally the most common language amongst all cruising folk as well as air traffic controllers and marine radio operators. In Germany one of my banking friends said English was even used in all their formal meetings so that they could grasp international trends.

I called my boat *Millefleurs*, French for 1,000 flowers, just to consciously break down that divide with French sailors, because they have a lot to offer. But when I'm in an anchorage and the French come by and discover that I'm not French, they rarely return. I'm not sure who is missing out.

My hero in sailing is Frenchman Bernard Moitessier who was the first man in 1968 to sail around the world solo, one and a half times non-stop and he inspired me to develop my own philosophy for oceaning.

I once listened to the famous actor Peter Ustinov talking about the most expressive languages in the world, particularly in matters of the heart and love. He said you may think of English or Spanish or even French as the true language of love, but it's actually Russian as that language has the richest nuanced words for the depth of all forms of love and relationships. Ustinov was obviously a deep thinker for he once famously said "beliefs are what divide people and doubt unites them" as well as "once we are destined to live out our lives in the prison of our mind, our duty is to furnish it well." I really liked the way he saw the world and the wisdom he was able to bring to my understandings of languages as the joiner or divider of all peoples.

The spread of the British Empire for example, bringing with it a common language for Africa, Asia, USA, Australia, India, Pakistan and many other countries, has been one of the greatest common connectors for humanity and world peace as a forerunner for worldwide communications. Having a common language encourages the rapid spread of new ideas and new word concepts for all of us to uptake. If we can communicate then we tend not to fight and the chances of random violence decreases. For example, it has been calculated that if one person spreads a new idea to another person and each of those persons spreads that new idea to another then the idea will only take 30 years to spread to all seven billion humans.

Maybe the ideas of increasing one consciousness language is because it's the best investment we can make in our happiness and understanding of ourselves and others will also spread in 30 years.

I come up for air and after a solid hour and a half in the water giving *Millefleurs* a really fastidious clean, I'm ready for some lunch and a well-earned rest in the sun whilst becalmed, enjoying some tasty food after all the exertion. I muse on the challenge I just passed as I'm sure there are many single-handed sailors who wouldn't get into the water and take a swim around just in case something went wrong. It is definitely a challenge to one's serenity, but I do know that when I let go of what I am, then, and only then can I become what I might be.

It seems that great truths always disguise themselves in contradictions and travelling alone encourages you to forget your tired old self and start laying the foundations for a newer better version. My better version is to create a new part of myself that stands strong and alone, happily morphing from a normally wandering nomad into a totally self-sufficient being. I want to go beyond all those learned fears of my being, not into a crazy fearless base jumper mood that was once my ideal, but into someone else who just enjoys being simple and uncomplicated, who appreciates the joie de vivre of life that arises from appreciating being anywhere, any place, any time, with a profound sense of a generosity of being that makes each day the best possible dream I can have. The contentment I feel sitting here naked in the sun upon a formless ocean is a movement from within that is attempting to get hold of me and draw me deeper into myself and humanity as source, and I feel the glow, the grace of it all like the nostalgia for Earl Grey as a warmth within my heart pushing me on.

The ocean is still and quiet with a low fading swell from the south west and absolutely no wind at all. In the desert only the wind makes a sound and it is the same on the ocean, they are reflections of each other where the wind is the only orchestra. We are literally a "painted boat upon a painted ocean," going nowhere.

I take my time putting away the gear and sit staring at the water to see if

I can see any of those tiny curious fish around the hull, but they're obviously hard to see with the sun reflecting off the water. Then as I stare I see something dart across the top of the water and realise it's some kind of tiny fast-moving critter that must live on the surface of the water. I go around the deck searching for more and I see another one, greyish and probably as big as a pea, but with quite long legs that support it on the surface. Maybe they're ocean "water spiders" who must live out here waiting for the ocean to go still, so they can hunt across its surface.

After spending more time watching for others and not seeing any I realise I'm hungry and a tin of fruit with some rolled oats and some nuts sounds delicious, along with the customary tea. I collect my rations and sit aft enjoying the stillness of the day after all the turbulence, enjoying being still without anything to do. I finish my food and drink and after checking the horizon, decide to take a long sleep while the time is ripe. I head below and am soon fast asleep in my bunk without the lee sheet interfering with my ability to stretch fully out with one foot over the edge of the bunk and the other over the end.

When I awake it's well past 1400hrs and I decide to take a look around, walk the deck, check for breeze of which there is none, nor any sign of it and go below to give the motor a run for some hours. I still have at least 20 gallons of fuel in the main tank and another 5 gallons in a container aft and that gives me a motoring range of 30 hours at 4.5 knots which is nearly 150 miles, almost half the distance to Horta. That's encouraging as I know that without wind and a clean bottom we'll be able to scoot along today, directly for Horta, giving the motor a good work out and getting the oil up to temperature.

I fire up the motor after opening the water valves and soon have solid water pumping out the exhaust and the motor humming sweetly.

I pull in the Jesus line, check for other lines in the water and I'm off like a wild stallion engaging forward gear and heading 80 degrees compass towards the distant horizon. We're soon skipping along, hardly making a wake at 4.5 knots which translates into 110 nautical miles per day and considering I've averaged only half that speed so far, I feel like I'm flying.

I stop *Millefleurs* for a few minutes, watching how she takes a long time to lose momentum with the really smooth bottom and go below to put on Kris Kristofferson, full volume on repeat, to sing above the sounds of the motor and we're off again with music blaring out the sides, the motor pumping white out the stern and the wake 100 metres behind and the sweet whiff of diesel. This is living, this is adventure, this is such fun. No more worrying about keeping my angle to the wind, no more watching the tell tales. We are making our own breeze and its dead ahead and boy are we powering along under an empty sky, a bright sun and much joy. Ah, the convenience of diesel over sail when you're becalmed.

We motor along like this for 5 hours and evening begins to take over and still there's no wind. We've covered nearly 18 miles and I decide to motor for another 10 hours which means we'll still have about 12 gallons of diesel for the run into Horta harbour.

The night closes in with bright stars overhead and the Pleiades big in the Orion constellation, with Scorpio hanging out in the south part of the sky. I always look to Scorpio as my "water diviner" star as I was a November child. I enjoy Scorpio as it's the biggest constellation in the sky, hanging there like a huge coiled serpent, seemingly discerning the nature of the universe, with a ready sting in its tail and the bright red star Antares, in its body.

I remember in particular Fred an American sailor from Texas, who I met in the Pacific in the early 1980s, who told me he was a special Scorpio, believing that there were 3 kinds of Scorpios.

He said there were Rasputin Scorpios who were devious, secretive and cruel while the ordinary Scorpios were discerning, loyal, loving but very sexual, and the spiritual Scorpios who were cosmic minded, searching for meaning and intensity all their lives.

He said he was the latter one, explaining how he had survived Vietnam and on returning to the states had become disillusioned with the small mindedness of society and had taken to the ocean as his solace, finding meaning in the Scorpio constellation as the only true reptilian symbol in the heavens. He'd followed the trade winds around the world keeping Scorpio over his left shoulder for good luck and regularly used Antares in Scorpio as one of his favourite navigation stars.

Fred was a character bigger than Ben-Hur who told me tales of his life in Texas and how he ended up in the military. He told me a wonderful story about the Vietnam war era where he had befriended an Australian soldier from Queensland and during one R&R flew downunder to see his Aussie mate Ken. Ken had quite a large farm by Australian standards of about 10,000 acres, but really a small ranch for Texas. Fred said, "I'd been farming all my life so I spoke his language and knew quite a bit about the land which is why we hit it off so well." The day after arriving Ken took me out to see the farm showing me with great pride the 30 acres stretch of wheat he was growing and I pulled out the old Texan trick telling him back home we usually have wheat in thousand acre lots. Then Ken took me to see his herd of Hereford cattle all weighing in at around 2,000 lbs each and were magnificent beasts, but I told him he should have Texan long horn steers as they handle the heat better and usually weigh at least 3,000 lbs.

He said they were beginning to understand each other by now. Soon we were charging along a side lane back to the farmhouse on our 4 wheeled farm bikes when suddenly a mob of 20 kangaroos dashed out in front of us, bounded down the lane and leapt the fence before charging off wildly into the bush.

I said naively to Ken "what were those critters?", knowing full well he'd spin me a yarn

And he said, "oh those are grey desert grasshoppers - don't you have any of those in Texas?"

I said "no, not yet but we do have Mexican fire ants and those blighters always start the worst bush fires, good job you don't have them here."

Ken enjoyed Fred's stories of Texas being bigger and better than any place in the world, but when I told Fred my Murray cod fishing story he said he'd alter that so he could fit that into his Mississippi brown carp tale.

The last time I saw Fred was a few years later with Dan and the American crew when we sailed back through Tonga in 1992 and in those 5 years he'd sailed around the world again, but he was still single, lonely and using Scorpio over his left shoulder. I wonder where he is now on his 36 foot fibreglass boat, *Francesca*, and ponder how much fun it would be to catch up today, to cruise in and sit for a while, share a beer and jaw over nothing and everything. He was one of those characters I remember well and when I'm sailing with the Scorpio constellation above, it often reminds me of when our paths crossed 20 years ago.

Two wandering Scorpios following our dreams to freedom, hoping we might find our infinity within the oceans or the heavens, and I shed a nostalgic tear for Fred and wonder when we'll meet again. We are all our stories, and Fred added glitter to life wherever he went, as I really resonated to his tales, which I've shared with many others.

I think again about Jake from Key West, similar to Fred in many ways, as that wise old man living in his hut, spending the winters down there and the summers in his hunting lodge in North Dakota. He was not a sailor like Fred, but both were rolling down their dreams. Jake had a fabulous lifestyle which he shared with me over a 3 month stop.

As we were walking around the waterfront one day, before I sailed to Panama in 1992, we were sharing tales about the ocean and travel and those things you do when you commune with a mate. Pointing to some seagull poop Jake asked me "what's the white stuff in that poop?" and I wisely said putting on my scientific hat, "it's lime Jake and big piles of that left in the weather makes great guano fertilizer."

"Right" he said, "I've got it, always wondered about that! "Now" he said, "what's that black stuff then?" and I said "I'm not sure Jake."

He answered with the laughing wisdom of Solomon, "it's just more shit!"

Jake was peculiar in that he received lots of mail but he wouldn't open any. It sat on his mantelpiece as a trophy for all to pick up, turn over and guess what was inside, but never open. As I slipped the lines in 1992 bound for Panama, Jake said casually, "good luck, fair winds and smooth seas Peter" and we hugged like we'd never see each other again, "and when you get to Australia send me back your bloody Australian flag!" that was flapping boldly off the stern pole. I promised I would, and I did, but I wonder if it is still sitting on his mantelpiece somewhere, also waiting to be opened.

As I motor along in the dark with the moon beginning to rise ahead I laugh to myself and make a promise that if I ever run into Fred and *Francesca* again, I'll tell him the beautiful story of my friend Werner, the wildest German I've ever met, who sailed with us from Hobart around Cape Horn and on to Uruguay in 1994. Werner decided he needed to explore South America by hitch hiking all over the continent, back packing, living on a shoestring budget and working for food wherever he could.

In 2000 Werner caught up to me again in Brogo in the state of New South Wales while I was building the castle, arriving out of the blue in an old clapped-out white Mitsubishi van, with a mattress in the back and lots of signs on the side including "no one knows enough to be a pessimist" and plastered across the back "I plan to live forever. so far so good!"

He came into my half-built castle, looked around, scratched his head, made a pot of tea out of dandelions, ginger and garlic and other additives and then sat down, as I lit the fire. Werner didn't drink alcohol as it sent him crazy, so I had some of his tea too and we just sat and communed about

South America and sailing in the Southern Ocean where we almost lost Werner as he went over on the Jesus rope for a wash and almost froze to death, his arms locked up, and he couldn't make it back up the rope. It took all the crew's might to get him on deck and carry him below to his bunk, to recover from the cold.

We sat into the night, I made a meal and we talked about his amazing tales of meeting a genuine shaman in a village in Ecuador who slowly walked around Werner 3 times and, via his son, who spoke English, was able to tell most of Werner's life history.

Then Werner told me about his most recent adventures. For the last 3 months after returning from South America he had got himself some wheels (the van), a mattress and some cooking gear and had headed north to see Cape York at the very northern tip of Australia. It's 3,000 miles up there from Brogo and the roads are very bad at the top and usually it is only attempted by 4-wheel drive vehicles but Werner had used ropes and blocks to get himself across rivers and out of mud patches and had enjoyed the challenge immensely. He said he camped on Cape York for a week catching fish and wild fowl, living the dream of self-sufficiency and freedom that he had followed after surviving as an orphan during World War 11 in Germany.

At the age of 18 he was rescued by an Australian soldier who brought him to Australia to work on his farm, eventually cutting cane and working in many sugar mills in north Queensland. This was Werner's chance to become his own man and he grasped it with both hands, eventually becoming a fitter and turner tradesman and setting up his own business in Melbourne in the 1960s, which was the beginning of a whole new life for him.

For Werner synchronicity ran his life as he loved taking any detour on the road to nowhere and anywhere. I asked what was the most notable thing about going to Cape York? He said he had had the most amazing experience crocodile surfing. Now I was all ears, I wanted to know more.

"Crocodile surfing, that sounds wild!"

And Werner said in his strong German accent "I meet this Yugoslav-Aboriginal man called Ozark coming back from the Cape, and we shared a beer and a fire on the banks of the coastal river where he had his camp. He had helped me cross the river and I felt obliged to share time with him.

After a few hours of sharing stories about life and travels Ozark said to me, "Werner you want to go crocodile surfing? I'm setting up an extreme adventure camp here and thought you might like to be my first client" and

I say "I'm in!" even though I'd never seen a live crocodile in my whole life before.

"So we had tea and then my new friend trains me how to crocodile surf. "I won't bore you with the details", says Werner," but very early next morning just as the sun was rising, we're drifting down the river in his tinnie (aluminium runabout) with the tide right down and the mud banks exposed, where lots of crocodiles were basking in the sun, asleep and taking absolutely no notice of us as we quietly drifted past."

Then Ozark says to me "Werner that's the one!" and I stare down his finger and see this large crocodile, maybe 18 feet long, sleeping close to a solid sand bank under the trees, just waiting for me to crazily turn him into a surfboard."

"We drift down to a bend in the creek and I get out in my wetsuit and gloves and sneak around behind the crocodile and as I'm standing behind him with all my senses on fire I say to myself 'Werner do you want to do this?' I say, yes and then go!

"I run quietly down the bank, gently across the sand and leap onto his back with my gloved hands grabbing him by the front legs, and hanging on like a limpet, giving him a loud smack on the back to hurry him along. Nothing happens for a second," says Werner, "while the world goes still and my heart pounds loudly I notice out of the corner of my eye all the other crocodiles are running flat out for the water and then we take off like a moving train and soon my croc is travelling at an amazing speed, overtaking all the rest with me hanging on, hollering out loud from the craziness of it all, which is my first arranged signal to Ozark that I'm on his back."

"Then we hit the water and we surf for maybe 20 metres across the top of the water, with the croc's huge tail thrashing out behind like a giant outboard, and then we dive and I know I've got to hold my breath for at least 30 seconds as we barrel through the water with me flat on his back holding on like crazy. Then we come flying up almost vertically and hit the surface again as the croc tries to get rid of me, and I throw myself off and roar long and loud again and Ozark comes racing in with the runabout and picks me up. This is crocodile surfing!!"

"F—k Werner" I say "you ever want to do this again?" and he says, "never, but at least the crocodiles seemed more scared than me, which was the real bonus."

I ask "is the guy still up there doing crocodile surfing" and Werner says,

"I don't know, but I did my promised part for his advertising campaign by going into the Cairns adventure sport office and telling them all about it, and they were amazed. They collected his contact details, my photo and they even gave me a free trip out to the reef for my story. In fact, there was a picture and story in the Cairns Post about me being the 'real crocodile man', going further and farther than the famous Paul Hogan's character Mick Dundee."

Now that's what I call a win-win.

Chapter 23

The 30th day

At midnight I stop and shut down the motor. I've covered over 40 nautical miles under power but I need to conserve my diesel for more motoring if this becalming lasts. I really need a sleep after putting up with the roar of the motor, the sweet smell of diesel fumes and the constant noisy helming. I go below, where the cabin is deliciously warm from the motor and collapse into my bunk full of joy for such a top day with promises of more to come, as the smell of Horta gets closer by the hour. I also know that these last few days to Horta will be difficult, as I begin to let go of the solitude and start to think about port arrival, planning for food, supplies and repairs. These last few days will get longer and longer and the hours will drag as I start expecting ice creams and beer and a warm dry bed, with long night sleeps. My mind will become a tyrant begging me to hurry up, to get a wriggle on and time will become more important again, but that can wait as I escape into these closer dreams.

    Today I'm into my 30th day and apart from the limited food everything is going sweetly, just like life on this wide Atlantic ocean. I sleep till dawn, the longest sleep I've had for the whole voyage and I get up just as the sun's rays begin to filter into the cabin and I go quietly on deck and look around. The ocean is flat, there's not a cloud in the sky and the sun is beginning to boom over the horizon. I sit aft and practise doing "quiet time" for a few minutes. Then I haul up a bucket of water, get out some shampoo and take a cold salt water bath, shivering in the cooler air but slowly being warmed by a huge sun that threatens to turn the day hot. I sit back on the stern lip with my feet in the water and meditate for half an hour with a smile for the beauty of it all written large across my face, content with the sheer joy of being free, being wild and being deep into my 30 days and nights of solitude.

By now I don't have to spend time waiting for thoughts to leave me alone before I meditate, they just don't come anymore, unless I'm planning to write or do a task or organise my arrival. On land everyone is obsessed by thoughts, now it's the opposite and I'm free from the mind games that often can go on all day long. It's quite a relief as I stare at things around, taking them in without having any noisy inner conversation. I intuit and feel, much more than trying to think my ways through things. The sense of stillness is all around me, I feel like I'm on the moon and a long way from the noisy metropolis of life.

The stillness stretches out to the horizon all around. There's a new me here, a feeling of being at home, feeling secure and rock solid, able to face any challenge by just being myself, without strings attached to any anchors. It is said "that man is poor, not who has little, but who hankers for more". I know deep down I have changed over these past 30 days and being minimalistic has been a real source of sustenance for my psyche.

I left my home, I left the big house and Mary my wife of 25 years and the two kids behind, not because of anyone's failings in particular, but because I had to go to grow. I had to finally become a seasoned world traveller, enjoying the beauty of life without trying to own it or anyone else and that was a steep price to pay. In the past I would have been born into a country, an identity and a lifestyle that would have owned me and all my friends for my whole life but after being a closet hippie of the 60's and a desperate escapee of the 70's, I began to realise that home is not a piece of dirt, but a piece of the soul.

Now I've joined those 220 million people in the world who live in a country other than their birth and feel at home, showing us that a sizeable percentage of the world's peoples are really on the move as the numbers growing constantly.

Home for me is this new person inside with a new identity, who like a snake has shed much skin to get here, but who is strong and capable and has consciously torn up all those old labels. I'm feeling full of potential and future possibilities and maybe I'll even go north when I get back to Australia and do some crocodile surfing with Ozark.

It's the mystery of life that now draws me on. I well remember Colin a great crew member who sailed with me from England to the West Indies in 1991, who indelibly expanded my vision of China and the sense of life's mysteries as they play out in our lives. He explained that he initially went to

China as a new reporter and over a couple of weeks he gathered information with vignettes of the lives of a number of locals and wrote a long article for an English newspaper that was considered a real snapshot of the typical middle-class Chinese worker, now living in suburbia.

After moving from the country this new city immigrant under the Chinese socialist ideal was finally fulfilling his family's expectations and expanding his vision for a better life. Colin said "I really thought I'd captured the Chinese spirit and I went home all excited and happy, receiving much back slapping and favourable comments on my ability to synthesise a whole new culture from scratch, and then like Marco Polo write wisely about it."

Then he remarked, "I went back to China after 10 years, married a Cantonese girl and lived there for another 10 years and every day has been the 'real mystery.' Every day has brought more and more mysterious inter-connected habits, sounds, aspirations and riddles for what living in a foreign land means. I have finally accepted that after 10 years the mystery is even bigger than I ever imagined with all those Chinese paradoxes, the screw ups, the face-saving habits, the nuances of gift giving, the importance of money and a thousand more reasons for their particular behaviours, that is way beyond my grasp of China as a foreigner"

He continued "their language and culture were so Eastern-nuanced that I didn't have a hope of capturing them, even in 10 books. I then began to realise that my first article of faith on China, written all those years ago, was an embarrassment, showing my ignorance of something so complex," he said, "I finally came to accept that the beauty of China was deep in the mystery rather than the knowing."

This morning as I sit here on the stern content in my day, I also realise the beauty of this ocean crossing is held intrinsically in the mystery and the magnificence of it all. Once I was obsessed with knowing all I could through thought and analysis about the oceans of the world, but after sailing over them many times I now know real ocean living is just accepting things as they are, going with the languid flow of pure salt water and being just content in the moment, with all the mystery.

There is no breeze nor signs of breeze, so I sit quietly and read for the first time on the trip. I make a cuppa and nibble a cracker and quietly read away, enjoying the sheer pleasure of having insights into others' lives doing wild things I'll never do. Through their books they are doing those things for me and I'm sure glad there are so many varieties of people living vastly different lives, having experiences, hardships and major events I could never consider. Of course, to really know something you need direct experience, while to read about something or study it even in minute detail, is to just have awareness of someone's vicarious experiences, but even that is enough for me today.

Noon comes but I don't take a sight as I'm sure of my position, knowing the dead reckoning I've used for years is very close to my real position.

Under the shade of the dodger I sit and relax in the sun playing some quiet classical music in the background, enjoying reading slowly and carefully as if it's the first book I've ever read, trying to feel the author as he vicariously leads me through Chicago looking to buy a sail boat in the great lakes.

At 1500hrs a new lighter cooler breeze begins to filter in from the north, but I can't raise the rig yet as there is no strength to it. It hardly ruffles the surface of the ocean but it has promise. It tempts me as it is cooler than the traditional south west breeze which gives it more oomph, but I think if we attempt to sail we'll just flop around causing more chafe than miles.

I spend time greasing the jib sail track and the mainsail track in preparation and then I go below to check on the motor oil level after it's long run and dip the fuel tank to see how many hours I have left. I ignore the tempting breeze, but after 2 hours I steal back on deck like a voyeur and I can feel it slowly increasing up to 7 knots, which makes steady sailing possible again, particularly if I head a little to windward which is fortunately on a direct course to Horta while gaining us some more latitude miles.

I put on some music and make a cuppa and hoist a full rig and soon we're slipping along at 3 knots on a heading of 40 degrees compass over a smooth sea. It's fun to be off again after that becalmment. Another long night's sleep would have been perfect, but what is is and I'm just happy to be on the road again with Willie Nelson rattling my tired cage, reminding me I must go back to the States again.

I dream and plan to get another van in Los Angeles and travel the northern states, going well up into Canada and the Lakes, across to Niagara Falls and back down the east coast again, probably making it to Key West where I'll sell the van, buy another small boat and head on down to Cuba just to see Fidel Castro.

Life is full of possibilities and another day of dreams, particularly as I realise this is the 4th of July, American Independence Day. I imagine myself amongst all those crowds celebrating and dancing and watching the floats and feeling the joy of being in the boisterous USA. Maybe I'll forget Fidel and go to New Orleans and hang out there listening to jazz and riding the street cars to the old town. Oh, the joy of choice!

By 2100 hrs the sun has gone down and we are in a solid 10 knot breeze from the north and rather than thump along on the wind, I'm heading due east by compass, with the apparent wind on the beam. We're rolling along at 5 knots, on a flat sea with the promise of another long night's sail and lots more miles to Horta on my mind.

I leave Willie playing on repeat as I don't trust leaving the helm and he wails away telling me about *"Lost Love"* and *"Seven Spanish Angels"* and *"Always on my Mind"* as I clap and dance and stand tall, enjoying the stars, the fresh breeze along with the splash and thump of a plunging bow. This is where beauty is pure appreciation of all around. I feel that we're on a railroad track going directly to Horta and I'm the fireman stoking up the wind, keeping the coals hot and enjoying each bump of the train as it speeds along the waves of time.

Each swell lifts me up on a gentle rise and we go down into the valley and on up again, repeating the same pattern endlessly, establishing the regularity of click and clack, lift and fall, bottom and top as the boat becomes another speeding train. I talk and sing to the driver, I cast wishes to the wind, I murmur soft feelings of pleasure as my lover drives me across the waters, remembering this "road to life" is only made by walking it. I look at the stars and imagine the day we discover some other intelligent civilisation in the universe.

We rage along and 2300 hrs comes and then out of the blue Sam sits down beside me and says, "Hi man" and the night takes on another dimension.

I say "Sam we're having a great sail, it's the 4th July for all Americans to celebrate; I've just had a couple of days being becalmed, Willie Nelson is playing solo below and best of all, you've joined us for the party, welcome."

Sam replies "I'm glad to be here, what a great time to visit to see how things are going. Let me have a look around and feel the flow while I tune into these moments before we can sing our beautiful duo with old Willie doing his best to imitate us from years ago."

We soon begin singing loud and long to Willie, almost for the whole album, not saying anything but communing all the same.

Then things go quiet and Sam finally says in a sombre tone "this may be my last visit as your sensitivity to inner realms will diminish as you get closer to the end of the voyage, where the constant streams of thought on rejoining life's melee will take over. Even your sense of humour will diminish."

"That's sad" I say, "your visits have been the real magic moments of this trip and I hoped we'd be able to enjoy the connections for much longer!"

"Sometime in the future that may be possible," says Sam, "put some music back on and let's just enjoy the cool night air, before this breeze runs out and leaves you becalmed again."

Then Sam says in a serious voice that seems to embed itself in my brain, "for no particular reason I'd like you to hold my story for at least 10 years, mulling over my visitations, balancing whether you'll hold yourself up for ridicule or for exposure. Only then talk about it if you dare."

I lock the helm, dash below and put Kris Kristofferson on repeat quite loudly and get back into the cockpit with *Millefleurs* still holding her course. We begin to sing and clap and I tap my feet as we share the familiar rhythm and beat of my favourite music and maybe Sam's as well.

I definitely can hear Sam's voice often much louder than mine as we rollick through song after song, mile after mile and then Sam's voice seems just above me and then behind and then it fades away and he's gone. I leave the music on and sit there enjoying all the images and fun I've received from Sam. He's so close in many ways and yet we travel all alone for the same reasons, knowing that as we travel down the lanes of life the most learning occurs when there are no distractions, when we are all alone.

I look at the time and it's near 0300 hrs and we have made lots of miles and had some great fun as well, but I do notice the sky is clear all round and the cool breeze has definitely eased in the last hour. It's down to 6 knots and I hook up more to the north east to keep *Millefleurs* rolling along sweetly. I decide to sail till dawn and then sit in the morning sun and take notes on Sam's visit, trying to capture his intent as much as his words. I'm trying to make sense of the puzzles his visits have brought, honouring our connections as if I'm giving myself a present, knowing that it'll be a long time, if ever, before I'm in a similar situation that somehow makes it possible to tune to another level of being. Perhaps this level is like the Aboriginal dreaming where the ancestors come bringing advice and purpose to their wanderings, giving deeper meaning to their walkabout life, adding a richer layer that modern man has lost.

Tomorrow can take care of itself, today I'm sailing with my stable mind cruising along as my special friendly companion, adding advice only when I need it, reminding me the wind is slowly petering out and soon we're going to be back to motoring.

At 0800 hrs the wind has virtually given up and the wind spurs on the water are becoming more isolated as I attempt to sail from one patch of wind to another, not because it gives me lots of progress, but more as a challenge, to keep the rig pulling for as long as possible. By mid-morning the sailing game is over for the day and I've taken down the rig and am sitting in the hot sun eating the last of my rolled oats and dried fruits with a little milk powder and the last of the honey. It seems that my food supplies are almost becalmed as well after 31 days and yet it'll be ok even if I have to resort to catching a dorado or more flying fish, which have been few and far between in the last few days.

I go below after taking that proverbial look around the horizon, willing that no ship comes by to interrupt my reverie and soon I'm in the bunk enjoying the becalmment, the sweet feeling of having to helm no more, the beautiful ecstatic feeling of being able to sleep for hours on end without any interruptions.

I wake at midday and go upstairs to check the horizon and inspect the wind situation. There's not a breath of air, we're definitely in the centre of a high that could last for a few days and I'm stoked. I take a walk around the deck, sit quietly in the sun, decide to take a bucket wash and dry off on the stern and then it's back to the bunk again. This is my lazy day, catching up on sleep, doing nothing and apart from having little food, all is well in my world. I do have a few crackers that are very soft and a small cache of peanut butter and after due consideration I reverently dole myself out one cracker, take a small teaspoon of peanut butter and sit quietly savouring the decadence of it all. I can taste lemon rind and fresh yogurt and orange blossom and fresh croissants and jam topped with whipped cream - it's all there buried in the peanut butter, I tell myself, just waiting to be revealed.

The feast takes a good 10 minutes and I ponder on all those other times I've wolfed down peanut butter and crackers without a thought, hardly tasting the food. But now the appreciation of just one cracker and some peanut butter makes up for all the others, long gone. I go back to my bunk satisfied, ready for another long rest.

I wake later dreaming of a ship hooting nastily as he bears down on me, the image is so vivid and frightening that I dive out of my bunk and race up shivering in fear to the cockpit, but there's nothing there. It must be my worries that's drawn that ship into my dreams. Maybe a rogue ship is one of my psyche's nightmares and sits on the sidelines and sneaks up on me when I sleep.

Maybe the worries of always checking the horizon have established parallel paranoid channels in my brain. It's in my hidden psyche somewhere, waiting to emerge when I'm vulnerable. I see we are going to be becalmed for quite a while so I decide to motor for another 6-8 hours rather than have another worried sleep, maybe making 30 miles or more. Then, if the wind hasn't picked up, I'll drift again and then sleep some more.

Horta seems a long way away without any wind.

I put the kettle on, check the oil, start the motor and let it idle for a few minutes before I pour a cup of tea and get into the cockpit for another afternoon's motoring session. I engage forward gear and soon we are clipping along at 4 knots on a slow 1500 revs to save fuel, heading north of east hoping to get to the next patch of breeze just beyond the horizon somewhere.

I decide I need some music to balance the hum of the motor and I indulge myself by slipping *Millefleurs* out of gear, waiting till she slowly stops and quietly going below and putting on one of the CDs that I so far haven't played this trip.

It's John Denver and by the time we're rolling again John is belting out *"Thank God I'm a country boy"* and I can relate to that feeling, after living in the bush as a country lad. Then John is *"Leaving on a jet plane"* and I wish him well and sing along imagining the fun I'll have over the next few days as I roll down the miles, getting closer to the safe harbour.

I pass bits of flotsam here and there as they're much easier to spot on the flat water. A ship comes over the horizon ahead and passes south of us not more than 3 miles away and I wave and wish it well, but of course no one on the ship can see me. I send greetings by offering up my cup of Earl Grey tea. We clip along without any sign of birds or dolphins or even flying fish. It seems that everything has gone on holiday for this calm time, settled down quietly, waiting for the next breeze.

The whole ocean is in repose and I feel out of place as I barge my way over it creating foam, whirlpools and boat swell across the stillness of it all.

I feel like the ocean is my mind and I'm a thought travelling across it, hoping to quietly slide over the horizon leaving no trace behind.

Chapter 24

Flotsam and life

As the voyage has progressed my head's constant demands for more entertainment, more comfort and greater security has diminished considerably. Now I can helm for longer periods of time without a thought challenging my wellbeing. Then it all changes in a moment as I sweep past some flotsam and find a big white buoy with a fishing net wrapped around it half submerged. My passing has disturbed something in the net, and it begins flapping wildly, jerking me out of my reverie. I stare at the flapping and realise it's a sad trapped turtle with its head emerging out of the mess around it and it stares forlornly at me like a prisoner, caught in some bastard's discarded tangled net, slowly dying of starvation and pleading for a favour from the universe.

I cut the propeller and swing around in a large circle using lots of rudder to slow our forward motion and glide up beside the buoy and stop. I turn off the motor so that the propeller can't get wrapped up in the net while the desperate plunges of the turtle cause me to rush down below, grab a sharp knife from the drawer and dive in beside the turtle.

I keep out of its flippers wild arc as it looks to be at least a metre in width and I begin to cut up the net, letting bits fall here and there and then sink. I chop up the net as best I can knowing I need to get closer to the turtle soon, as he'll probably take off dragging remnants behind him with me in tow and then I'll never be able to cut him free. I'm working cautiously and then I have a better idea - get up on the stern lip, attach a rope to the net and haul the turtle closer from a more solid position, where I can cut him free. I do just that using the boat hook to pull the mass alongside the stern lip and a rope to hold it there when I realise I'm panting heavily from all the exertion or lack of food, but as I get closer to the turtle it suddenly breaks free and swims off diving deep into the ocean.

I continue to pull in about 6 metres of net attached to a buoy and I cut it up into smaller pieces and let them drift away until I have the single buoy attached to about 6 metres of black strong line which I finally cut off, bringing the buoy and line on board. At least I have some treasure for my efforts and the turtle has his freedom. I wipe myself down and resume my position in the cockpit, where I restart the motor and slowly head east again.

The ideals of humanity that forced me to stop and rescue that turtle are surely our reliable guides to proper behaviour, as we drift across our own oceans of life, forming synchronistic events when we are forced to see how close we come to those ideals. I know that had I just motored past that trapped turtle, my mind would have called me to account forever, as the existential tension of my conscience would have visited me at 0300 hrs for years to come.

I've never met a killer of some innocent person, but I guarantee they can't walk away unscathed. I'm sure the tension they create in their mind, the guilt they generate, must cause their nights to be plunged into long terror sessions. There's no way they can sleep soundly anymore. Wisdom says when you kill someone even in war, you kill 2 people, them and yourself, and that turtle incident definitely showed that to me. The whole exercise only took about half an hour which is just 2 miles of progress and yet it filled me with an inner glow for being kind to the universe.

I turn off my Johnny Denver CD as he seems a little too trite for the lessons of the day and continue motoring along till 1700hrs when a breeze begins to build from the south east and soon we're in an 8 knot fresh breeze again. I gladly stop the motor, lock the shaft, hoist another rig and head north east on a beam reach. This breeze has filled in so quickly from a point of the horizon that I surely didn't expect, and it reminds me that I am in a part of the ocean called the horse latitudes, dominated by sub-tropical highs to the south and spent lows to the north.

The consistently warm, dry and sunny conditions of the horse latitudes as the summer builds are the main reason for deserts on land. The old sailing ships spent days and even weeks stuck right here, becalmed, with their inability to take advantage of the light airs at this time of the year, while food ran out for the animals. They had to historically push the dead horses over the side in their hundreds.

Fortunately, I can take advantage of the lighter airs with my Bermudan rig and I clip along at 4 knots again without the droning noise of the motor, but I do feel dreadfully hungry after all the exertions of the day. I know that I'll soon have to have something to eat otherwise my stomach is going to become a tyrant again. I do have a few cups of rice left, so I rig lines to the helm and hold course from the galley as I cook some rice in one third sea water and the rest fresh, giving it more taste, and then I plan to accompany it with another spoonful of peanut butter to add to the ambience. I put on the kettle so I can feel like I'm getting a 3 course meal, and while the rice cooks I take my cup of Earl Grey into the cockpit and remind myself that ever since the age of 20 when I was living as a student in rented accommodation in Hobart, I've been Earl Grey's most avid fan.

It was one of those seminal moments in life that changes your attitudes, because the old Polish lady who owned the accommodation knew we were all poor students. One day she offered me a cup of Earl Grey tea, telling me the health benefits of bergamot oil as a tea additive and hunger suppressor. Traditionally the Chinese flavoured their teas with various herbs including bergamot, and Earl Grey was apparently an "illegal copy" of that. The Earl Grey blend in England was named after Charles Grey the British Prime Minister in 1832 who supposedly invented a mix of strong black tea and bergamot oil, and it's popularity has gone world-wide since then on the back of the entrepreneurial British Empire.

I raise my cup to the Chinese and thank them for the gift they gave me via England. In some countries I curiously observe that there are mainly coffee drinkers and in others mainly tea drinkers. The coffee drinking countries do seem to be more agitated and hyper, as I'm sure it's quite as strong a social drug as tobacco. In fact, after oil, coffee is the biggest industry in the world money-wise, and it all goes through the New York stock exchange which helps make the USA the commercial coffee capital of the world.

But here's the twist that happens in most human behaviour. The coffee in the USA is the worst coffee in the world and I can understand them having that bottomless coffee tradition, as there are few who really want more than one. There must be a word for coffee addicts as I've certainly sipped my share, once drinking up to 17 cups regularly in a day while sailing. Maybe we call them coffee-ites, or percolators or beaners and that brings me to common words between languages and how useful would it be to have more shared common words across all countries.

I'd like to have a word that describes the state of the ocean right now other than quiet or settled or still, maybe "seeble" meaning warm and friendly, that we could all share.

As I sail along wondering about this immense mind world we live in I remember that the most common word amongst all languages is OK. It has the same meaning from Russia to America to New Zealand. Another word that seems to cross all languages is f..ck, said with the same explosive breath, meaning "what the heck".

New words that have topped popularity and entered our languages in a wave of modernity are 'tweet' in 2001 and 'WMD' in 2002. Wouldn't it be nice to have more world words to share between languages, particularly about those same things that we all commonly share under the same sky.

I guess what gives science its influence is that all scientists have to share the same concepts and often the same words about the phenomena that they are studying, so the mystery can be tested and verified. There's nothing like the need to solve a problem and a one world language would help a lot.

We sail into the night with the breeze holding steady and the stars twinkling away above. I'm battling again to keep Horta out of my thoughts. The night is dark with only a late moon and the pole star hangs well up in the sky to the north with Castor above Orion and Pollux below and the Big Bear stretching across the sky, keeping his eye on us all. All the cities of the world, all the buses and trams and computers and airlines all seem focused in my Horta vision, along with coffee and baklava and spanakopita and wonderful freshly cooked bread. I seem to smell them all, even from out here.

I know I'm about 250 miles out as a ship comes over the horizon a little north of my track and steams past me heading east. That tells me I'm getting back into the southern shipping lane across the Atlantic, confirming my guestimate position on the chart.

There's a real struggle in my mind as I feel the familiar pull of the stars reminding me I am as attached to them as they are to me and that cosmic part of my humanity, my DNA, is definitely resonant to their magnificence. And then there is the pull towards civilisation with all its wonders and connections and comforts, its music and arts and architecture and writings that I'm never likely to let go. I can understand all the milestones of civilisations past but the majesty of the heavens is a real puzzle, that most of us never consider when we are living our confined city lives.

We hardly ever survey the immensity of it all because the lights of our civilisation blur it out.

The most incomprehensible thing Einstein said about the majesty of that huge universe up there, is that it is ultimately incomprehensible to us. And this illustrates another axiom that whatever meaning we give to that universe has personal value and must be real, because that's how our consciousness operates, going from within rather than without. Like a laser from the mind, making those things we focus upon literally glow in the dark, as the sky does for me now.

I'd like to make another cup of tea as I have ample tea bags, so I complete the delicate and slow process of attaching lines to the helm and rushing below to pump some water into the kettle and then stand in the companionway watching the black tell tales to see if we're still on course, always applying some correction every few seconds. Then back to the metho stove to prime the burner and look up to steer and back again to light the primer and look again to make corrections. And then the critical moment is to turn on the metho valve and light the burner before the primer runs out, otherwise the operation has to be repeated between course adjustments. There's no way I'm ever going to have another spirit stove, I'll settle for gas everytime.

I put on the kettle and wait for 10 minutes as metho is a really slow way of getting heat into the water and then dash down again, pour some hot water into the cup, do a course adjustment and bring the cup into the cockpit, take off the steering lines and sit back waiting for the tea to steep. After doing it for a thousand times, I've become quite efficient and it's become my silent mantra for correcting the patience I lack. No matter how pedantic and slow the process is, I do end up with a cup of tea that is invaluable on night watch. I often laugh at the stupidity of it all and treat it like I'm a circus clown making magic, while holding course. I often call out the steps to my silent audience asking them to improve my sequences and encouraging them to clap the finale, particularly as the kettle whistles and the whole mantra is close to being done.

I do promise myself though that this voyage with the metho stove is my own wise pill moment, and I'll never have such a pathetic slow form of cooking again. If the metho wasn't so poisonous I think I'd drink it and leave out the tea bag!

I'm not sleepy tonight and as midnight flows past and a half moon begins to rise, I slip below not to sneak a biscuit, which I don't have, but to put on some music and enjoy the beat standing in the cockpit tapping my feet, talking to the wind, being in time to the roll of the elements and keeping my thoughts in a locker under the helm.

Daylight begins to colour the morning sky and the breeze holds steady from the south east at 8 knots pushing us onto a beam reach, heeled 5 degrees with the sails driving us on, over a flat sea. I turn off the music and stand and meditate in the morning sun as it climbs steadily above the horizon, just hoping it will suppress my appetite that has to survive for the rest of the voyage on a few spoonfuls of peanut butter and a cup of rice. My shoulder blade has been aching for days and the long hours on the helm have to be interrupted by continually repositioning my shoulder and arm. I don't have any pain tablets to take so it's like the stove saga, grin and bear it. I promise to get myself some Tiger Balm in Horta.

To compensate for the sore shoulder, I've been practising steering with my feet, pushing myself back into the cockpit coaming and extending my leg across the helm. It's nowhere near as easy as hand steering, but it does relieve the shoulder somewhat.

Nature definitely has an increased volume out here and with my lack of inner talk I've been able to delve into matters of the psyche I've never considered before. I'm amplifying the courage to make this journey after giving up sailing, I'm revelling in my new-found certainty, I'm walking within the Tao of just being.

Oh, what a gem that life deals when you take a dive into an ocean of uncertainty and emerge more sure of yourself. I've been able to challenge assumptions and illuminate my fears without anyone to hold my hand. I'm beyond the hushed tones of the forest, beyond the idle clack of a stick along the railings of suburbia, beyond the distant roar of traffic and into some deeper resonant murmur of the ocean that burrows down into my core coming from nowhere and going everywhere. The deep blue ocean is the heart of the earth and it provides so much contentment for us all, particularly when we are sitting on the shoreline watching the waves rolling in. The contentment seekers say "when you cease thinking and begin accepting, when you cease dividing and begin connecting, when you cease worrying and begin loving, only then you will have arrived" and I feel that I have arrived through connecting to this amazing ocean between two great continents - balanced between the old world and the new.

I sail through the morning as if in a trance with the sweetness of nostalgia coming through the music, showing me how quickly pleasure can pass, while contentment lasts forever. There's a flame here that reveals itself only in stillness and I feel that I have slowly merged into the sea, the sky, the stars and the horizon. I become aware of the power and infinite beauty of the whole globe as I float upon this immense, wild, untamed rock in the infinity of the universe, giving me comfort and meaning for all that I am doing. This is all me, all mine, my inheritance as an earthling where I can wage unlimited experiences for the rest of my days. Ecstasy is within my grasp, one breath at a time, no closer no further away than this single moment of awareness.

Memories of those thousands of past ocean miles flood in, allowing me to string my feelings together like a tapestry hanging on the walls of life, resonating to those wonderful movies one has created just through being out there. Looking back and seeing life as a movie, made by past experiences in coloured threads alone.

Even my hankering for cheese or peanut butter or hot chocolate comes through as a form of pleasure from the past, and I know that even if I never get any of these pleasures again the memories alone could sustain me for a lifetime. There is a deep joy that comes when I stop denying the painful aspects of no food or the long hours on the helm or the complications of the furler and just accept my lot. It's a privilege to be free, to be out here getting closer to my mountain top, to just appreciate what I have.

So I push on steadfastly trying to close the gap to Faial, promising myself I'll stop for a noon sight tomorrow, day 33, to get that final confirmed run into the safe harbour of Horta.

I happily sail on into the evening with the light leaking from the day, taking with it those sharp images and clean lines replacing them with shadows, mellowing with the soft light falling on the screen from another day's movie, fading into oblivion. I realise I'll soon have to stop to rest otherwise my shoulder is going to drive me crazy, as it's cries for help are getting louder and louder, drowning out the desire to make hay while this wind blows. I need sleep as much as I need relief from the shoulder and both are beyond any desire for food or cups of tea.

I'm pushing myself to the limit again and I really don't know why I just can't relax and let the voyage take its own shape, rather than the impulsive me trying to take it by the scruff of the neck and shake the last few miles out in haste.

Up ahead I see something glowing strangely, bright pink in the fading light and it looks intriguing, so I let the main right out and the jib fly as we slowly lose momentum and cruise up to this new mystery. I reach for the boat hook and luff up so the "pink thing" bobbing up and down ahead dives under my lee bow and wonder of wonders it's a big white laundry basket floating upright with bright pink handles. Well, how the hell did that get out here, I wonder aloud?

As it begins to come alongside I can see there's a fish in the basket. He's black and about a foot long and through my mind flashes the loaves and fishes story. I reach out with the boat hook to snag the handle and secure my dinner. Manna has somehow arrived on my shores in the shape of a laundry basket and mystery fish! Then I see about 10 other similar dark fish all around the basket, hiding in the weeds hanging off it and at that moment my pet dorados swim out for a look, scattering the fish in all directions.

My heart goes out to the one left in the basket who is obviously sharing it with the others, probably taking turns to feel secure in their own private "lucky ocean home". I drop the boat hook as we glide past, telling myself its probably a fish that you can't eat anyway and I feel guilty for disturbing their freedom, living happily around their "protective shell" where they all obviously hide when the big boys come around. I wonder how long they've been growing with that basket, eating the food it provides, living in the kelp below and regularly getting inside for a secure sleep. They've discovered a fish Eden and I'm glad I didn't upset their existence.

I slowly crank in the jib sheet, pull in the luffed main and scuttle off to the east with my nosey dorados in toe. My loaves and fishes story will have to be replaced by a spoon full of peanut butter instead!

Night closes in and I promise myself I'll stop sometime in the night for a long sleep as I gently massage my shoulder pain. That's the one thing I don't seem to be able to deny. I need sleep more than I need food or pleasure or entertainment. That shows that a rested mind must be the most important thing we have and its periods of unconsciousness seems to outweighs all others. The mind's need to take a break, to go unconscious seems to determine our daily patterns of living where research has found that we all need about 7-9 hours' sleep per night regularly.

Yet for the last month I've rarely slept longer than an hour at a time, waking far too often, too early, even when I'd like to sleep more. But I feel refreshed and my judgements seem fine even though the researchers have found that chronic sleep loss makes sustained focus nearly impossible. I'm sure that we are all very different, but I also know I'd love to sleep for 8 hours tonight and for the next month just for the sheer pleasure of it all.

During all my sailing journeys though I've always been fortunate enough to wake at the least change in the boat's motion and then fall asleep almost instantly. Mothers seem to be able to do that too, otherwise the lack of sleep would be a big biological problem for them with their newborn babies.

Maybe sleep is controlled more by the mind than we suspect, being more malleable to the environment than any timetable, but at this moment I know I'm ready for another session of sleep after I've sailed on for another few hours. At 2230 hrs I decide I must sleep, I actually don't decide, it decides for me. I've been sleep-driving for the last hour, trying to hold course with one eye open, while responding to the jib by listening to it fluttering when I get too far off-course. Unlike the dolphin that can shut off one side of the brain at a time, I try to deliberately practise listening, rather than watching, but I find myself being woken when I get too far off-course, just by the jerky motion of the boat and it's just no fun.

I lock the helm and stagger up to drop the main and almost fall over the side. By the time I realise what has happened I'm half way over the rails with one leg caught in the lazy sheet and my head pointing down the hull with my hands desperately flailing for anything I can grasp, all in slow motion.

I'm a car wreck in progress, I'm sliding down a wet road totally out of control and I'm not sure how I got here. That definitely wakes me up with an ice-cold clammy hand running up my back particularly with no Jesus rope out the back, which I've suddenly remembered I'd forgotten to restore after the turtle rescue. I would have been history if I'd fallen in.

My right leg has luckily snagged the lazy sheet and fortunately it has been cleated tightly back in the cockpit to stop it falling over the side. I gradually and carefully haul myself back up onto the deck and lay there breathing hard. I realise I'm also not wearing a harness as it confines me too much and I don't particularly like the idea of falling over the side being tethered to the boat and unable to get back on board anyway. That would even be worse than drifting away, so near and yet so far. My worst fear is of the boat sailing away leaving me floundering around in my wet weather gear trying to catch up. That could have been realised just then and I make a serious mental note not to get too tired again, and to always, always, put out the Jesus rope when rolling along alone. It may slow me down a small amount and unconsciously that's probably why I didn't put it out, but the consequences could have been devastating.

The jib slaps and bangs as we go off course and we swing beam-on to the breeze as it's noisy tugging on the lazy sheet reminds me in no uncertain terms that I have to get it down immediately before I start contemplating what could have happened.

I drop the jib with a greater sense of awareness and go below ever thankful that I'm inside the cabin safe and secure, rather than over the side lost forever, with family worrying what had happened to me as I disappeared from the face of the earth. The thought of wasting those last few spoonfuls of peanut butter causes me to laugh out loud as I climb into my bunk. It's a sober reminder of how vulnerable we all are and how life often hangs on a thread. I happily fall asleep with a big smile on my face.

I'm a little wiser about the fact that more sleep is definitely needed as I get closer to port. I wake at midnight and go on deck to look around. I note the breeze has dropped again and is down to 5 knots, but more from the south so I head back to my bunk for another few hours' sleep. I know I can't be more than 200 miles out and who cares if I'm another day out here, sleep is the most valuable thing I need now.

I wake at dawn without dreams, feeling dehydrated and amazingly tired. The second sleep has not been refreshing but rather a sombre affair, and I feel heavy gloom approaching. I rush on deck to confront the next "phantom ship" whose been running down my lanes of sleep, rolling over the top of me, creating nightmares in my psyche. There's nothing there again and I hope this doesn't get worse as we close port. I realise the greater prize here is endurance as the more the pressure builds for a safe landing the more concerned I become. I have to conquer these runaway feelings that are emerging from my psyche as the pressure of being run down gains more momentum. It's like that old saying," it's not if, but when" and the big basket of doubt still lingers there strongly.

Those long, lonely nights early on when I was in the shipping lanes with rain squalls all around and visibility down to a few hundred metres have caused these doubts to grow into a tsunami. Evolution is something of a handyman whose long DNA fingers keep reminding me of the dangers of a possible avalanche in my mind as my unconscious fears get "ansy." The longer I stay disconnected from normality the more the chances of slipping over the side seem to grow.

My body's batteries are running down, I need sugars and sunshine, long mooring lines and the hands of love on my shoulders. There's a lonely man inside who is restless and agitated, nervous and worried when he should be happy and content with where he is right now. He is not happy when I nearly let him fall over the side or didn't take care to get more sleep.

He is constantly saying "get a good meal inside you, put on some music and invite friends around for a party." I remember this has happened before when I've been short of food and I'd lost the rapture of rising above it. I have sailed on from it before through necessity and it's either going to wear me down now or I'm going to have to face the reality that food is definitely my big Achilles heel. I remember the Sufi story of the tyrant-general who rides into his newly conquered town and finds everyone has fled. He smiles, knowing that his reputation for savagery has preceded him, but as he approaches the town square there is still one old man sitting on a seat quietly and stoically, feeling just like I feel. The general slides down from his horse, takes out his sword and walks up to the old man saying "do you know I could run this sword through you without batting an eyelid?"

And the old man replies, "do you know I am the only man in this village who could be run through with your sword, without batting an eyelid!"

I know I am that old man and I have to shake off these blues, stop feeling sorry for myself, stand up to the approaching ships, push back the thought avalanche, get my bum off the cockpit seat and get a rig up at least as an act of defiance to those negative realms. Happiness is not about reaching out for more pleasures but also about letting go of the need for them. Forget that spoonful of peanut butter, or the cup of tea and get rolling, only action is going to quell the psyche and settle the nerves, only doing is going to settle my being. I'm soon out of here, "on the road again, going places I've never been" as I prepare a bigger rig to get on the roll.

I hoist the full mainsail in 7 knots of wind from the south and then the big jib, then the mainsail backs but I refuse to complain as I run back to the helm, focusing on the need to be careful and not fall this time, just to get her rolling. I wheel her around in a big circle and gybe the mainsail again and head east north east at 3 knots.

As I complete the circle I consciously throw all my negativity into the ocean without "batting an eyelid", reminding myself I'm off to visit all those neighbours in Horta soon.

I feed out the Jesus rope that is lying on deck behind the main-sheet traveller, feeling blessed once again to be out here having come so far, appreciating the long road I have carved across the ocean that solely belongs to me and I positively switch my attention to contentment which in these last few days may be my greatest treasure. There will be a long time before I can enjoy solitude like this again and in that self-sufficiency stream of living I have to let go of my likes and dislikes, realising I am neither cold nor hot, neither hungry nor full, neither lost nor found, but flowing wild like a wave with life.

I don't have any desire to control anything, particularly the weather between here and Horta, nor ships or more dolphins. That's not my business now really, I'll just get on with the job, take a sight today, sleep when I can, absolutely enjoy my last saved cup of rice and look forward to what life has to offer. I'm a lot better off than that old man sitting waiting out his fate in his conquered village.

I finally appreciate the rapture of the morning sun charging my batteries, sweeping away the loneliness and the dark clouds of doubt and I even imagine that I feel the waves of gratitude flowing from that freed turtle, who is now free to go where his instinctive journey leads. Maybe to mate somewhere in the tropical cays of the West Indies or another 8-10 years living the dream of turtle solitude, wrapped up in mother nature, that provides all the food and comfort the turtle could possibly want.

At 1115 hrs I drop the rig and decide that today is the day I must shave and get ready for this last big position sight, that will hopefully have me pinned down solidly on my dead reckoning chart, maybe a lot closer to Horta than I think.

I want to keep rolling, to make more miles, but I also have to remove my beard and hair again and get social. I set up a bucket of warm soapy fresh water in the cockpit and I collect a mirror and set it up in the corner of the helmsman's seat along with some sharp scissors and lots of razor blades that I have put away for this momentous occasion.

I trim my beard with the scissors and it falls away in clumps that I throw overboard, rather than let collect in the cockpit drains, and a thin faced, white skinny me finally emerges from that rough hairy vagabond look. I soap my face and start the rough process of wearing out five razors before I'm clean shaven, except for my moustache, which I also trim with the small scissors. Then I cut my hair the best I can, turning this wild vision into respectability, watching the old teacher emerge with his suit and tie and disciplined approach to life. I trim the hairs in my nose and ears and my eyebrows and shampoo my hair again rinsing off with the remaining clean warm water.

I watch the blood trickle down from the many shaving cuts that sting horribly in the salty water.

I don't want to float my boat but maybe the warrior has been reduced down to the clerk, and there's a sadness there, like when I awoke from my morning sleep this morning. Maybe I'm sad to be going back into the tyranny of fitting in where all pilgrims face the same pangs of adapting to the rigours of being cloistered again.

I clean up the evidence and throw the soapy water overboard for the dorados and I catch a brief glimpse of them as they lazily emerge from near the stern to check out my contributions to their world. It's small beer but later today or tomorrow I'll get out my shore-going clothes that will obviously be damp and air them out again on the stern, ready for fitting on the last day into Horta.

I'll gather up the boat sneakers that I've hidden in the aft cabin and I'll get out my jeans and tighten the belt a little as I see I've lost a lot of weight. I started out at 78 kilos but I imagine that I'm down to about 70 kilos now, the lightest I've been for at least 20 years. My paunch has gone, there's no flab around my gut and my arms are skinny lengths of well-used sinew and muscle.

I'm enjoying listening to the Eagles blasting their way over the waves from my trusty CD as I get that *"Powerful easy feeling"* of these last few tequila sunrises, realising this journey will soon be over. And the realisations of being alone remind me of the conversations I've had with Sam that were often life changing and mind expanding and that only happens when we go out on a limb, out on the edge and see beyond the west horizon. Bliss is not a place anymore but a state of being where going with the flow, melding into the forces around and enjoying the moment is the real gift of aloneness.

Vulnerability is a two-edged sword - I didn't want to feel it but I had to accept my fate and feel vulnerable and still content in it knowing that I'll eventually make it out of here, a better person than when I entered.

At 1145 hrs I begin to take sights and times, watching the sun carefully as it slowly rises to its zenith and then timing it's fall, getting good sights as

I rock the sextant to let the sun kiss the horizon, right at the bottom of each sweep. Soon I am keenly working out my position, using the nautical almanac corrections to get noon latitude and time corrections to get longitude. I check and re-check and then my calculations placed on the chart give me a lovely reward, yes, yes, yes. I happily see I am a little ahead of my guesstimate position, hooray.

I'm at least 10 miles closer to paradise, two horizons closer to reaching my summit.

I'm 37 deg 30 n latitude and 31.10 w longitude and I have to get to 38.30 n and 28.38 w which puts me 60 miles south and 152 miles west of Horta which is just fantastic. Only another 3 days at the most and even if I only do 50 miles per day I'll be in by midday on the 36th day.

I make a cuppa and take another teaspoon full of peanut butter, which I slowly lick off the spoon, enjoying every nuance of taste there is within its creamy golden folds, spreading it out over half an hour, deliberately taking my time before I get rolling again. While I'm enjoying the peanut butter, I decide to cook the last cup full of rice and stretch it out over the last 3 days to go with the one last teaspoon of peanut butter that I can scrape out of the empty jar, to give it that extra unique flavour.

At 1400 hrs I excitedly hoist my rig and soon we get sailing again, heading 65 degrees at about 3 knots, well off the south west wind that has slowly moved back into its customary position, with another high obviously passing well south of us. We sail all day quietly from one horizon to the next and then onto the next, until I see a huge black shape ahead that quickly shrinks into being rather closer than I thought. As we get near to it I see it's a floating tower about 30 feet high with a large black radar reflector on top and a large steel platform below. Maybe it's a ship's channel buoy that has been washed out to sea, or an oil well marker or some weird contraption that maybe transmits current data to the satellites. I do know though that if I ran into it, it could do quite a bit of damage to my rig. It has been out here for quite a while as the base is completely covered in seaweed and barnacles. I see my dorados checking it out and I hope they stay with it, rather than follow me.

Just imagine that you're floating out here after falling off your boat and you come upon this life saver.

You'd be caught between the devil and the deep blue sea, because no one is coming to check on it, every ship is going to avoid it and soon you'd run out of eating barnacles and seaweed. It would just prolong the agony and I think I'd rather just drown and get it all over. The thought doesn't warrant too much traction though and I promise myself to keep the Jesus line out just in case, and not get into surmising on the blues.

A fishing boat hoves into view and we slowly gain on him as he drifts south, fishing for something quite deep in the water and as I pass only a mile away, the crew waves and go on fishing, poling away in the deep. I could radio asking for his position but language would be a problem and I'm confident of my position. They'd have to come from Horta for sure, even though I can't see their registration name. They have a flag up, just like me, but we pass slowly and I feel like home is not too far away. If these fishermen are out here maybe a day's steaming away, making a living and only going back to Horta when their freezers are full, then it has to be very, very close.

Chapter 25

Closing land

Today the passing wind whispers, nothing urgent, nothing necessary, none of this before that, just let things be as they are. It speaks in soft tones, whispers quietly through the rigging, wonders why I'm here, smiles with appreciation and wanders quietly ahead. There are small swirls of breezes tattooing the waters here and there in random patterns, offering clues through distant traces of where I should head. There are many more birds around as we slowly close land and I'm really enjoying their antics. They're hunting surfacing schools of fish and they look to be big energetic frigates, but it's only when I begin to see gliding skuas that I'll know that land is very close.

A bosun bird comes fluttering along like a lonely drunken sailor, checking out my wake which is pretty ordinary at 3 knots and he flies around for a long while seeing if he can settle on my rigging. I make loud sounds by banging the winch handle on the chopping block and eventually he loses interest and goes away further down the line looking for more friendly customers, hopefully those fisherman.

The wind is light and the seas are flat as we continue to slowly sail along at 3 knots. I'm thankful for the low swell that doesn't knock the wind out of our sails and kill momentum. The sails have stood up well to this voyage, but when we get in I'll wash them down in lots of fresh water and happily wrap them up in their sail bags for the next long leg to Lisbon. I'll check the mainsail for batten chafe and wear on the leech line, but apart from that modern sails provide thousands of miles of wear and tear, quietly dragging sailing boats all over the world. Quietly is the key word as it's difficult to appreciate the beauty of the ocean when it's drowned in the noise of motors.

The ocean is one of the quietest environments on the earth when the wind is light, as there's no rustle of grass or whispers through the trees, it's just like the quiet flow of air across a desert, where the sounds of silence are almost deafening and at night the universe can be heard ringing, while the ocean whispers quietly in the foreground and the two make a fine symphony that few ever experience. It's the sounds of silence and freedom all wrapped together, of mystery and wonder as the universe gently taps our frontiers of perception and sailing along at 3 knots where the boat makes little if any noise at all, with a soft gentle free wind in the rigging is something only a deep ocean sailor can truly appreciate as the water closes around you and no one but yourself knows you've even been this way.

I decide to sleep before the sun goes down so that I'm visible to any passing traffic and with the mainsail still up I heave-to, with the jib backed and the main sheeted hard in, with helm half to port, so if we do move, we'll only go around in circles. I go below promising myself that when I wake I'll have some rice spiced with whatever I have left and again sail deep into the night to gain those extra miles to land.

I go below and am soon drifting in dream land imagining all the changes Horta will bring, all the flurry of things to do, all the gathering of information, mail and emails, catching up with the family and making new friends.

Oh, the joy of a landfall as every extra day out here makes it even more savoured.

I wake as the sun is going down and come on deck to find the breeze is still light from the south west while the air is warm and I'm ready for my last ocean feast. I gather a couple of tablespoons of cooked rice and add some black pepper and some olive oil with a little cinnamon while making a cup of Earl Grey tea and sit back contentedly, imagining that I'm the King of the world.

I have my own ocean, my own spaceship and I have everything here needed to get me around the world, as I mentally plan the next long voyage further south through the West Indies on to Panama and then across the wide beautiful Pacific Ocean and on to sunny Australia.

Firstly, though I'm going to explore some of the 9 islands around the Azores that were settled in the 14th century by the Portuguese. Then I'm going to sail to Lisbon in Portugal and hang out there for a while, enjoying the culture and history of such a vibrant city and try to understand why the

Portuguese see themselves as so very different to the Spanish, even though they are basically and ethnically the same people. I'll moor in the centre of the city and establish a pattern where I'll walk to the city square early in the day and find the art galleries and explore the monuments and buy sangria wine to mix with squid meals and make new vibrant friendships.

I'll listen to music, maybe find some great buskers and drop a few euros into their cups and take ferries and buses, extending my mud map of it all. Then I'll sail over to Seixel, a town just south of Lisbon and hang out there, anchoring free in the river as friends have told me is possible. My mind is at it again, it's out exploring and hunting, leaving me to just sit in the cockpit and enjoy my rice, taking a really long time over each small taste, savouring the future taste of squid and pork crackling and fresh oven bread, mixed with freedoms dreams.

I reluctantly break the spell as port calls, and I put away my empty bowl and back the main and get *Millefleurs* slowly heading north-east again, going slowly downwind in this south wester, hoping the breeze will swing more ahead to help pick up my pace. After half an hour of really slow progress I track back to the south-east and even though I'm heading slightly south of Horta, the motion is much better and our speed is a little higher.

Who knows, the breeze may change considerably in the next few days as we near land, so I tell myself that trying to hold course directly for Horta may not be the best plan.

As night closes in and the hours drag I try to put Horta out of my mind. That's impossible, it's like trying not to remember elephants in the next two minutes. So, I accept the lure of the mind and just go with it making Horta movies and Lisbon stories and then some Gibraltar and south Pacific images as well, gladly letting them all flow together into a smorgasbord of the things that land will finally bring, as I change from being a nomad of the sea to being a tourist again, enjoying all that civilisation has to offer.

2300 hrs comes and we're still slowly heading south east. I know that if the wind stays the same tomorrow I'll gybe north again and continue downwind slowly connecting my dead reckoning dots till I close the gap to Horta, or the wind changes to give me that better angle into the island. The night is really dark without any moon and the stars are amazingly loud with all the big constellations of Orion and Cassiopeia, the Big Bear and my favourite Scorpio singing in the sky. I spend time watching the Pleiades trying to see the 7 stars clearly when someone sits down in the cockpit beside me and I say "Sam, you're back!" and he doesn't answer. I continue the one-sided conversation to try to get some response, but there's none. It's definitely another "flying carpet man" but it's not Sam, and I feel kind of honoured that there's someone else here who can slip into my energy field so easily.

I question whether it's my grandmother who I was very close to, or my dad who died just a few years ago, but I get no resonance there either. This person has a different resonance to me as we're not communicating, but he hangs there in a neutral state, neither threatening nor friendly, finding his own comforting space in my cockpit.

Maybe I should ask him for rent and then I get an image of him as a Japanese flyer from World War II, he's lost his plane and is roaming the ocean for it. There's no logic to my intuitions, no tests of objectivity or supposed truths but I feel these images as they arise spontaneously, satisfying my need to know.

I try to communicate again but he sits there and I can hear him breathing quietly and steadily but he doesn't want to talk, so I just steer and commune, happy to have another unexpected mate. I begin to sing quietly, reinventing *"Goodnight Irene"* as I don't know all the words, but my singing brings no response either. Then I begin whistling quietly as he sits there in a kind of limbo, hopefully enjoying my auric presence, just as I am perceiving his.

Maybe he's a lost pilot who has died over the ocean, running out of fuel, crashing and wandering lost, just trying to get back home. Maybe he's a suicider who just needs some company or a kamikaze pilot who missed his target. He is a part of humanity though, just like me, like that trapped turtle, so I do have a responsibility to accept him as he is and just sail on doing my thing, without any judgements at all, without any annoyance. I begin to send him lovely feeling vibes, as I smile and imagine that I'm telling an old friend how this Japanese guy visited me in the night, and he's telling me I'm losing it.

I begin talking loudly to "Mr Tokyo" as if he is an old friend who's just returned, explaining where I'm headed and where I've come from and other snippets of information that I can add, and then, after half an hour he's gone. Poof, he's out of here, the cockpit is empty, there's no more breathing and he's off to some other party in town. I wish him well and I'd like to go with him if he's heading for Horta to get some fried chicken.

I intuit that I'm having a two-way conversation with this bit of the universe within my horizons and it's on another level to merely being an observer because as I tune to the bigger fields around they also tune to me. There are strong contributions from other parties unknown to me and I am just the information gatherer peering over the edge of the mystery, seeing a little further into my infinity and it strikes me that maybe this is the hidden reason we all go on long voyages alone. This voyage has definitely been first and foremost an act of self-discovery.

I've gone deeper within and time has slowed as a greater intensity for being and another depth of feeling has emerged. My taste buds are richer, the colours around are sometimes emotional and the serenity is powerful. Oh to be a lone sailor on my sea.

Living on the edge is intense, wild, magical and I know I am richer for the experience. Richer, spiritual, transcendent, alive and one of the fabulous senses of being truly alive inside myself will come from having a continuity of memories to which I can feel entitled, later down the tracks of life.

The breeze is hardening a bit, it's up to 8 knots and, wonder of all wonders, the universe is favouring me by letting it swing to the south some more, and I can now sail due east. Maybe my Japanese visitor was one of the wind gods checking me out and he's out there now swinging the breezes in my favour, because I've been kind to him. I was thinking about calling it a night before the breeze hardened, but now I'll use this breeze as best I can and continue rolling along into my 34th day, marking off mile after mile, like a big countdown.

Yeah, I'm now 'the countdown kid'.

We roll past midnight and into the early hours of the dawn and I'm cautiously optimistic that the breeze will hold and we'll be in soon.

I look for planes but the sky is empty of those civilisation signallers and what I wouldn't give for some passing plane to drop me that longed for croissant filled with ham and cheese. I try hard to imagine how it could happen, but eventually realise some things are even beyond the tall tale scenario. There's no chance I could make up such a story with a twist in it that would have any credibility. My friend Terry who sailed with us on *Sundancer* in the late 1980s and is now a big boy pilot, said he could remember when "sex was safe and flying was dangerous" showing you that things can change quickly, particularly in our day and age.

Instead I get another spoonful of spiced rice and add the last scraping of peanut butter and some more olive oil, taking all of 10 minutes to balance the helm and get the feast together, while all the while questioning why

I'm doing it, as soon I'll have more food than I can possibly handle. Sitting back in the cockpit under a rising small moon I realise it is all worthwhile as I savour the tastes again like an old friend. realising that food does bring great pleasure in life, certainly not as intense as sex and love but still fantastic, while those who rush into their food like I've often done in the past are missing out on an awful lot of pleasure.

If I had been smarter I should have stocked up on more food for this voyage as going on a long haul and sailing as a minimalist is courting disaster and missing wonderful cuisine pleasure. I take another spoonful of rice and some extras and sit quietly watching the night sky, checking for ships and fishing boats, listening to the gentle murmur of the passing ocean bathing under a sinking moon and try to see how I can consciously extend these food flavours.

I've heard of restaurants without lights where you eat in semi-darkness and apparently it is amazing how sight and the size of the eye's bandwidth in the brain suppresses many of the flavours in our food.

Perhaps the old cave man cooked his meat outside and then dragged the spoils into the cave to be shared in the dark, enhancing his sense of smell within the whole salivating process. That kind of image certainly passes muster, whereas the plane dropping me a meal doesn't.

As I take the last small spoonful of rice and peanut butter I promise myself that I'll take time to savour it always, refusing to think or talk as I extend its powers, following my now intense taste buds to some oasis under palm trees where contentment lives "lime marinated" in south seas trade wind breezes, amid a lazy island lagoon surrounded by noisy reefs quietly reflecting the moon.

I decide to heave-to for an hour and get another lazy hours sleep. I turn on the masthead light, lock the helm and go below thankful that I'm so close to finishing this leg of the voyage, remembering that during the hurricane I was even considering turning back to New York to fix my self-steering gear, maybe getting another GPS, replacing the furler gear before getting on the road again. I'm pleased that didn't happen because I'd still be weeks away from here.

Perhaps the hurricane and the self-steering loss was just synchrony messing with my plans to have an easy ride across the Atlantic, once again supporting my ideas that too many plans get in the way of enjoying life as it unfolds, while we all are desperately trying to stay in control. Bernard

Moitessier once said after his historic long voyages at sea, that the greatest discoveries are those we make about ourselves. So synchronicity, or the guiding hand of fate may be one of the greatest discoveries we could tune into in the future, where we go into a portal for adventure, list all our details and it chooses where we'll go for our holidays.

It'd be a brave man who lists minimalism, solitude, adversity and hunger as his top priorities, because this is what fate has dealt me this time, and I'm really grateful for all the memories it has provided, but I don't plan to repeat the exercise anytime soon.

I wake at 0300 hrs and get some more warm clothes on and go up to the cockpit to take stock. The masthead light kills my night vision and I go below and turn it off and emerge keen to get a better sense of the sailing conditions without the light to spoil the beauty. It's day 34 and my calculations before sleep showed me I was about 110 miles out, meaning my average 60 miles per day will get me in in 2 more days.

That's just beautiful as I am disciplining that urge to hurry up. I want to take it easy, sail when I'm ready, sleep often and cruise in better than when I started. I boil the kettle, check to see that I have about 3 teaspoons full of cooked rice left and I debate whether to eat it now or wait till later. After some long deliberations between immediate satisfaction and later joy, I decide to save it for tonight's feast, with the last few scrapings of peanut butter and truly celebrate another long day done.

I make myself a cup of tea and go up to the cockpit and sit still for a while, searching the heavens for aircraft, the ocean for ships and anything out of the ordinary. I note the pole star is very big and bright and cold tonight as it's twinkling lights beckons me to take a sight which I could do even under this pale, weak moon, as the horizon is crispy clear. I eventually decline, trusting in my dead reckoning navigation as I plot the miles and angles coming slowly down. I don't need any more confirmation that my landing is close. I hoist the rig for the thousandth time, getting the mainsail up first and then the jib, tensioning the halyards, occasionally lubricating the tracks and working my way back to the helm and get rolling off to the east.

We're beam reaching to an 8 knot southerly that is warm and friendly, filling the rig with optimism and purpose, taking us happily on the last legs of this journey. We're soon rolling along at 3.5 knots and I know that if I were to put up the no.2 jib we'd be doing 4 knots, but the effort isn't worth it as it would just make me even greedier for more miles.

Dawn is getting closer and the change in the moon's lasting influence and the sun's overwhelming power is now balanced on a knife edge, and then I hear a flapping on the side deck and I know I've been handed a flying fish who has flown into the cabin side while the moon was reflecting off the cabin port lights.

I lock the helm and sneak up along the deck like a big tabby cat, following the occasional rustle till I find my wonderful prize lying stunned beside the deck coaming. He's about 10 inches long and I gleefully gather him up, snap his neck and take him back to the bucket in the cockpit for a later very welcome snack. He's longer than my hand span and will certainly satisfy my appetite for a whole day, particularly when added to the rice. How lucky was that, maybe that Japanese flyer sent me a flying fish to warm my heart. Sayonara!

Dawn comes and I stand in the sun naked and brown, getting some colour in my face after the shave and feeling like an ocean warrior who has just discovered he is totally self-sufficient. The breeze feels light with a little cloud to the south west, perhaps heralding more wind later. I've got that old thousand yard stare going on as I survey the scene, the morning is wide and bright and honest and I'm trying to take it all in at once.

Farmers get that long stare and so do fishermen and today it tells me the ocean is ready to take a breather. I meditate, slowing my breath and drawing in the sun forgetting all thoughts, feeling fantastic knowing this day could be one of the most valuable days of my life. All the hard work is done, I've climbed near to the top of my mountain and am looking over the edge deciding where to land.

I've just got to keep sailing towards each horizon without expectations, keep the wind in the sails, keeping content with that generosity of being that fills up the whole boat contentedly, making me King of my world today.

I can't ask more than that as I stand on the side deck watching ahead for more flotsam as there is something odd and bright white ahead, reflecting off the sunlight and then disappearing in the swell. Treasure I think, maybe a net with fish in it, maybe a box of bananas, a Mike hat or a hamburger in a polystyrene box, left for me by the gods. I get closer and closer and the excitement rises as it's definitely out of the ordinary again. I reach for the boat hook to scoop it up but as it passes the bow I see it's just a poor dropping from civilisation, out on its own journey. Damn it's just a white polystyrene plate, floating upside down, tossed casually aside by some passing fishing boat crew and left out here as a crumb marker for my trail to Horta.

I thank them for it, smiling happily at the possibilities it arouses in my imagination of what it once held and I'm sure as I close land there will be many more signs of modernity upon the waters.

A cloud of flying fish take off heading south-east up into the breeze and I imagine my dorados are still with me, rather than staying behind with that floating marker and are hunting those flying fish off the bow. These are the first flying fish I've seen for days and maybe there's a warm current around the Azores that brings them this far north. Then a pod of dolphins swings by from astern catching up to me and playing around the bow.

I run down and put on my Willie Nelson CD and begin to entertain them as they gambol and cruise around coming alongside the cockpit, where I begin tapping out the beat on the hull with my hand and whistling like a wild man again. They appreciate my efforts as they play around me going along at my slow pace, rolling over and diving alongside and then suddenly barrelling out to the side and leaping full bodied out of the water. These dolphins are smaller than the big tropical bottle nose dolphins, they have white markings along their sides and their tails have greyish speckle patterns.

I have seen them before as they are the same size as the tropical spinner dolphins, but shyer. In fact, there are about 38 different kinds of ocean dolphins and 5 river dolphins, so not knowing which type one is seeing is to be expected.

These guys are more nervous than the big tropical fellows and soon they've grown impatient with *Millefleurs* and are off again heading on to the same horizon as me. I even wave them goodbye, thoroughly enjoying all the intense activity that is blossoming around me today.

Today is 8th July and we're in mid-summer with the sun very strong overhead, forcing me to put on a t-shirt and wear my Panama hat as I crouch under the bimini,, sitting on the side of the cockpit coaming, steering with my bare brown feet. I slip below and change Willie for Kris Kristofferson and sing along happily, whiling away the hours till noon, as the breeze begins to pick up to 10 knots and we are finally doing 4 knots straight to Horta.

I trim my fingernails and rub some oil into my dry skin and my face, remembering that it's soon time to fit in and look my best. No good arriving in dreadful shape looking as if I've swum all the way, dragging the boat behind me. When I land I want to be in the best shape possible. Clean clothes, hair combed, teeth cleaned and wearing new underwear. In fact, in my Sunday best as grandma used to say, feeling like you "own the place".

When we came into port off long passages on *Sundancer*, I always had the crew dressed in their best, showered, washed and looking fantastic and that way the customs never gave us trouble or delayed granting us visas. I always thought a good impression comes from wanting to fit into land again, leaving the bad impression of those past historical hard drinking, fighting sailors behind.

Chapter 26

Horta ahoy

In the afternoon the wind begins to drop again and soon I am battling to keep the rig full, as this soft gentle breeze falls below 6 knots. I am trying to move from one eddy to the next and then having to finally drop the jib, as it's continually trying to wrap itself around the forestay. I clean my freshly delivered flying fish, taking off the scales, throwing out the gut and marinating him in soy sauce and oil, finally leaving him in a bowl in the sink.

I hope this becalmment doesn't last too long. So near yet so far, but at least I'll be able to sleep and be easily seen as I leave the mainsail up in such a light swell, vanged (tied down) to midship and occasionally belly flopping as we gently roll and creak. I go below to sleep holding the pleasant intention that when I awake I'm going to cook the fish and use the last of my rice to make a beautiful meal.

I leave the hatch wide open in the warm air and am soon enjoying being gently rocked to sleep before another pleasant night's sail, if the breeze returns. I wake before dark and after taking a look around get out my trusty pan and cook Mr flying fish till he is near crispy, adding the cooked rice in the last few minutes to get it warm, and then tipping the marinade all over it. I make a cup of tea and take my feast upstairs and sit quietly enjoying the last of the day as the sun dips below the horizon. I'm taking my time over the absolute last of my food.

I thought the trip would have taken me about 25 days so I have done reasonably well to have food last another 10 days. The flying fish is so delicious and crunchy compared to the rice, that is soft and spongy and the two add another level of texture to such a fine meal. It's my last supper I trust before Horta and I even imagine I'm having some sangria with the fish, disguised as water.

I promise myself that when I get in I'll buy a fish and a bottle of wine along with some greens and more herbs and have a really fine feast. Night closes in and the wind is still rather fluky from the south and I don't expect there will be much action tonight. I work out that I have about 20 hours motoring at 4 knots, so I start the motor and promise myself to motor till midnight and if there is no wind to stop and sleep till it comes knocking on my door.

With the wind being fluky at 4 or 5 knots from the south I use the main to help drive us along as we create our own breeze and soon with the help of the motor at 1600 revs and the mainsail we're skipping along at 4.5 knots, quietly motoring down the remaining hundred miles that'll take us at least another day.

We motor on till midnight with the night so dark I can hardly see the sails, and after making another 20 miles, I stop. If I had enough fuel I'd motor at least till dawn when the wind is likely to return and Horta would be only about 50 miles away.

I turn on the masthead light and go below for another sleep sojourn. Another couple of nights at the longest and the struggle will be all over. If only I had more fuel I'd be in earlier, but it is what it is. I wake after maybe an hour and there is another "mind ship" bearing down on me. I rush up to the cockpit to see with relief the lights of a fishing boat to the north of me tracking well away from my position.

There is still little wind, with a clear sky and the stars are huge with a small feeble moon part way up the eastern sky. I trek below and light up the stove to make a cup of tea while hunting around the galley to see if I've missed something exotic, like a biscuit or piece of chocolate or a muesli bar, but after the third time of doing this I realise the cupboards are bare, and solid reality has come to trump hope.

I let my mind wander off around Horta and the surrounding islands trying to remember details from the last time I passed through there in 1994 as we were heading for England on *Sundancer*, after coming up the Atlantic from Brazil. Both Brazil and the Azores are part of the old Portuguese empire that faded in the 17th century. We spent a week in Recife, a northern Brazilian harbour, recovering from the long haul from Hobart, Tasmania, around the Horn, onto to the Falkland Islands and then on up the coast of Brazil.

There inflation was running at 12,000% but things weren't cheap. A tube of silicone cost US$20. I thought that with the huge rise in inflation things may be cheaper if we held US dollars, but the reverse was the finding. The valuable US dollars had to be changed into fading local currency before we could buy anything, while the banks were undoubtedly swinging things in their favour with their dreadful "last week" exchange rates. I asked a businessman how he survived and he said he changed the prices of all goods every week and altered wages every two weeks and if he borrowed $10,000 dollars today in a year he'd owe over a million dollars.

That was a real eye opener to how government policy can implode a country's economy, so it was such a relief when we arrived in Portuguese Horta after suffering Brazil, to find that the currency was stable and stores were much cheaper, even though most things were being imported from Portugal.

I hitchhiked around Faial island which was full of hard-working farmers and found the most amazing blue hydrangeas which were introduced to the island centuries before. Every island has a different coloured hydrangea due to the rich volcanic soils.

Horta has a population of about 15,000 and was originally an historic whaling port with scrimshaw (tattoos on whale bone) still being one of their biggest tourist bonanzas. Being the capital city of the island of Faial, Horta is a safe harbour for any yacht on their Atlantic crossing.

Now there's even a bigger harbour marina for all the visiting yachts and it is a very cosmopolitan place, drawing thousands of international yachtsmen every year. This is my memory target and the longer this breeze plays dead, the further away it seems. Apart from dreaming of land and looking for other indications of land, I am effectively stopped and waiting for the train to leave the station again.

So, I go back to my bunk and sleep some more, waking without any more feelings of impending doom, taking another look around and again going happily back to my bunk. This is such a luxury and I feel as if I am in a time warp quietly waiting for the clocks to run again when I'll be off on my way.

Dawn drags itself up from the horizon and the sun begins to wake up each wave, giving it a sparkle as it gently rolls by from the south west, offering hope for another good day's run.

I walk around the deck looking for more flying fish and consider having a swim but decide that if there are any nasties in the water, being this close to land means we could possibly meet. Then I notice a Portuguese man-of-war gently drifting around with his purple sail held high, hoping for a breeze to blow him along as well and I can see his tentacles hanging below him for at least 5 feet. I'm pleased I didn't go in for that swim as brushing those tentacles can deliver a powerful sting that other sailors have told me is like pouring boiling water on your arm, and unless it is washed in vinegar to neutralise the stings, large welts are often seen for days afterwards. Their sails are a beautiful pink held up above the water as they drift along and their major predator is the loggerhead turtle whose skin is too thick even for their fierce stings.

He's actually the first man-of-war that I've seen on this trip which means there is definitely a warmer current sweeping up from south, which the whales used to relish after leaving their Arctic feeding grounds.

They would then calve in the warm Azores waters where there used to be a big whaling industry.

Three dolphins, the same species as yesterday, come by with their mottled skin but they don't stay long as they're heading south east, eager to be on track to some unknown place, way up ahead of me. I feel envious that they can travel freely without the need for wind, going faster than I can go and picking up food on the way. Apart from needing company they are self-sufficient and I wonder if humanity is connected to the dolphin consciousness in some way as our DNA came from the ocean, thousands of years ago. Maybe we grew arms and fingers that have given us the ability to conquer the land while the dolphins have brains as big as ours while needing no manipulative skills to conquer the ocean.

Could humanity's hands and fingers, as extended probes for the brain, along with our sharp decision making, give us such an edge on evolution? Or could our search for meaning give us a more valuable edge in becoming self-aware.

Our search for meaning only becomes self-fulfilling when what we reach for, eventually reaches back, giving us our freedoms and abilities I suppose, way beyond what the dolphins or whales have.

I ponder awhile and then over the next 20 minutes the first ruffles of a breeze catch the surface of the ocean in various spots and after another 20 minutes they all begin to connect up and we have a steady breeze from the south again, that fills in at the usual 8 knots.

I'm busily running around getting up the new rig, spinning *Millefleurs* around to be on track to the north east again and galloping off with my thoughts and my cup of tea, celebrating by standing in the cockpit with the helm firmly grasped between my knees, while Willie Nelson plays softly below.

It's 1100 hrs and at 4 knots we're down to our last 100 miles and only a day's steady sailing from port. It's day 35 and my antennas are up for signs of land. I'm watching for birds like the skuas or insects floating past or clouds over the land. It's long been realised that the antennae of insects, the feathers of birds, the tails of animals and even the vertebrae of man are intricate receiving stations necessary for navigating, feeding, flocking and escaping predators. Even if we took away all the modern navigation tools I'm sure we'd still be able to navigate on our 6th sense as the Pacific Islanders do or the African tribes or the Australian aborigines.

My 6th sense is saying land is ahead just like the great Polynesian navigators did as they cruised the Pacific for centuries trading between islands, extending their territory to all the smaller islands and even down to New Zealand. The Australian aborigines walked the deserts from water hole to water hole for hundreds of miles using their 6th sense alone with the stars as their guides along with messages from their ancestors keeping themselves positioned in those trackless wastes.

I'd somehow like to continue their tracks and learn more about how they do it. They were able to remove the shoulds, the ifs and the maybes and work on the whys and that's me today tuning into when I should hit land tomorrow. Perhaps my energy field is fusing with Horta as I can almost feel land slightly to the left of dead ahead and I steer more to the left trying to follow my nose that has often led me to land when I've been out of sights before. I'm like a blue heeler sensing something is changing and I'm on to it! There's dog food somewhere ahead!

I pass another fishing boat, the crew waves and I know I'm definitely getting there as I spot more bits of wood and plastic in the water and even a tennis ball that has escaped its owner and bounced away to sea. By 1600 hrs I'm seeing big cloud banks ahead but there's no sign of land and by 2000 hrs I still seem no closer to the clouds, but I can definitely smell diesel smoke.

I heave-to with the rig up and do some more dead reckoning on the chart. It says I'm about 30 miles out and I decide to sail on till maybe I can see some lights of Horta or catch other signs of land.

I sail on full of hope and expectation knowing that even though I'm hungry, tomorrow will bring every bit of food I need and more. I cruise on for another 4 hours and after passing another squid boat with his lights glaring brightly across the ocean, I wait for him to disappear and then I stop for a sleep. It's past midnight and I get ready for my last sleep with the masthead light on and the radio turned low in case I hear any traffic. I even leave the rig up, hove-to for these last few hours and go to my bunk ready for the big day ahead.

Memory moments come to me of all those days ago of the hurricane and when I was lying in my bunk waiting for the end and then being brought back to reality by being squirted in the face with water coming through the hatch boards. At that stage of life, I was down a set and the weather was serving aces. But I struggled back and if I was meant to die then that would have been the moment in this trip.

I remembered that other awful moment in the Pacific in 1990 when the winch handle skewered me and I thought it was all over as well and still I came back. I even remember floating in the waters off Tasmania in 1971 as my friend's 6 year old boy had fallen off the boat, and now was crawling all over my face, as I was treading water trying to rescue him. I had all my heavy gear on and was desperately trying to get a hold of something solid on the side of the boat, causing me to sink even further. I was running out of air but I eventually pushed him away as Alan his dad closed in on us and grabbed him. I managed to get to the surface and take my sea boots off, allowing me to swim again.

Phew life certainly challenges us all and it's nice to know that when the end does eventually come, it's always quiet and gentle and without the urgency that we imagine will overtake us.

Right now, I feel all the beauty and thrills in having survived my latest water ordeal and am close to completing the long run into a safe harbour. The fruit of experience is surely the ecstasy that feeds the soul and I feel full up and overflowing with the natural high of surviving this long, lonely trip. The ocean has tested me on many occasions, taking me to the edge but not quite over and the search for my limits were always within rather than without. That was comforting.

Even if I was a millionaire and owned all the toys in the world, not one of those things could have saved the day in those desperate moments, and now I am here ready for a sleep, ready for the big day, ready for an end to this long haul that has been casting the daily dice for too long. I now know the veil between reality and unreality can easily be ruptured when you're sailing alone, but fortunately I've kept my marbles and can smile at the tales I'll be able to tell.

I come on deck at 0230 hrs and take a close look around hoping to see the glow of Horta but the sky is so clear it's hard to see if it's lighter in any direction. I sit on the water containers at the stern and rest my chin on the rail, stare into the distance and feel life's deep exuberance as I put the final brush strokes to this sailing mural. Then a falling star streaks across the sky like a long flash of lightning and sinks into the horizon just ahead and I know for sure that Horta is just over that north-easterly horizon, synchronicity has spoken again.

I feel expansive and light and cosmic and then I hear Sam's voice a long way off laughing and he faintly but clearly says, "made it man, I'm sending you a blessing" and there's more far away laughter as the universe goes quiet again.

And I smile and raise my arms realising that everything we do eventually increases our chances of knowing something more. I go slowly and reverently back to my bunk. I sleep for a few more hours and wake at dawn, and I feel fantastic, just like on Christmas morning as I get up and put on some warm clothes and go on deck.

It's 0500 hrs and I can definitely see the glow of Horta against the darker land clouds away to the northeast and that says it's not more than 30 miles away. I'm back, as I stand in the cockpit I smile the biggest smile I can, for a long, long, time and the feelings that come when you stop banging your proverbial head against the hard wall, are just beautiful. After this longest and loneliest journey on my own, with the breakages and failures of gear that have made it a third longer than it should have been, I'm almost done.

They say that any noble adventure absorbs huge amounts of energy but it is always worthwhile when it repays that investment with interest. And after the long struggle with the uncertainty of ships and dodgy weather creating more turbulence than I was expected to handle, I have finally opened to both the ocean's unpredictability and magnificence as my own well-earned interest.

As I swept aside my expectations and uncertainties and deep fears the ocean has opened to me and that is the difference that has made all the difference. That virtuous circle of opening to the universe, that we all need sometime in our acceptance of the "nobility of living" has turned my fraught and painful adventure into a beautiful personal odyssey. Now it all feels worthwhile. The critical juncture was my mind's search for meaning and an inherent trust in my being for inner harmony that have fused magically together. They have melded into a fusion of acceptance and understanding where I feel a much better person for the trying. They say that when life becomes more fractured than it should and things go haywire much further than they could, then it becomes a way of the soul.

That creative spirit resting within, waiting to stretch us to our limits, calls time out at the peak of our desperation, making us more profoundly whole again. After all, why should the human spirit call us to regularly stretch ourselves, unless there wasn't some profound personal growth within the exercise?

I make a cup of tea, possibly the last for the voyage, and sit quietly watching the cloud bank over land, waiting for the sun to shine through, maybe glinting off a high point on the hills, or the dark of a forested valley, letting me know with certainty that we have arrived. The wind is still light, having dropped off to about 5 knots from the south and the water is flat indicating that another high is over us and this becalmment may last for days.

My ace card is the gallons of diesel I have in the tank, sufficient to motor at least 50 miles. I get the scissors and razor out and after polishing my tiny hand mirror I tidy up my hair and snip the eyebrows and overgrown moustache so I'm harbour ready. I hold the mirror close and take a long look and see that there are bags under the eyes and tiredness written all over the face.

There's a 57 year old man here who looks 10 years older. I can make this man smirk and I can make him smile, flair his nostrils or even weep, but I slowly let acceptance and joy creep into his countenance. I know this morning I must leave his image alone, let him be, there's enough on his mind and he's not really me - there's someone else inside, different to when I set out months ago. I've just become the voyeur and I'm forced to set all assumptions aside and take a longer look at myself.

A tsunami has happened behind this lined face exposing the best and the worst in stark detail and it's something I need to live with, to share and enjoy and carry with contentment, right into my old age. I smile again and bid him adieu and put the mirror away - life lived hard is so revealing and yet so rewarding.

I give the cabin a thorough spring cleaning, making up my bunk and check the motor for oil and start her up. Yanmar diesels are so reliable and this one is my third, so I'm familiar with its magic and soon we hoist the mainsail and begin motor-sailing to Horta.

We roll at a steady 4 knots on a 60 degree heading with the Australian kangaroo flag flapping out the stern and the courtesy European flag flying from the starboard spreader. I don't want any music to drown out my impressions of coming in off the run, coming into port with all its magnificence, with the buildings growing in stature and the cars racing along the road and then people standing and watching another single-hander making landfall, possibly wondering where he came from.

This is my day for personal glory, for self-adulation, for appreciation of the being that I am, for living on that edge again, and I intend to enjoy every moment of the slow wind down.

I intuit that this journey is not so much a subject to be examined but a lens for seeing something more, beyond all those sail changes and long hours at the helm. There is an old truism that the more difficult the adventure, the more rewarding the experience. I intuit that because this journey has been full of puzzles and tangles, mazes and ladders that have varied each day, at the end of it all I will not be the same person who began. It has certainly been an exercise for seeing what is possible, when there's nothing more to leave behind. I certainly feel a deeper connection to those vicarious theatres of life where we see every man framed in his own microcosm of living, battling with his weaknesses to rise above the common frailties of life, and that's maybe why we go on long and lonely retreats to experience the same with our own lives.

Fortunately I've been framed through my own lens and as I lift my eyes I see the loom of a lighthouse slightly to port and somewhere in the near distance, I slowly swing towards it and measure the timing of the sequence of flashes.

It is intermittent and irregular, meaning I'm right on its loom and a little further out. If I go below and find that light on my paper chart and search all the details it will tell me precisely the sequence. But that's not what I want, it's just confirmation that I'm on course for Horta, telling me I am here, close to the end and we have made it.

That beautiful, oh so sweet feeling from my first solid confirmation of land, makes my brain tingle with joy as ecstasy sweeps over me, and it becomes another monumental skittle in this long single hander's game. I gladly raise my nearly empty cup of tea to the light as it flashes again, passing a message across, "I've been found!" I'm back, I've been discovered by civilisation again and the long trek across this water desert is nearly over. I am arriving with a newer mind, a cleaner approach to life, lots of realisations, totally wonder struck, gathering up those generosity of living moment and tasting it right down to the bone, knowing this is the magical transformational time of the whole trip.

I'm home, I'm here, I'm done with not sleeping and the lack of food and being a slave to the helm. I'm done! Yeah, I'm back.

I meet a small fishing boat going out to sea and the crew waves and I laugh and I pump my fist high and point to the kangaroo flag flapping astern and the Jesus rope bouncing along in front of the float. Maybe they think I've got a fish on the line and I'm playing him in, maybe they think I'm crazy to be out here alone, but we enjoy each other's humanity for a few moments and then they are gone from my mind, as I eagerly gaze ahead for more signs of land.

We motor along sometimes reaching 5 knots, galloping when the breeze hardens for a few minutes, giving me a lovely home bound beam reach, as the apparent wind moves forward onto the beam.

We are closing the distance, slicing away the miles, straining to see more through the haze over the land, hoping for that gorgeous first glimpse of greenery from amongst the constant blue and grey. And then it happens, the magic of landfall just for a wee moment and then another and another as I begin to focus on seeing emerald green hills in the distance through the rising mornings sea mist, and then it breaks clear and solid like a mirage growing real, and we're nearly there.

I stand tall and raise my arms and laugh long and loud and shout for joy and even whistle and dance. And then I begin to cry like a baby as the tears roll down my cheeks and I can't stop them, nor do I want to. I cry loud and long like a baby seal with joy and appreciation as if land is momma coming back from a long hunt.

It's not the removal of the struggle that brings all the tears but the opening and realisation of a deeper vision that's not so self-centred or adverse to the pain of going deeper. It is the grasp of an intangible aspect of life that rarely reaches out far enough to open our eyes until we are really on the edge. It is wrapped around the mystery of living that the migrating swallow faces each season. The mystery to which we are drawn before we are born. The mystery of why we need to get closer to that hidden person inside our psyche who eventually will take us to the cosmos. Who is greater than the sum of our parts, who is there at the deepest core of our being beyond all the machinations of the mind.

Perhaps the whole journey has been all about those heart moments when I have stepped beyond form, fears or limitations and have grown into the grace of acceptance, into a bigger understanding that freedom and being unsettled ride the same wild stallion.

Now I really appreciate and support that old saying by Hunter S. Thompson "life should not be a journey to the grave with the intention of arriving safely in a pretty and preserved body, but rather to skid in broadside in a cloud of smoke, thoroughly used up, totally worn out, and loudly proclaiming "Wow! What a Ride!"

I drop the revs and dash below, put on my Willie Nelson CD and return to the helm and pick up my speed again. I'm *"Crying in the rain"* with Willie wondering out loud if there's room in the harbour for a trans-Atlantic bird coming home to rest for a few days. Oh, the joy of living well, oh the fun of winning my Wimbledon after being two sets down, the absolute joy in the generosity of living as land hoves into view and I know it's almost done.

That promised "quiet sleep and sweet dream when the long trek is over" sweeps over me and I feel like I'm King of my world. I go quiet and alert and still within and the old - new me pops out to say "well done." I feel Lao Tzu's words float through my being, "he who is contented is rich", I've gone to the edge, looked over and I am back, deeply contented.

I close land slowly, running along from the first point where I was headed, to another point 5 miles further to starboard, where I can eventually see cranes and buildings and more signs of life. As I motor-sail along the shore a few miles off I see small farm buildings and vehicles on the road and I know the whole world has gone about its business oblivious to my journey, but there's little out there that is important compared to what's happened within.

I'm flying over the ocean now rather than counting the white caps on each monster wave where I opened this story, as hurricane Barry bashed down my door, and now I want to end it with peace and quiet, savouring these last joyful moments of coming home safe and sound. I begin to really know that travel is more of a journey of the spirit than the body, as it seeks authenticity and knowledge and experience.

The reflections in my soul's mirror of the unfamiliar were unlike any other ocean voyage, as this one was entirely alone and my fruits gathered from persistence and patience and clarity of being, should last me a lifetime and more.

I am glowing from within with a newer clarity for bigger expressions of my being and the oceanic voices blowing through my mind from past voyages are resonating loudly on this big old sunny day. A brief squall comes from seaward as patchy rain falls across the salt stained bimini and splashes warm across my bare arms as I hide in my fresh new clothes under the dodger, like a pilgrim hiding from modernity, keeping dry.

A jet boat passes with absolute raging raw power after sneaking up from behind me, startling me with a thunderous roar that I haven't heard for a month or more, and I see vapour trails pouring from its exhausts as it speeds towards the port ahead and I roll drunkenly in its wake.

The toys of the "Azores boys" come creeping in as I motor on and the harbour gets nearer and civilisation gets bigger and bolder. I cruise around the port outer harbour and notice it's well past noon and I haven't felt any time passing as a local cruise boat comes directly towards me. I have to put my mind into gear now to remember to pass him port to port. Rules and etiquette are back. There are lots of tourists aboard and they wave as we pass and I feel the warmth of fellow travellers as they reach out and grasp me with their arms of friendship. Boy I've missed that and my skin prickles with the pleasure of being held, even if it's in the hands of strangers.

I swing around the inner harbour wall and line up for the entrance to the yacht harbour and then I remember I have to stop and get the Jesus rope in, before it catches on something and causes me a lot of grief. I haul it in and as I drift I see other yachts anchored all the way up to the entrance, probably saving harbour fees as I've often done before.

But today I am a rich man and the port fees will feel like money well spent as I lie quietly to a pontoon watching life go by, out of the swell of the ocean and deep in the arms of Horta.

I get out my fenders and mooring lines and purposely take my time, quietly drifting, in perfect harmony within the still harbour entrance as I prepare the deck for coming alongside. The moat of the Atlantic has been breached by me alone and now I can finally own it, gather it up and deal it down in daily dibs, that add to my own small victories in life, but I know for sure that once is enough.

I swing into Horta's inner harbour and spot the customs pontoon where I'm to clear customs and I quietly head for it. The end is almost nigh, I'm coming in low now, my wheels are lowered and the flaps are down. Then it's touch down as I bump the pontoon gently, hitting reverse slowly and pulling up quietly, while dropping a springer line over the bollard and attaching bow and stern lines. I turn off the motor and go below to get my passport and ship's papers and comb my hair and wash my hands. It's almost all over as customs officers knock on the side of the deck and I go up and shake hands and invite them down. They smell of perfume and the city. We laugh and joke and then they clear me into Europe and send me up to get port clearance and other details, before going into the harbour. Yes, I'm back.

I go to the port office and get a visa for Europe and a marina berth position on the outside of two rows of yachts and then I'm back in the fold.

As I motor slowly down the line of yachts from all over the world someone shouts Aussie, Aussie, Aussie from the inner row, obviously recognising my kangaroo flag. I wave and shout cooee and give a big smile and thumbs up and prepare to tie up with the help of other sailors coming out of their boats to welcome me in.

And then I'm home.

Tourists accept, travellers select and here's my spot alongside two bigger yachts, that'll absorb any surge, as I turn off the motor and someone asks loudly "where did you come from?" and I say "Norfolk, Virginia!"

He says, "how long?" and I say "36 days," with pride.

He replies "you took your time" and he winks and claps!

I climb off the boat with a big smile, dancing gently across the line of other boats and someone helps me gingerly ashore and stands me up on the wharf. A feeling of immense relief slithers over my forehead and flows down my back, drips off my hips and out onto my bare feet.

Pure relief, it's over, done, wrap it up, close my arms around the bundle of memories and let them transform into touch stones for the future. That's the legacy of any voyage.

I feel the aches and pains in my body that I've neglected, I feel the unfamiliar earth swaying beneath my feet and I want to dance and shout, but custom doesn't allow it.

My lion has roared, I've walked off the edge and I'm back in suburbia, amongst humanity, measuring distance in metres rather than miles, focusing on things much closer than the horizon, listening to sounds of traffic and car horns and people shouting and kids running and dogs barking at nothing.

I smile the biggest smile and more tears run freely down my cheeks, so much so that I'm even slightly embarrassed. Suburbia feels amazingly safe and warm and close and it's so good to know I can sleep for as long as I like, forgetting about ships and wind direction and sail changes.

Home is the sailor, home from sea, and the hunter home from the hill.
Robert Louis Stevenson.

For tomorrow will bring coffee and chocolate, pastries and choices galore!.

Epilogue

After sleeping for 16 long hours I emerged into the bonhomie of a foreign port where other sailors understood my need to sit quietly, undisturbed and feast my senses upon the sideshows all around. Then we began to share stories and talk about the damage in the USA from hurricane Barry that no one else had been through, and the extent of the doldrums this year that seemed to be running further north.

John and Susie from Bontemps, a 38 ft Erickson yacht had just arrived from Brazil and we shared the state of affairs in Recife and the problems encountered clearing into Brazil without payola. Then Clarkson and Andrew who had sailed up from Venezuela on a 40 ft catamaran delivery job, advised me not to close the coast down there as I was heading for Panama, as piracy was increasing with the deteriorating political crisis. The days in port filled me up with news from around the Atlantic and soon I was back in the fold and my crossing became another blur amongst the stories of others who were out there seeing the world from their differing perspectives.

I rested in Horta for a week replacing both my self-steering device and GPS while doing work on the furler bearings, a task which needed the assistance of two others to haul me up the mast to unshackle the forestay. Then I cruised south eastwards through the other islands of the Azores for another 3 weeks, taking the advice from others who had been in the various anchorages. It was great enjoying only day sails, sometimes sleeping through the whole night and getting ready for the next long haul of a thousand miles to Lisbon.

That passage from Ponta Delgardo in the Azores to Lisbon took another 11 days as the self steerer again broke down after 3 days and I was back on watch for more long hours of helming, sail changing, and navigating.

It was another slow and frustrating journey, particularly through lack of sleep as the numbers of ships increased dramatically closing the Spanish coast. I had one strong blow from the northwest that reached 40 knots for a few hours and then down to 25 knots for a day and that drove me further than I wanted down the Spanish coast. I never reached the absolute worn out state I experienced from Norfolk, Virginia to Horta in the Azores, as I was battle hardened and I'd also stocked up on more peanut butter, honey and lots of chocolates.

Sadly, there were no more visitations from Sam.

I finally cleared in at Lisbon, anchoring south in the Seixel River where I slept and rested for three days. I spent 3 weeks there enjoying the food, wine and other sailor's tales as I slowly recovered, coming to understand that the ocean tells you more about who you really are, rather than what you'd like to become. It's spaciousness, it's quiet acceptance of your passing, those vast daily horizons finally allow you to happily grow into yourself. And these lessons often take a lifetime to discover on land.

Kaye, my partner from Tasmania flew in to help me, sharing the sailing burden after Lisbon as we cruised down to Gibraltar and on across to Madeira and then the Canary Islands where we found a wind-vane self steerer, that eventually became our new best friend. From there we headed south through the Cape Verde islands for Christmas 2007 and then had another long 28 day haul on to Barbados.

This was Kaye's first introduction to oceaning and sharing those nightly 3 hour watches, but she was tough and uncomplaining, enabling us to establish a rhythm that suited us both although we were always tired and worn after each leg as every oceaner is. Afterwards we sailed across to the Dutch islands of Bonaire and Curacao. We particularly enjoyed the inland lagoon in Curacao that offered perfect cruising anchorages away from the ocean.

There we intended to stay for a few more months just relaxing and sharing in the local sailing community but as usual another crisis emerged when we heard about troubles in Panama and were advised to get there as early as possible to facilitate our transit into the Pacific.

In Panama we were held up for 6 weeks in early 2008 along with 160 other yachts, as the Panama Canal pilots went on strike. The unexpected bonus to that situation was the great fun of meeting all those cruisers who were preparing to cross the beautiful Pacific ocean. Most intended to sail all the way to Australia and many Europeans were continuing on around the world. They were truly birds of paradise stretching themselves for their own Everest through the promise of living wild and free between continents.

I well remember as a group of us yachties, about 20 boats in total, waiting late in the afternoon for the last gate in the Panama locks to open and admit us into the Pacific. As it swung open in desperately slow motion, the joy of freedom rediscovered flooded our being and we all broke out in song, singing New Zealand's unofficial national anthem, "Oh Pokarekare Ana". As the song echoed around the sailing fleet led by an all-female New Zealand crew and their onboard sound system, we began our vast Pacific journey in joyful anticipation.

Our entry to the south Pacific in late May 2008 led us to cruise further south to Ecuador and then on to the Galapagos Islands, then westwards to the Marquesas, taking 29 days to do that passage and then on to the Cook Islands, Tonga and Vanuatu. Kaye flew home from Vanuatu for the birth of her second grandchild and Clive McCarthy, from Beechworth, Victoria, a former crew member of *Sundancer*, flew in to help me sail home. We arrived in Brisbane Australia, in November 2008.

Sailing downwind across the vast south Pacific introduces the long-haul wow factor where the winds are a steady 15 knots, the breeze is always south easterly and warm.

There are very few strong blows to alter the steady rhythm of the ocean, which day after day is the secret to blue water ocean sailing. And at night when you lean your head back and take in the sky there's an endless parade of bright stars that reflect across the phosphorescent waters in long streaks of fireworks that dance and cavort in your wake. The Pacific gave me back my appreciation for ocean cruising that the Atlantic had nearly shattered and once again I felt at home, connected to all, riding downwind, home. What was a slog to get to the Azores was now a downhill slide through the fabled Pacific islands full of coconuts and bread fruit, paw paws and flying fish and Kaye loved it all.

There's the Southern Cross, the big body of Scorpio and the brightest star in the sky, Sirius in Canis Major, all doing their long night vigil against the Milky Way, giving you stars to steer by and guide posts for tomorrow. And then there's the long low swells of the big south Pacific ocean, languid, long and gentle, unlike the short sharp jerky Atlantic mounds that forever keeps you on your toes. As I distance myself from the Atlantic I hold up a massive finger to its temperamental nature. Yes it stretched me, it was a rough Everest to the Azores and a better, quicker stride down to the European coastline. I feel some dignity in acknowledging that once across the higher latitudes of the Atlantic solo is enough. After Kaye joined me it was gentler treks (mostly, except for some wild weather across the Atlantic), no more on my own, with someone to talk to, laugh with, share cold bucket salt water showers, stand a watch, tell forgotten stories and take a photo.

How fantastic it was to be back in Australia with time spent in the Brisbane river, down to the Gold Coast and then further south to Coffs Harbour, the Clarence River, Lake Macquarie, Ulladulla, Eden and then Hastings in Victoria before tackling Bass Strait. This was another short solo sail as Kaye needed to transport our car from Melbourne to Tasmania on the Spirit of Tasmania ferry.

We enjoyed 3 months on the wharf in Wynyard, close to our families and then headed to Hobart via Wineglass Bay, Binalong Bay and other beautiful spots down the east coast of Tasmania. Constitution Dock in Hobart was fun with visits from many family and friends eager to hear tales of *Millefleurs*' journey.

We then spent another year cruising up and down the east coast of Australian enjoying the many beautiful towns and anchorages along the way and forming new friendships. We joined the boating community living on the water in the Brisbane river where we organised a party in the nearby Botanic Gardens to celebrate my 60th birthday in November 2009. We invited all the local yachties and enjoyed a memorable day with other members of the cruising community.

Going home is the best journey, going back to the familiar and the shared, seeing the same lighthouses, hearing the weather on the ABC or Macca over Australia on Sunday mornings. And in the end we realise that we travel so that we can value-add when we return, that's the reward for every home bound traveller.

We sold the ever-reliable *Millefleurs* in 2010, estimating we had done over 20,000 nautical miles in her. She was definitely an honest and solid sailing machine, suitable for any ocean passage and I'm sure it was fate that delivered her into my hands when I was earnestly searching the Chesapeake Bay area for that one honest needle in the haystack. To that end I am ever grateful to Mr Hunter for his solid, hand laid fibreglass production boats of the 1980s, that probably lie around many marinas of the world, out of date and sadly neglected because they were never seen as worthy contenders for long ocean passages.

After selling *Millefleurs*, Kaye and I went back to the USA in 2011 and bought a small van in Los Angeles and toured much of the USA, going well up into Canada and back down the east coast to the Chesapeake Bay area where we bought another yacht - an Irwin 42.

We then sailed *Dancing Brave* back through the Bahamas, Cuba, Panama, Ecuador and on across the Pacific to Australia via New Zealand where we sold her in 2015.

For the leg from Panama to Tonga I was joined by Tasmanian friends Rod Walker and Maureen as Kaye's third grandchild had been born while we were away so she took the opportunity to visit her son, Matt and his family in Frankston, Victoria.

My daughter, Caroline and her Texan husband, Clay, together with their Texan friends Dan and Tyson flew in to Tonga and enjoyed a week's cruising around the islands with Dan staying onboard for the hair-raising ride to Opua, in the Bay of Islands, New Zealand.

Kaye joined me again and we had a fantastic time cruising the Bay of Islands and the Great Barrier islands and then fell in love with the town of Whangarei.

On the last leg from the Bay of Islands in New Zealand I was joined by another former *Sundancer* crew member, Greg Warton, from Sydney. This was a really tough leg which found us clearing in to the country in Eden and not our original destination of Sydney.

Kaye and I sailed north to Sydney where we headed for our favourite anchorage, Blackwattle Bay from where we enjoyed playing tourists before sailing north to Broken Bay and the Hawkesbury river where we spent the winter months in reasonably moderate temperatures.

While in the area we sold *Dancing Brave* and were delighted to see her bought by Leo, a fellow Tasmanian. Yet another former crew member of *Sundancer*, Terry Calley, joined me in sailing her south to Lakes Entrance where Leo, the new owner hopped onboard and we crossed Bass Strait together heading for her final destination of Port Sorell in north western Tasmania.

Kaye and I then opted for an easier life of travel which involved vanning around Australia. It's similar to sailboat cruising but the anchorages are better and not as weather dependent.

We continued to enjoy living the life of freedom and change, finally settling in Wynyard, Tasmania where we bought an old house and are into rebuilding, gardening and enjoying the local community.

For now long haul sailing is done, but the memories live on forever.

The End

About the Author

Peter Keating is now retired and living with his partner Kaye in Wynyard, Tasmania.

He has a degree in psychology from the University of Tasmania and spent time teaching maths and science in Hobart, NSW and London in the 1970s and 1980s.

He became an international sailor, owning 5 yachts ranging from 34ft to 104ft and completed over 200,000 ocean miles, sailing deep into the Pacific and crossing all the oceans of the world. He circumnavigated, using only a sextant, both east-about and west-about.

Returning to Australia in the late 1990s, Peter built a stone castle as an esoteric and healing centre, but returned to oceaning again, as his first love, which is where this story begins.

He has 2 children, 4 grandchildren and has been a maverick, adventurer and wisdom seeker throughout his life, always regarding himself as an international citizen.

Peter is now enjoying a quieter lifestyle, building, gardening, writing and playing his ukulele.

If you would like to contact Peter about this book, or his wider sailing exploits, please email him at keatingontheroad@hotmail.com

Acknowledgements

There are a number of people I must thank for reading the manuscript and making recommendations that enabled me to reduce my initial text from 370 pages of A4 down to what you now hold in your hands.

Thanks to Jonathan Samiec for his initial proofing and his encouragement to keep going and also to my lifelong friend Andre Legosz, for a more detailed proofing.

Then to my partner Kaye Dunn who spent many hours making sense of my wandering tale and assisting me in providing a workable manuscript, with it finally emerging after two years of constant headwinds.

To say that sailing the Atlantic was difficult is an understatement, but certainly condensing my journey into mere words was much more so.

Glossary

Anti-foul	toxic paint to kill algae growth
Aussie shagged	exhausted
Beam on	lying sideways to the wind and seas
Becalmment	no wind on the ocean
Choofing whale	blowing steam like a train
Dodger	covering over the cockpit
Furler	device on the forestay that winds the sails in and out
Going to windward	sailing with the wind forward of the beam
Gunkholing	anchoring around the bay
Gybe	change direction downwind, so boom swings over to the other side and headsail is reset
Harleys	Harley Davidson motorbikes
Hove to	stopped with sails still up, rudder to windward and headsail backed
Lying a hull	drifting without sails.
Oceaner	sailor who goes beyond 100 miles offshore
On the run	sailing with the wind behind
Pooped	wave landing on back deck
Port tack	wind coming in over left side of boat
Push-pit	rails around the bow
Reaching	sailing with wind on the beam
Reefed down	sails reduced in size
Rolly	hand rolled cigarettes
Starboard tack	wind coming in over right side of boat
Tell-tales	strips of material hung in rigging to indicate wind direction
WMD	weapons of mass destruction
Vanging	tying rope to boom to stop it lifting

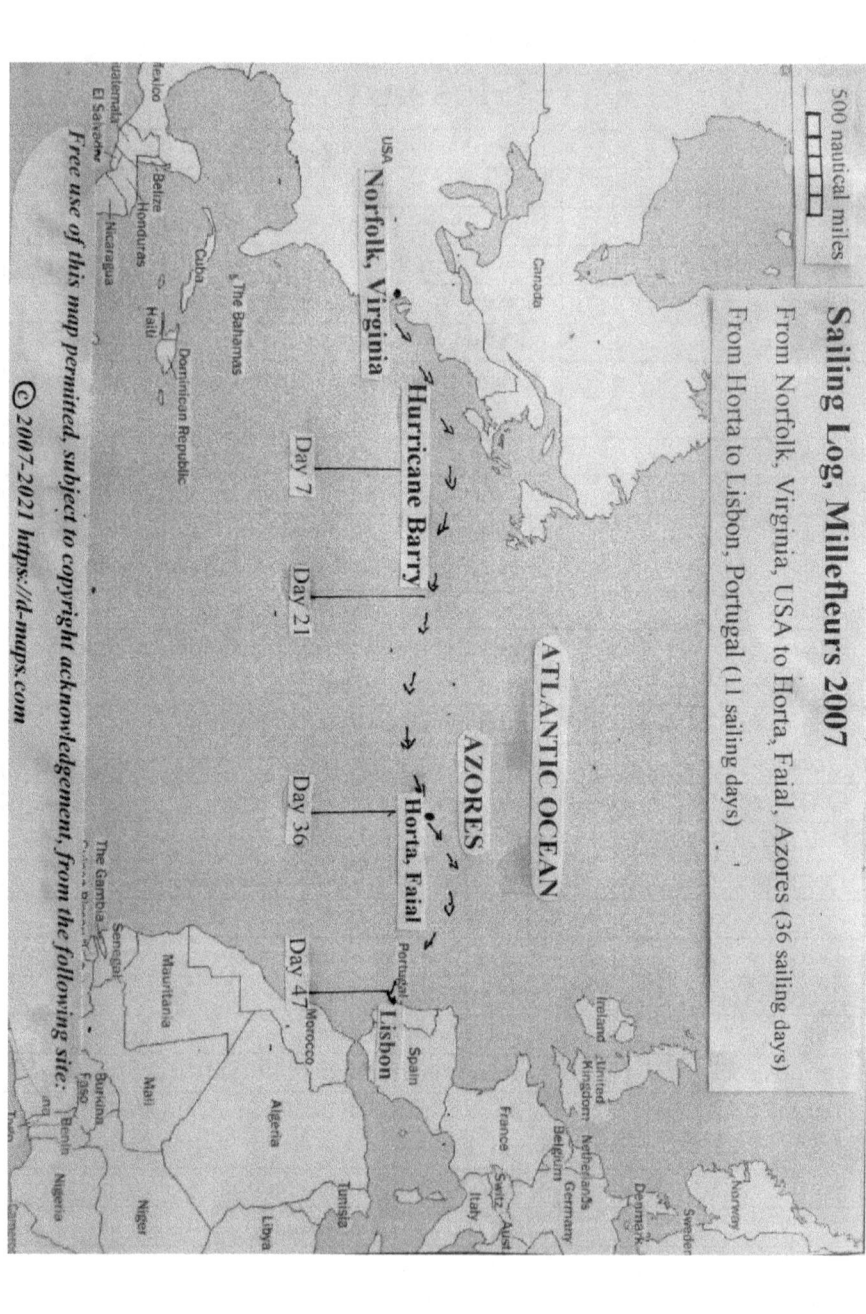

www.ingramcontent.com/pod-product-compliance
Lightning Source LLC
Chambersburg PA
CBHW071956290426
44109CB00018B/2042